PRAISE FOR
BIOETHICAL CHALLENGES AT THE END OF LIFE

"The culture of death has tightened its grip during the COVID-19 pandemic. Combining a comprehensive overview of the personalist foundations of end-of-life ethics with magisterial references, Fr. Weimann equips readers to advance the culture of life, by guiding them through such extraordinary means as euthanasia and assisted suicide, and offering insightful contributions to more recent controversies surrounding brain death, organ donation, and alkaline hydrolysis."
—**JOHN A. DI CAMILLO**, The National Catholic Bioethics Center

"Christianity is a message of hope. It shows the path that does not end with death, but leads to eternal life. Therefore, the right way of dealing with dying and death is crucial. In view of the challenges involved, Prof. Ralph Weimann's book offers a fundamental ethical and moral orientation of the greatest importance for Catholics, but also with an ecumenical dimension. This scientifically thorough but accessible book deserves wide distribution."
—**CARDINAL KURT KOCH**, President of the Pontifical Council for Promoting Christian Unity

"Today, death and dying are increasingly seen as technological problems concerning utility, rather than moral issues regarding meaning. As with our attitude toward living, so our attitude toward dying will largely depend on whether we understand ourselves as transient products of blind evolution or as creatures of a wise and loving Creator having an eternal destiny. In his highly recommendable volume, Weimann advocates the latter, providing a panoramic vision of current end-of-life issues in the broader context of what it means to be a human person from a Catholic perspective."
—**STEPHAN KAMPOWSKI**, Pontifical Theological John Paul II Institute, Rome

"In the context of a culture under the lash of economic, media, and post-modern pressures, this timely, well-researched, and lucidly argued book poses questions about end-of-life care sure to benefit Christians, bioethics experts, and people generally. Fr. Weimann focuses on modern presuppositions about the human person which have led us astray from authentic Christian ethics. Forms of euthanasia, assisted suicide, and therapeutic obstinacy are distinguished from authentic principles of Catholic teaching. A stimulating critique of brain death criteria, organ transplants, and burial and alternatives to it, further enhances this major work."

—**FR. GEORGE J. WOODALL**, Emeritus Lecturer in Moral Theology, Regina Apostolorum, Rome

"Father Weimann offers Catholics a substantial and mostly non-technical study of the issues surrounding euthanasia ('making a good end') and suicide—whether self-inflicted or assisted—and usually enacted as a means of securing the 'dignity' of the human person and respecting his 'quality of life.' Largely adapted from the teachings of John Paul II and Benedict XVI, it provides a challenging introduction to an important part of the culture-war between the partisans of the 'Culture of Life' preached normally (but not always) by the Catholic Church and the 'Culture of Death' preferred by abortion-mongers and those eager to save money and trouble by eliminating the elderly who, as they see it, are now 'past their shelf-life.'"

—**JOHN RIST**, Emeritus Professor of Classics and Philosophy, University of Toronto

BIOETHICAL CHALLENGES
AT THE END OF LIFE

Bioethical Challenges at the End of Life

*An Ethical Guide
in
Catholic Perspective*

RALPH WEIMANN

Angelico Press

First published in the USA
by Angelico Press 2022
Copyright © Ralph Weimann 2022

All rights reserved:
No part of this book may be reproduced or transmitted,
in any form or by any means, without permission

For information, address:
Angelico Press, Ltd.
169 Monitor St.
Brooklyn, NY 11222
www.angelicopress.com

paper   978-1-62138-821-0
cloth   978-1-62138-822-7

Book and cover design
by Michael Schrauzer

To all who are committed to defend and promote the value and dignity of human life from conception to natural death

TABLE OF CONTENTS

Abbreviations. xiv

I. INTRODUCTION. 1
   A Positive Approach to Bioethics 1
   General Introduction 4
      Bioethics is About Human Life — 5; Bioethics as an
      Interdisciplinary Subject — 7; The Main Problems
      with Bioethics — 9; The Magisterium of the Church
      on Bioethics — 11

II. CULTURE OF DEATH 17
   General Introduction to the Concept
     "Culture of Death" 17
   Some Aspects Regarding a Culture of Death 21
   A New Prototype 26
   The Culture of Death. 30
   Spiritual Combat Against the Culture of Death. 34

III. ANTHROPOLOGICAL FOUNDATION 37
   The Anthropological Problem 37
   Looking for a Reference Point. 40
   Some Basic Considerations Regarding the
     Concept of Man 45
      Some Basic Distinctions — 46; The Human Person
      — 52; The Person is an Individual — 53; The Person
      is a Rational Being — 54; The Significance of the
      Concept of Man — 55
   Anthropology in Our Time 57

IV. SOME ASPECTS ABOUT THE END OF LIFE 61
   Some Introductory Considerations 61
   Definition of "Euthanasia" 64
      Antiquity — 64; Christian Influence — 67; Renais-
      sance and Enlightenment — 70; Modernity — 71;
      Post-Modernity — 74
   A Look at the Current Situation in Some Countries . . 78

V. EUTHANASIA   85
   Direct (Active) Euthanasia (Killing on Request) 87
      Voluntary Euthanasia — 93; Non-Voluntary Euthanasia — 93; Involuntary Euthanasia — 93; Ethical Evaluation of Direct Euthanasia — 95
   Indirect (Passive) Euthanasia 101
      Ethical Evaluation of Indirect Euthanasia — 106; Principle of Double Effect — 110

VI. SUICIDE AND ASSISTED SUICIDE 115
   Suicide 115
      Christianity and Suicide — 116; Definition and Ethical Evaluation of Suicide — 119
   Assisted Suicide 123
   Final Moral Evaluation 129
   Summary 130

VII. ORDINARY (PROPORTIONATE) AND EXTRAORDINARY (DISPROPORTIONATE) MEANS 131
   Preliminary Ethical Reflection 132
      To Do Everything Possible — 134; To Do Only the Possible — 136; To Do Things in the Best Way Possible — 140
   Conserving / Prolonging Life 141
      Ordinary Means — Some Basic Considerations — 143; Extraordinary Means — Some Basic Considerations — 145; Approaching a Definition and Its Consequences — 147; Nutrition and Hydration — 149; Permanent "Vegetative" State — 153; Suffering — Palliative Care — 156; Concerning the Living Will — 161; Advance Healthcare Directive as a Guide — 162; Guiding Criteria for an Advance Healthcare Directive — 165

VIII. DEATH — BRAIN DEATH 167
   Some Basic Considerations Regarding Death 169
   Psychological Effects and Death 173
   Death from a Philosophical Perspective 175
   Death from a Theological Perspective 177
   Determining the Moment of Death 181

Brain Death—Death of the Whole Person? 184
The Magisterium of the Church and Brain Death
— 187; A Critical Analysis of the Brain-Death Definition — 190

IX. ORGAN DONATION 197
Some Historical Notes 198
Terminology 199
Defending the Life of the Donor and of the
Recipient — 202; Protecting Personal Identity — 203;
Informed Consent — 204
Position of the Catholic Church 206
Legal Situation 209

X. CREMATION—BURIAL—ALKALINE HYDROLYSIS . . . 211
Historical Development 211
The Influence of Christianity — 212; Modern Age
— 215
A Philosophical Perspective 217
A Theological Perspective 218
A Technical Perspective 220
Cremation — 220; Alkaline Hydrolysis — 223
An Analysis of Burial, Cremation, and
Alkaline Hydrolysis 224
The Church's Position 227

CONCLUSION 231

BIBLIOGRAPHY
Magisterial Documents (chronologically ordered) . . . 237
Other Literature (alphabetically ordered) 240
Online Sources (alphabetically ordered) 252

ABBREVIATIONS

AAS	*Acta Apostolicae Sedis*
AL	Apostolic Exhortation *Amoris Laetitia*
BSG	*Bioethik in einer säkularisierten Gesellschaft*
c.	canon
CV	Encyclical Letter *Caritas in Veritate*
CCC	*Catechism of the Catholic Church*
CDF	Congregation for the Doctrine of the Faith
CIC	Code of Canon Law
DCE	Encyclical *Deus Caritas Est*
DE	Declaration on Euthanasia
DH	Denzinger Hünermann
DNA	Deoxyribonucleic acid
DP	Instruction *Dignitas Personae*
DV	Instruction *Donum Vitae*
EV	Encyclical Letter *Evangelium Vitae*
FR	Encyclical Letter *Fides et Ratio*
GS	Pastoral Constitution *Gaudium et Spes*
HV	Encyclical Letter *Humanae Vitae*
LF	Encyclical Letter *Lumen Fidei*
LG	Dogmatic Constitution *Lumen Gentium*
LS	Encyclical Letter *Laudato Si'*
NCBQ	*The National Catholic Bioethics Quarterly*
NDD	*The New Definitions of Death*
RH	Encyclical Letter *Redemptor Hominis*
PB	*Personalist Bioethics. Foundations and Applications*
PL	Patrologia Latina
PVS	Persistent Vegetative State
SB	Letter *Samaritanus Bonus*
SS	Encyclical Letter *Spe Salvi*
STh	*Summa Theologiae*
USCCB	United States Conference of Catholic Bishops
VS	Encyclical Letter *Veritatis Splendor*

I

Introduction

A POSITIVE APPROACH TO BIOETHICS

Pope John Paul II began his papacy with the words "non abbiate paura" ("do not be afraid"). The same motto should be applied to this book on bioethical challenges regarding the end of life. It is important to address bioethical issues and we shouldn't be afraid of being overburdened. We need to face the problems and we need to be able to offer valid solutions since death is always part of human life, not only in times of the so-called coronavirus. The progress of technology is challenging and whether we like it or not, we need to accept the challenge. Bioethics is related to life issues, and certain decisions and the use of new technologies are going to have an impact on life and even on eternal salvation. Saint John Paul II wrote in his first encyclical letter *Redemptor Hominis* that Jesus Christ is "the continuous spokesman and advocate for the person who lives."[1] This attitude has to be the basic attitude for anyone who wants to study bioethics, whether Christian or not. It might be easier to understand the purpose of this book from this perspective, which is meant to offer ethical orientation within a rapidly developing new science.

The tremendous progress of science, technology, and medicine provides new means and opportunities, all of which are accessible to the people. Furthermore, many—even practicing Catholics—are already using these different means, and since they do not receive much bioethical formation they use them according to their own principles or according to the information provided by the mass media or certain institutes. The question has to be raised whether the provided information is sufficient? Whether these new technologies and opportunities are justifiable or not according to an ethical perspective? These questions are not insignificant since they touch the question of eternal salvation.[2] It is unfortunate

---

1 John Paul II, RH, 13.
2 The Letter *Samaritanus Bonus* from 2020 underlines the need of salvation and that the "Church regards scientific research and technology with hope,

that this important subject is mostly excluded from bioethics; nevertheless, it should be at the core of any ethical evaluation. According to Saint Thomas Aquinas eternal life consists in the enjoyment of God Himself.[3] In order to reach this goal, it is important to follow the way Christ has shown us through the Church. It is necessary to remember the words of the Gospel of Saint Matthew: "Go, therefore, and make disciples of all nations, baptizing them in the name of the Father, and of the Son, and of the Holy Spirit, teaching them to observe all that I have commanded you" (Mt 28:19). This would be the right attitude needed to embark on this book *Bioethical Challenges At the End of Life*. It is important to see that the various technical or medical procedures do have an impact on the question of eternal salvation.

Considering bioethics in general, the impression is given that it is for most people a big mystery because it includes a broad spectrum of problems and challenges. According to Elio Sgreccia, who served as the director of the Bioethics Center at the Gemelli School of Medicine and Surgery from 1985 to 2006, the academic treatment of these subjects needs to be divided into three distinct areas:

a. "*General bioethics*, which is concerned with ethical foundations, is discourse about the original values and principles of medical ethics and the documentary sources of bioethics (international law, codes of professional ethics, legislation)."[4]

b. "*Particular bioethics* analyzes major problems, which are always approached from a general perspective, both in the medical field and in the biological field: genetic engineering, abortion, euthanasia, clinical experimentation, etc." Sgreccia concludes: "Particular bioethics, therefore, can do nothing unless associated with the conclusions of general bioethics."[5]

c. "*Clinical or decisional bioethics* concretely examines what values are at stake in medical practice and clinical cases; to put it differently, clinical or decisional bioethics assesses

---

seeing in them promising opportunities to serve the integral good of life and the dignity of every human being." CDF, SB, Introduction.

3   Cf. Thomas Aquinas, STh, II-II, q.17, a.2.
4   Elio Sgreccia, PB, 23.
5   Ibid., 24.

Introduction

the right ways of determining a course of action without altering such values."⁶

This subdivision is helpful since it is the goal of this book to offer an ethical orientation that aids discernment. Any clinical or particular bioethics must be associated with the ethical foundations, otherwise it will be impossible to provide orientation. Today, many people speak about discernment, but only a few people offer clear orientation. There is no discernment without an ethical foundation, which is the necessary condition. Bioethics needs to provide answers and—as Pope Benedict XVI said—there are principles, "which are not negotiable." Among them is the "protection of life in all its stages, from the first moment of conception until natural death."⁷ Only in the light of this will bioethics not remain a "mystery," but a source of orientation and inspiration.

There are some basic aspects related to general bioethics that have to be mentioned before one can start considering specific bioethical challenges, which have an importance for most bioethical problems. Without any doubt, bioethics can be very complicated. The main reason for that consists in the problem that the general overview in order to understand the big picture is mostly lacking. This overview is increasingly missing regarding the different challenges concerning the end of life, due to an ever-progressing specialization. Some decades ago, doctors used to take into consideration the human person as such, with all its dimensions and differentiation, when making their diagnosis and making a decision. It was important to consider the well-being of the spiritual, psychological, and medical dimensions. Today, doctors are almost exclusively putting their emphasis on the medical dimension, having submitted to the economical standards and rules, concentrating ever more on their specialization. They no longer consider the whole person with all its dimensions. This ongoing specialization has some advantages, but it relieves the doctors from any ethical considerations. If someone considers the human person according to a materialistic perspective focusing only on certain

---

6 Ibid.
7 Benedict XVI, Address of his Holiness to the Members of the European People's Party on the Occasion of the Study Days on Europe, 30.3.2006, in w2.vatican.va/content/benedict-xvi/en/speeches/2006/march/documents/hf_ben-xvi_spe_20060330_eu-parliamentarians.html [15.1.2022].

functions, the big picture will get lost and he will not be able to see the forest for the trees. Therefore, it is not a priority of this book to deal with the special issues and biomedical technologies, but to demonstrate principal guidelines that are helpful in order to classify the individual problems.

GENERAL INTRODUCTION

This book is not meant to be an introduction to bioethics; nevertheless, it is helpful to call to mind a few aspects of importance to understand the problems we are going to face.

In the post-modern age, relativism has become the new dominant philosophical paradigm. Historians, theologians, and scientists—especially those dealing with bioethics—face this difficulty. Thomas Dubay underlined that this becomes a real issue when dealing with morality and ethics. He affirms that for many today there "is no such thing as objective good and evil. [...] What is good or true for one, may be evil or false for another. Subjectivism leads logically to relativism."[8] This rapidly spreading tendency has a great impact on bioethics, even regarding the very definition.

The term "bioethics" was created in the United States and is attributed to Van Rensselaer Potter († 2001), an American biochemist. He coined the term to describe a new subject that sought to integrate biology, ecology, medicine, and human values.[9] According to Potter, scientific and technological progress was endangering humanity and the very survival of life on earth. For that reason, he called bioethics the "science of survival." Tristram Engelhardt († 2018), one of the pioneers in bioethical research, wrote in a foreword to Potter's book entitled *Global Bioethics* that new words are often not very precise, lack clarity, and are ambiguous. "This has been the case with 'bioethics.'"[10] Therefore, it should not be surprising that regarding the definition of bioethics there is not much consensus among scholars. However, certain aspects can be highlighted which indicate the way to an objective and less ambiguous understanding of this term.

---

8 Thomas Dubay, *Faith and Certitude* (San Francisco: Ignatius Press, 1985), 46.
9 Cf. Van Rensselaer Potter, "Bioethics: The Science of Survival," in *Perspectives in Biology and Medicine* 14 (1982): 127–53.
10 H. Tristram Engelhardt, "Foreword," in Van Rensselaer Potter (ed.), *Global Bioethics: Building on the Leopold Legacy* (East Lansing, MI: Michigan State University Press, 1988), vii–xii, here vii.

Introduction

Regarding its etymology, bioethics derives from the Greek *bios* meaning life and *ethos* meaning ethics. The ancient Greek word βíος (*bíos*) is a term both complementary and opposed to ζωή (*zoë*). Primarily, at least in the Attic period, *zoë* was limited to physical life,[11] while *bios* indicates the fullness of life, including a metaphysical perspective and relation to God, as well as to the concept of death, soul, immortality, and eternity.[12] Today, there is a type of reduction of life to *zoë*, to the physical dimension of man, which could lead to serious consequences. If a person is reduced to his material life, it might be easy to deprive him of his rights and dignity. Regarding the bioethical challenges at the end of life, a one-dimensional reductive view of the human person must be avoided. It will be necessary to learn from the Greek and to explain life including the perspective of the *bios*, which would lead to a wider perspective on moral and ethical behavior and ethical evaluations. In any case, the concept of bioethics has to include an ethical reflection, which necessarily surpasses the biological dimension.

The term bioethics has experienced large growth.[13] It can include the environment, and therefore animals, plants, and humans, as well as a political ethic, genetic engineering, reproductive medicine, and more. Originally, genetic engineering and reproductive medicine did not have much to do with bioethics, but through the advance of technology, they gained a greater approximation. Some delimitation will be necessary.

Bioethics is About Human Life

To simplify the following explanations, this book will consider bioethics as related only to human life. Many things are technically possible, but—this question must be raised—are they also ethically licit? This is one of the most fundamental questions that bioethics seeks to provide an answer to. Bioethics is about how to

---

11   Cf. Aristotle, *On the Soul*, in Jonathan Barnes (ed.), *The Complete Works of Aristotle*, 6th ed., vol. 1 (Princeton, NJ: Princeton University Press, 1995), Book I, 403b, 16-18.
12   Cf. Angela Maria Cosentino, "Vita (Sacralità, Inviolabilità, Indisponibilità)," in *Enciclopedia di bioetica e scienza giuridica*, vol. XII (Naples: Edizioni Scientifiche Italiane, 2017), 853-84, here 855.
13   See the explanation offered by H. Tristram Engelhardt, *The Foundations of Bioethics*, 2nd ed. (Oxford: Oxford University Press, 1996), 3-134.

deal with human life in the different stages of human development concerning the new technologies offered by science. Technology has acquired a new influence, dominance, and even dominion over human life, which increases continuously and affects the human person above all at the beginning and at the end of life.

At this point, it has to be mentioned that most bioethical issues are dominated not only by technology but also by the economy. This is a giant market worth billions and very often the money indicates the way and directs political decisions.[14] Two examples are worth mentioning; one regarding the beginning of life and the other regarding the end of life:

a) There is a whole industry supporting so-called In Vitro Fertilization, which was expected to reach $21.6 billion globally by 2020.[15] Money often dictates or dominates research and even ethical evaluations. This is a sad reality and corresponds perfectly to the Machiavellian principle "the end justifies the means." This principle will be applied whenever economic interests dominate the decision-making process. Then the most profitable is going to be justified because it is simply the most profitable, even though it might be immoral and illicit.

b) Something similar can be said regarding the demographic situation of many countries, especially in Europe.[16] The shrinking populations in many European countries have a strong economic impact. Generally, elderly people do not work anymore, they are not productive, and often they need help and support. Further, the increased number of retired people increases the economic pressure on the working population. The state and especially the economy will look for ways to reduce the number of people in need of care; the sick or nursing cases, the handicapped, and elderly people. The pressure is increasing to use euthanasia and similar means as a solution regardless of their being immoral. The influence of economic issues cannot be overestimated.

---

14 Cf. Manfred Spieker (ed.), *Biopolitik: Probleme des Lebensschutzes in der Demokratie* (Paderborn: Verlag Ferdinand Schöningh, 2009).

15 Cf. "In Vitro Fertilization Market is Expected to Reach $21.6 Billon, Globally by 2020," in www.alliedmarketresearch.com/press-release/global-in-vitro-fertilization-market-to-reach-216-billion-by-2020.html [15.1.2022].

16 Cf. Franz-Xaver Kaufmann and Walter Krämer (eds.), *Die demographische Zeitbombe: Fakten und Folgen des Geburtendefizits* (Paderborn: Verlag Ferdinand Schöningh, 2015).

Introduction

Bioethics as an Interdisciplinary Subject

As part of the introduction, it is necessary to mention that bioethics is an interdisciplinary subject. The constellation of subjects involved in bioethics can vary according to the different experts. There is no consensus about the subjects among scholars; it is only clear that there are many diverse subjects involved. This mixture of different disciplines is also responsible for creating the impression that bioethics is so complicated, for nobody can be specialized in everything.

Nevertheless, there are good reasons to propose a number of core subjects, which can be considered an integral part of bioethics. In his book entitled *Personalist Bioethics: Foundations and Applications*,[17] Elio Sgreccia proposes to subdivide bioethics into five faculties: medicine, philosophy, biology, theology, and law. But a brief look makes this proposal more comprehensive. Elio Sgreccia presents an integral understanding of the human person in order to solve the problems posed by scientific progress, medicine, and law. For that reason there is a need for:

a. Medicine: The starting point of bioethics is the medical data, which bioethics has to examine. Medical aspects are inevitably involved.

b. Biology: Together with medicine, the biological data serves as a starting point and has to be taken into consideration.[18]

c. Philosophy: Anthropology, as a philosophical discipline, takes into account the human person as a whole. It has to be ontologically grounded in order to be able to justify man's intrinsic value.[19] Philosophical anthropology provides the framework within which an ethical evaluation regarding procreation, suffering, sickness, death, etc. becomes possible.

d. Theology: This subject is probably the most controversial and most often omitted among scholars. Nevertheless, theology provides answers for the most important questions in life, afterlife,

---

17 Under the pontificate of Pope Benedict XVI, Msgr. Elio Sgreccia had been appointed cardinal, mainly due to his outstanding achievements in the field of bioethics. He co-founded a "personalistic bioethics" and promoted it through his many publications. Among other things, he wrote the standard work on bioethics published as a handbook, now in Spanish, French and English. Cf. Sgreccia, PB.
18 Cf. ibid., 29.
19 Cf. ibid., 24-25.

and regarding the dignity of man. Even though some of its applications are above all to be considered within the community of faithful, many of its conclusions happen to coincide with those of ethics and moral philosophy.[20]

e. Law: This faculty needs to include the juridical system, legal norms as well as the development and application of those norms. These are distinct from moral and ethical norms and might differ from country to country.[21]

This interdisciplinary study will work only if every science works within the parameters defined by the science itself. Bioethics is not only about presenting different ethical positions. It must provide objective answers based on rationally valid criteria, which facilitate a decision making process. This will be possible only by interrelating the sciences that contribute to a fuller understanding. It must be remembered that bioethics affects human life not only in its physical dimension but also in its psychological dimension and—this has to be included—in its spiritual dimension.[22] A new awareness should be created that many people suffer in different fields because of wrong decisions that have been made. This is reflected mainly on the mental and spiritual level, and therefore bioethics should be related also to the spiritual/psychological faculty of man. For that reason, priests and religious, but also physicians and psychologists, must understand that only an interdisciplinary approach will provide valid answers. This can also serve as a bridge to promoting the sacraments, especially the sacraments of confession and the anointing of the sick. While a psychologist can help to suppress or hide the sins, he cannot absolve them. The burden of sin can be taken away only by a priest. Everyone working in pastoral care needs to be aware of what is going on in order to be able to help. Therefore, it will be necessary to overcome a one-dimensional view and consider the human person as it is, with all its different dimensions. Thus, the proposal of Elio Sgreccia remains valid. However, it still needs to be fully developed since he offers an objective reflection which is built upon a metaphysical foundation.

---

20 Cf. ibid., 26.
21 Cf. ibid., 22.
22 See Harold G. Koenig, *Spirituality in Patient Care: Why, How, When, and What*, 3rd ed. (West Conshohocken: Templeton Foundation Press, 2013). Cf. Stephen P. Kliewer and John Saultz, *Healthcare and Spirituality* (Oxford: CRC Press, 2006).

Introduction

The Main Problems with Bioethics

To complete the overview of this general introduction, it will be necessary to address the main problem with bioethics, which will become fully evident throughout this book. There is a growing gap between technical progress and ethical-moral responsibility.[23] The development of technology has made a great deal possible. But scientists, physicians, politicians, and even different religious leaders no longer know what is good and what is bad for people. The people, however, due to a lack of any real guidance, often believe the frivolous promises of progress. Moreover, from its historical origins bioethics made people believe that only professionals and specialists should deal with these topics and that everyone else had to trust in what they said. This mentality of delegating the responsibility to specialists has become more and more absolute, with most hospitals and even governments employing "bioethics committees" in order to deal with possible ethical objections or arguments.[24] They hand over all the responsibility to specialists, which is a serious problem. What criteria do they use to make their decisions? Who is going to be part of the committee? Is the common person no longer responsible for his own decisions? The Catholic Church tries to form responsible faithful, who, according to the invitation of the Second Vatican Council, take a clear stand. How much more are religious, priests, and bishops urged to do so:

> Laymen should also know that it is generally the function of their well-formed Christian conscience to see that the divine law is inscribed in the life of the earthly city; from priests they may look for spiritual light and nourishment. Let the layman not imagine that his pastors are always such experts, that to every problem which arises, however complicated, they can readily give him a concrete solution, or even that such is their mission. Rather, enlightened by Christian wisdom and giving close attention to the teaching authority of the Church, let the layman take on

---

23 An overview regarding this problem at the beginning of life is presented in Debra Evans, *Without Moral Limits: Women, Reproduction, and Medical Technology* (Wheaton: Crossway Books, 2000).

24 Cf. D. Micah Hester (ed.), *Ethics by Committee: A Textbook on Consultation, Organization, and Education for Hospital Ethics Committees* (Lanham: Rowman & Littlefield Publishers, 2008).

> his own distinctive role. [...] Since they have an active role to play in the whole life of the Church, laymen are not only bound to penetrate the world with a Christian spirit, but are also called to be witnesses to Christ in all things in the midst of human society.[25]

This is going to be a crucial task, especially regarding bioethics. Many basic ethical principles and values such as "human dignity," "person," "human nature," "the beginning and end of human life," and many others, are not recognized anymore. In a multi-religious and multi-cultural society, criteria, which derive historically from Christianity, are usually turned down. A new nominalism arises, according to which certain terms such as "person," "dignity," "marriage," etc. are still in use, but their real content—with its ethical and normative foundation—has been lost. Moral relativism is gaining ground in place of objective standards. Cardinal Ratzinger described this process in the following way on April 18th, 2005:

> Today, having a clear faith based on the Creed of the Church is often labeled as fundamentalism. Whereas relativism, that is, letting oneself be "tossed here and there, carried about by every wind of doctrine," seems the only attitude that can cope with modern times. We are building a dictatorship of relativism that does not recognize anything as definitive and whose ultimate goal consists solely of one's own ego and desires.[26]

This has a great impact on morals, ethics, and bioethics and it has increased since.

A false understanding of tolerance helps to reinforce these relativistic tendencies and is already causing a great deal of damage to humanity. Especially those who are innocent suffer the most; those who cannot defend themselves, the unborn, the old, and the handicapped. When relativism becomes the dominating philosophy, one's own opinion becomes the measure of all, which leads inevitably to the law of the jungle. This is reflected not only

---

25 GS, 43.
26 Joseph Ratzinger, Homily *Missa pro eligendo Romano Pontifice*, 18.4.2005, in www.vatican.va/gpII/documents/homily-pro-eligendo-pontifice_20050418_en.html [15.1.2022].

in the ideology of gender[27] but in almost every bioethical field.

To have a personal, objective, and well-founded position is a necessity and the only possible way to confront the actual problems. We always have to be prepared to give an answer to everyone who asks us to give the reason for the hope that we have (cf. 1 Peter 3:15). This demand is valid also for bioethics since it is not enough to say some nice words nor is it enough to know some complicated theories or medical issues. Clear and objective principles are needed to provide answers in a field dealing with life and death. Nobody who has to make important decisions can afford to be ambiguous or vague. Most of the bioethical issues are about life or death and therefore it is extremely important to make the right decision. In times dominated by relativism, some are afraid to tell the truth and they prefer to bring forward ambiguous and meaningless phrases. Regarding theology, this would do great damage to the Church's teaching; regarding bioethics this could be unforgivable. A wrong decision or a lack of clarity could provoke the death of someone. A doctor who needs to make an urgent decision about life or death needs clarity, otherwise, the patient might die. If, for example, a priest is consulted whether a person in the vegetative state should still receive food or not, he must know what to say. Any type of moral relativism will collapse in this situation. People need orientation, they need guidance, and every Catholic is called to give them the answers.

The Magisterium of the Church on Bioethics

At this point, no detailed overview can be offered, regarding the different magisterial interventions on bioethical issues. Nevertheless, it might be helpful to mention some key documents and figures, related to bioethical topics.

Pope Pius XII welcomed new technologies and offered a reliable orientation. In more than 100 speeches he referred to bioethical problems, without using the word "bioethics" explicitly, which indeed did not exist at that time. Whenever new technologies or scientific inventions, which were important for the lives of the faithful, came to his attention, Pope Pius offered orientation and

---

27 Francis, AL, 56. See also Gabriele Kuby, *The Global Sexual Revolution: Destruction of Freedom in the Name of Freedom*, trans. James Patrick Kirchner (Kettering: Angelico Press, 2015).

gave clear answers. One of the most important principles related to his person, which still provide guidance today, is the so-called "principle of totality."[28]

This principle, also stated by Paul VI in the encyclical letter *Humanae Vitae*, affirms that the best interests of the part are subordinate to the good of the whole. Thus, if it serves the good of the whole, a part must—at least on some occasions—be "sacrificed." This happens, for example, in the case of an amputation since the human organs are removed or its functions are limited for the benefit of the whole. For the whole of man is not only his physical function, but the whole person, with its physical, mental, and spiritual faculties. The welfare of the individual has to be seen and recognized in this perspective. Pope Pius XI had already implicitly mentioned this principle when he spoke about surgical sterilization, which is only allowed if it is for the good of the whole body.[29] Nevertheless, it was Pope Pius XII who frequently made reference to it. This principle of totality is of fundamental importance, especially regarding the bioethical challenges at the end of life. When considering, for example, suffering and pain, it is important to adopt a holistic approach, taking into account the different dimensions of the human person. Otherwise, the end would justify the means, which would lead necessarily to a reductive view of man, and would pave the way to justifying direct and indirect euthanasia.

It is important in this context to know that Pius XII formulated this principle and from that moment on it has found its way into the Magisterium of the Church. In times of increasing specialization, this principle is of great significance since its application

---

28 Cf. Pius XII, Allocutiones "Societate internazionali Hematologiae," in AAS 50 (1958), 732-40.
29 Pope Pius XI makes reference to this principle, without giving it a special name. He says: "Furthermore, Christian doctrine establishes, and the light of human reason makes it most clear, that private individuals have no other power over the members of their bodies than that which pertains to their natural ends; and they are not free to destroy or mutilate their members, or in any other way render themselves unfit for their natural functions, except when no other provision can be made for the good of the whole body." Pius XI, Encyclical Letter *Casti Connubii*, 31.12.1930, in w2.vatican.va/content/pius-xi/en/encyclicals/documents/hf_p-xi_enc_19301231_casti-connubii.html [15.1.2022], 71.

prevents one from carrying out reductionisms and helps to overcome mistakes and negative developments. In his encyclical letter *Humanae Vitae*, Pope Paul VI defended this principle against misunderstandings.[30] Modern society, however, tends towards making concrete and practical solutions, but often loses the overview. The whole question of eternal salvation is part of the necessary look at the big picture and unfortunately this vision has been lost. Pope Paul VI tried to explain the doctrine of the Church about contraception from this perspective, but he was not understood and even many priests, bishops, and episcopal conferences opposed the document with dissent.[31]

Regarding general principles for an ethical and moral evaluation, there are above all two encyclicals which are of great relevance for this topic. Even though these documents are quite extensive, it would be well worth it to explain them in detail. In 1993 Pope John Paul II issued the encyclical letter *Veritatis Splendor*. In it he explained the position of the Catholic Church regarding the most fundamental positions in moral teaching. The Pope offers a response to moral relativism, affirming the moral authority of the Catholic Church. He provides important clarifications with regards to topics such as human freedom and divine law, natural law, the importance of the conscience and the judgment of conscience, the fundamental option, etc. He also explains the reality of intrinsically evil acts and offers central principles for any ethical evaluation. The *Splendor of Truth* "will set you free" (Jn 8:32) and, therefore, he encourages all people of good will to follow the path that will lead to eternal life. Already this brief explanation shows clearly that the Pope inserts morality into the bigger picture, which necessarily has to include eternal life.

In contrast to modern science, the Church considers the human person in all his different dimensions and it becomes more and more evident that reductionism does tremendous harm to mankind.

---

30 Cf. Paul VI, HV, 17.
31 Ralph McInerny has shown that the strong opposition faced by the encyclical letter *Humanae Vitae* originated above all in the clergy. This is all the more astonishing as the clergy are supposedly not affected by the use of artificial contraception. Cf. Ralph M. McInerny, *What Went Wrong with Vatican II? The Catholic Crisis Explained* (Manchester: Sophia Institute Press, 1998), 108–9.

Pope Benedict XVI highlighted this in his encyclical letter *Caritas in Veritate*, when he stated:

> The new forms of slavery to drugs and the lack of hope into which so many people fall can be explained not only in sociological and psychological terms but also in essentially spiritual terms. The emptiness in which the soul feels abandoned, despite the availability of countless therapies for body and psyche, leads to suffering. *There cannot be an holistic development and universal common good unless people's spiritual and moral welfare is taken into account*, considered in their totality as body and soul.[32]

The other important encyclical letter regarding general principles for an ethical and moral evaluation is *Evangelium Vitae*, issued by Pope John Paul II on March 25, 1995. John Paul II was an advocate of life. He promoted a vision strongly inspired by and based on the Gospel, but also shaped by his own experience. In his youth he had experienced the dramatic consequences caused by godless ideologies. Therefore, he wrote this encyclical letter, directed to the bishops, priests, men and women religious, lay faithful, and all people of good will on the "Value and Inviolability of Human Life." Already in the introduction, he mentioned that believers in Christ must especially defend and promote the right to life:

> aware as they are of the wonderful truth recalled by the Second Vatican Council: "By his incarnation the Son of God has united himself in some fashion with every human being." This saving event reveals to humanity not only the boundless love of God who "so loved the world that he gave his only Son" (Jn 3:16), but also the incomparable value of every human person.[33]

The encyclical was the result of an Extraordinary Consistory of Cardinals that met in 1991 to address the problems and threats to human life. The Cardinals asked the Holy Father to reaffirm with authority the value of human life and its inviolability. This was necessary, since already in 1991 the dignity and the value of human life were under attack. This is a surprising fact since in

---

32 Benedict XVI, CV, 76.
33 John Paul II, EV, 2.

Introduction

1990 the communist dictatorships had already collapsed. Nevertheless, there were, and continue to be, new threats. The letter was meant to reaffirm the value of human life. As the Pope stated, each faithful has to defend and promote life, "from conception to natural death."[34] This is part of the mission entrusted to each Catholic, and this view should be ensured by laws and institutions of the state. *Evangelium Vitae*, the Gospel of Life, is not just another document, it points towards the essentials of Christian belief; life and eternal life. John Paul II affirms:

> In Jesus, the "Word of life," God's eternal life is thus proclaimed and given. Thanks to this proclamation and gift, our physical and spiritual life, also in its earthly phase, acquires its full value and meaning, for God's eternal life is in fact the end to which our living in this world is directed and called. In this way the Gospel of life includes everything that human experience and reason tell us about the value of human life, accepting it, purifying it, exalting it and bringing it to fulfillment.[35]

This has to be the central point for all bioethical issues: they are related to life and somehow to eternal life. Whoever is opposed to life, will also be opposed to eternal life. This is reflected in a discourse that Pope John Paul II gave in Denver at his arrival ceremony before the World Youth Day in 1993:

> The culture of life means respect for nature and protection of God's work of creation. In a special way it means respect for human life from the first moment of conception until its natural end. [...] The *culture of life* means thanking God every day for his gift of life, for our worth and dignity as human beings, and for the friendship and fellowship he offers us as we make our pilgrim way towards our eternal destiny.[36]

It is one of the most important tasks of the Magisterium of the Church to form the consciences of the faithful, offering a

---

34 Ibid., 93.
35 Ibid., 30.
36 John Paul II, Address at the International Airport of Denver, 15.8.1993, in w2.vatican.va/content/john-paul-ii/en/speeches/1993/august/documents/hf_jp-ii_spe_19930815_congedo-denver-gmg.html [15.1.2022], 2.

vision that goes beyond the realm of the material, as the pastoral constitution *Gaudium et Spes* affirms: "Hence the focal point of our total presentation will be man himself, whole and entire, body and soul, heart and conscience, mind and will."[37] To achieve this goal the Magisterium has published several documents, which are supposed to offer objective criteria. Besides the documents quoted above, the *Catechism of the Catholic Church* has to be mentioned as a general and precise guideline, as well as two instructions regarding bioethical issues. The instruction *Donum Vitae* from 1987,[38] which is about respect for human life from its origins and on the dignity of procreation, and the instruction *Dignitas Personae* from 2008, which is a continuation and an update of *Donum Vitae*. This instruction on "Certain Bioethical Questions"[39] reaffirms once again that "the dignity of a person must be recognized in every human being from conception to natural death."[40] These very helpful and well-done documents issued by the CDF are not well known, sometimes not even by priests and bishops. Throughout this book, however, they will serve as reference points.

---

[37] GS, 3.
[38] CDF, DV.
[39] CDF, DP.
[40] Ibid., 1.

II
Culture of Death

GENERAL INTRODUCTION TO THE CONCEPT "CULTURE OF DEATH"

Problems concerning life are also influenced by the dominating culture. It is therefore important to know the surrounding reality, which will make it easier to provide answers. Each culture takes a certain stand regarding the issues of life: some cultures are inclined to life, others to death. According to Pope John Paul II, the dominating culture is strongly inclined to "death" and sometimes even opposed to life.[1] This often becomes clear when decisions regarding the beginning and end of life have to be made. Before examining these tendencies, it is worth saying a few things regarding the concept of "culture" as such.

The term "culture" derives from the Latin verb *colere*, "to cultivate." In antiquity, the use of this term was extended to those behaviors that imposed a "care towards the gods." The word "cult" is related to the verb *colere* and has to do with culture. A culture implies a certain knowledge of the gods and includes a religious dimension, to which the ethical principles and different behaviors are somehow related.

Today it has become very difficult to define a culture. The multicultural and multi-religious aspects seem to be of such great importance that any type of definition becomes difficult. There is a tendency to extend the "democratic principle" from politics to culture. As people are considered equal, their cultures must also be equal. Since a "cultural imperialism" needs to be avoided there is a tendency to accept any culture without discernment. According to this false premise, which excludes the distinction between "good" and "evil," "right" and "wrong," any culture is considered similar, even though some cultures might be—referring to their moral and scientific standards—hundreds of years behind. Christopher Dawson affirms that historical relativism "is not limited to the material and political aspects of culture; it

---

[1] John Paul II, EV, 12.

extends even more explicitly to its spiritual traditions."[2]

At the same time, in a globalized world there is no homogeneous culture anymore and everything is somehow mingled with different customs and beliefs. This makes a definition very difficult, especially in times in which relativism has become the dominating philosophical current. Currently culture, therefore, refers above all to social behavior and certain norms found or recognized in society. In any case, there is less and less agreement about these norms and behaviors. Juan Gabriel Ascencio offers a description of culture with which he tries to approach a definition. The following explanation will rely partially on his description, which is going to be modified in some ways. In any case, they can be helpful to come to an approximation of what a culture is. Ascencio compares culture to a flower. The flower has a peduncle, a petal, and—if it is still alive—it has roots.[3] Through this image three dimensions of a culture can be described and analyzed.

Starting with the roots: they reveal the theological or religious foundations. Each culture—unless it is a superficial and dying culture—has to find a deeper meaning to life. For that reason, a culture has to consider questions about the meaning of life and about eternal life. All great cultures tried to offer answers to these questions, either from a religious point of view or from a philosophical point of view. The roots of a flower are important; without them the flower will die. A flower in a vase looks great even when the roots are cut off, but only for a short time. After a short while, it will be thrown away because it has died. The same will happen to each culture cut off from its roots. From this point of view, it might be interesting to note that the dictatorships of the last century excluded God and created immediately a culture of death, spreading death. Therefore, it is important to consider the roots of a culture. When a culture is no longer capable of offering answers to questions such as the meaning of life, then it

---

[2] Gerald J. Russello (ed.), *Christianity and European Culture: Selections from the Work of Christopher Dawson* (Washington D. C.: Catholic University of America Press, 1998), 87.

[3] Cf. Juan Gabriel Ascencio, *Il pensiero culturale: Tra filosofia metafisica e razionalità postmoderna* (Rome: Casa Editrice Ateneo Pontificio Regina Apostolorum, 2004), 18ff.

will perish.⁴ As a result, each government has the responsibility to enforce these roots because they provide vital strength and real inspiration for a culture, they keep a culture alive. Today it seems that many cultures are deprived of their roots and that is one of the reasons why parts of society fall apart or simply disintegrate.

A second dimension to consider is the stem/peduncle, which is intrinsically linked to the roots. Considering a culture, the peduncle can be compared to ethical principles. The vital energy is transported through them. All members of a culture do have certain ethical principles, which are expressed, for example, in the Ten Commandments. The stronger the ethical foundation is, the more the petals will flourish. Whenever considering a culture it will be significant to take a look at the ethical principles: how are they expressed, how are they grounded, how are they known, how are they applied in society, and how are they expressed in laws. Strong roots will provide a strong peduncle, and weak roots a weak peduncle. There is a close relationship between them.

Finally, a flower has flower petals. They usually express the beauty of a flower and are the most visible part. Relating this image to the concept of "culture," they could be considered as their expression in a concrete way: they contain behaviors, laws, customs, and any type of practical realization, in which the social life takes place. They are related among themselves according to different sectors, such as family, education, friendship, economy, rights, arts, business, etc. Some elements are continuously present, such as family and economy, meanwhile, others are just occasional, such as feasts, etc.

Whenever the roots are cut off or replaced, the outcome will be different, and the flower petals will change. For example: The Basic Law for the Federal Republic of Germany begins with the following preamble: "Conscious of their responsibility before God and man."⁵ These words have lost their meaning and most politicians of the German parliament, the so-called Bundestag, today refuse any reference to God. In consequence, the ethical

---

4 A good overview is offered by Donald de Marco and Benjamin D. Wiker, *Architects of the Culture of Death* (San Francisco: Ignatius Press, 2004).
5 Deutscher Bundestag, *Basic Law for the Federal Republic of Germany*, last amended 28.3.2019, trans. Christian Tomushat et al., in www.btg-bestellservice.de/pdf/80201000.pdf [15.1.2022], 13.

principles necessarily change and therefore their expression and practical application as well. This will affect not only decisions regarding the beginning and the end of life, but any ethical evaluation as well.

Within every culture there are material elements and also spiritual elements; both are important and related. The material elements are, for example: production, technological progress, everything which is artificial, and it includes also raw materials and cultural achievements. Nevertheless, these things are always related to spiritual elements. The spiritual elements are more important than the material because they determine the use of the material elements and their application in each culture. They find their expression in values, norms, and customs. In other words, the use of material elements, the progress of new technology and technique reflects certain values or—in the worst case—anti-values. At this point, it usually becomes evident whether a culture of death or a culture of life is favored. One example might make it clear. The BBC published an ethics guide in 2014 in favor of abortion. The arguments are:

> women have a moral right to decide what to do with their bodies; the right to abortion is vital for gender equality; the right to abortion is vital for individual women to achieve their full potential; banning abortion puts women at risk by forcing them to use illegal abortionists; the right to abortion should be part of a portfolio of pregnancy rights that enables women to make a truly free choice whether to end a pregnancy.[6]

These arguments reflect a spiritual attitude that is echoed in the material application, in this case abortion. In this circumstance, the spiritual attitude is not only hostile to life, but it denies also the value of human life for some. A similar attitude was reflected in the dictatorships of the last century. For example, the national socialists declared certain ethnic or political groups unworthy of living. In other words, there are always spiritual and material elements in each culture, the spiritual pave the way. Hence it is crucial to consider first of all the roots of a culture, then its

---

6   BBC, *Ethics Guide: Arguments in Favor of Abortion*, 2014, in www.bbc.co.uk/ethics/abortion/mother/for_1.shtml [15.1.2022].

stem/peduncle, and finally its flower (petals). A mere sociological consideration, focusing on the petals, is in any case insufficient.

The so-called "culture of death" presupposes that the roots are poisoned or even cut off. The German philosopher Josef Pieper made an interesting observation. He wrote already in 1968 that in our language when referring to the death and dying of human beings we focus on the simple fact of the end of physical life, and he calls affirmations based on this reductionary view "remarkably meaningless."[7] He concludes:

> We may hazard at least this: our thinking runs afoul of the human experience embodied in living speech, afoul of reality itself, as soon as we leave out a single one of the following aspects: that death and dying mean both end and transition, both terror and liberation, both something violent and something maturing from within, something happening to us but also something we ourselves perform, something natural and occurring by nature but at the same time something that runs counter to all natural volition.[8]

Whenever considering a culture and its stand regarding life issues, it will be essential to remember these three elements, because only in this way can reductionary views be avoided and justice be done to the dignity of man.

SOME ASPECTS REGARDING A CULTURE OF DEATH

Throughout history, there were many "cultures of death." It might be enough to remember the reign of communism in the Soviet Union. The first concentration camps were founded right after the Bolshevist revolution and they were called Gulags. They were legally established by a decree. The internment system grew fast, reaching a population of more than 100,000 people already in the 1920s.[9] The Nazis went to the Soviet Union in order to learn how to build and run them. After the defeat of Germany in 1945, several German concentration camps continued to be used

---

7 Josef Pieper, *Death and Immortality*, trans. Richard and Clara Winston (South Bend, IN: St. Augustine's Press, 2000), 15.
8 Ibid., 21.
9 Cf. Nicolas Werth, *Cannibal Island: Death in a Siberian Gulag*, trans. Steven Rendall (Princeton, NJ: Princeton University Press, 2007).

by the Soviets, including more than ten in the Soviet Occupation Zone of post-war Germany. The former Nazi concentration camps were transformed into Gulags. According to estimates, more than 65,000 people were murdered there after the war, from 1945 to 1950. Most of the victims died of starvation, some had been beaten to death.[10] These darkest sides in human history correspond perfectly to a culture of death, which always existed—due to its roots—but which started to spread with new rigor and strength especially during the last century. The ideology of the communist dictatorship was based on Marxist-Leninist atheism. Marx had denied the existence of God and man deprived of God is a truncated man. Marxist atheism was at the root of the Soviet Union with its anti-religious posture. The vacuum left after eliminating "God" in a materialist understanding of the human person reduces man to different modes of production. Religion was considered an "opium of the people," the abolition of religion was a logical consequence.[11]

Marxist atheism promoted not only the abolition of religion but was considered at that time to be "scientific." The impression was created that religion had finally been substituted by scientific knowledge. The well-known definition from Immanuel Kant, enlightenment is "man's emergence from his self-incurred immaturity,"[12] was applied according to an ideological perspective, and in order to justify the rupture with the cultural roots. Accordingly, the communists called their new roots "scientific atheism," which substituted not only religion, but in consequence introduced a new vision of man, new ethical principles, and new behavior. Scientific atheism tried to explain the origin of religion and everything else according to the criteria of science, using the evolution hypothesis and other theories to justify their decision.

It is important to mention this since certain aspects repeat themselves again and again in history. It seems that today many people have a limitless faith in science, which in the German

---

10   Stephen Kinzer, "Germans Find Mass Graves at an Ex-Soviet Camp," *New York Times* 24.9.1992, in www.nytimes.com/1992/09/24/world/germans-find-mass-graves-at-an-ex-soviet-camp.html [15.1.2022].
11   Cf. de Marco and Wiker, *Architects of the Culture of Death*, 121–34.
12   Hans S. Reiss (ed.), *Kant: Political Writings*, trans. H. B. Nisbet, 2nd ed. (Cambridge: Cambridge University Press, 1991), 54.

language is expressed in one word: *Wissenschaftsgläubigkeit*. It refers to a new type of "faith," no longer based on divine revelation, but instead on the results or hypotheses presented by science. In any case, science is not capable of answering the most important questions about life, nor is science capable of offering ethical principles by itself. Whenever this is intended, one would invert reality. It would be expected that the flower petals provide ethical principles and even the religious foundation. Whenever these attempts were undertaken, they failed. The results were devastating. According to Norman Davies, it is unlikely that under the tyrant Joseph Stalin the number of people murdered is below 50 million.[13]

In this context, we did not mention the concentration camps run by the national socialists with devastating results, nor the massacres in China in 1950–1951 and so many others. It becomes clear that a culture of death does not defend the dignity of all men, nor does it respect life from the beginning until natural death, but it promotes death. It is surprising that most of these incredible crimes—committed in the last century—are already forgotten or not known at all, even though millions of people suffered a great deal, their lives were destroyed, and their dignity trampled underfoot. Nevertheless, it is not enough to consider only the dictatorships of the past; we must learn from history. There are certain elements of Western society that are promoting a culture of death once again. This time, though, it is not done under the premise of scientific progress, but under the premises of freedom, equality, and quality of life.

In parts of Western society, there are two competing worldviews, which becomes more evident considering the situation in the United States. "America is divided between those who believe in a sanctity-of-life ethic and those who proclaim a quality-of-life ethic."[14] Thomas Glessner describes this division as follows:

> Under the first ethic, all human life has value regardless of physical condition, condition of dependency, color of skin, or physical handicap because all humans are made in the image of God. Under the second ethic, human

---

13   Cf. Norman Davies, *Europe: A History* (London: Oxford University Press, 1996), 964.
14   Thomas A. Glessner, *The Emerging Brave New World* (Crane, MO: Anomalos, 2008), 1.

beings are valued only to the extent that they experience a certain level of quality of life and are productive to the rest of society.[15]

Simplifying a more complex situation, it can be said that the ethical approach, which makes reference to the sanctity of life, is necessarily linked to the origin of sanctity: God. The quality of life approach is contrarily man-centered, it makes the human person—according to his own quality—become the reference point of all ethical evaluations.[16] This might include even the killing of the unborn or ending one's own life. Referring once again to the three dimensions of culture, it becomes more evident what is at stake. Sanctity is related to the roots, which nourish the culture. Quality of life is nothing else than *one* flower petal. Whenever it becomes the only reference point for ethical decisions it must necessarily lead to a reductive view of man with all its consequences. This can be seen clearly if one considers the practice of abortion, or to be more precise, induced abortions. In contrast to spontaneous abortion, also known as a miscarriage, the so-called induced abortion is caused purposefully. Birth control, proposed by powerful governments, for example, China and organizations such as Planned Parenthood, causes each year around 56 million abortions in the world.[17] These estimations do not include the pill or intrauterine devices, which can also provoke abortion. Not all abortions are registered, such as the so-called "unsafe abortions." This concept refers to abortions performed by unskilled people or with insufficiently sanitary facilities or equipment. According to existing statistics they cause about 47,000 deaths each year.[18] In 2008, 40% of women in the world had access to legal abortion without limit.[19] Institutions

---

15 Ibid.
16 The difficulties regarding this new approach are presented in James J. Walter and Thomas A. Shannon (eds.), *Quality of Life: The New Medical Dilemma* (Mahwah, NJ: Paulist Press, 1990).
17 Cf. Gilda Sedgh et al., "Abortion incidence between 1990 and 2014: global, regional, and subregional levels and trends," in *The Lancet* 338 (2016): 258–67.
18 Cf. World Health Organization, *Information Sheet. Unsafe abortion incidence and mortality. Global and regional levels in 2008 and trends during 1990–2008* (Geneva: World Health Organization, 2012), 1–8, here 2.
19 Cf. Kelly R. Culwell et al., "Critical gaps in universal access to reproductive health: Contraception and prevention of unsafe abortion," in *International*

such as the World Health Organization promote and recommend "safe and legal" abortions for all women.

It is not the topic of this book to talk about abortion, but it must be said that science has clearly proved that an embryo is a human person at the beginning of life.[20] In any case, the embryo is a human person and must be treated as such. It is striking to know that according to official statistics around 56 million are killed every year by means of abortion. The rights of the women—their quality of life—is placed over the right to life of the unborn. Even worse, their right to live is denied.

Whenever such a reductive vision of man is applied and combined with the new methods of bioethics, for example, the preimplantation genetic diagnosis (PGD), the consequences are dramatic. The unborn are selected according to certain qualities or preferences. A eugenic mentality is spreading fast.[21] A similar process can be observed at the end of life. Whenever the "quality of life" becomes the new criterion—even though it is no ethical criterion at all—life is submitted to arbitrary criteria.[22]

These few examples describe that a culture of death is rising again, a culture whose roots are either dead or do not even exist anymore. What the former German federal judge Ernst-Wolfgang Böckenförde had stated in the 1970s becomes true: the secular state lives from preconditions that it is no longer able to guarantee by itself.[23] Whenever humans decide over others according to subjective and arbitrary criteria, life will be at risk. Some might receive the right to live, while others might be doomed to die. Since these considerations are of great relevance regarding bioethical challenges at the end of life, it is worth considering this problem at its roots.

Journal of Gynecology & Obstetrics 110 (2010): 13-16.
20   See Juan de Dios Vial Correa and Elio Sgreccia (eds.), *The Identity and Status of the Human Embryo. Proceedings of Third Assembly of the Pontifical Academy for Life*, 2nd ed. (Vatican City: Libreria Editrice Vaticana, 1999). See also Weimann, *BSG*, 78-85.
21   To this topic, see ibid.
22   See the study by Wesley J. Smith, *Culture of Death: The Assault on Medical Ethics in America* (San Francisco: Encounter Books, 2000), 33-80.
23   Cf. Ernst-Wolfgang Böckenförde, *Staat, Gesellschaft, Freiheit* (Berlin: Suhrkamp Taschenbuch Verlag, 1976), 60.

A NEW PROTOTYPE

At this point, it is necessary to understand the basic problem of an age that can be described as "post-modernist," and which has a profound impact on bioethical decisions. The encyclical *Laudato Si'* mentions twice the word "postmodernism." It says: "Amid this confusion, postmodern humanity has not yet achieved a new self-awareness capable of offering guidance and direction, and this lack of identity is a source of anxiety. We have too many means and only a few insubstantial ends."[24] The Pope talks about confusion, which characterizes the postmodern world because of its lack of identity. In #162 of the same encyclical letter, the Pope states:

> Our difficulty in taking up this challenge [the responsibility regarding the lifestyle] seriously has much to do with an ethical and cultural decline which has accompanied the deterioration of the environment. Men and women of our postmodern world run the risk of rampant individualism, and many problems of society are connected with today's self-centered culture of instant gratification.[25]

Loss of identity and—as a consequence—ethical and cultural decline are the main characteristics of postmodernism, accompanied by a mentality dominated by egoism and consumerism. The postmodern person has lost his roots and is therefore constantly afraid of almost everything. Faith transmits hope, security, and future; meanwhile, self-centeredness leads to a constant fear of losing parts of the quality of life. This "post-modern mentality" dominates bioethical decisions and discussions.

Already in 1952, the philosopher and theologian Romano Guardini outlined this process, which is now picking up speed. Guardini was one of the most outstanding figures in Catholic intellectual life in the 20th century. The analysis provided by Romano Guardini is somehow prophetic because of the precision of his thought. He published an article, written in German, about the "acceptance of oneself," a beautiful masterpiece. In his analysis of the development of modern times he said:

> In modern times something peculiar becomes evident, which must affect everyone who is capable of seeing the

---

24 Francis, LS, 203.
25 Ibid., 162.

essentials. Man—more correctly, many people; those who set the tone regarding the spiritual dimension—are turning away from God. They declare themselves autonomous, that means, able and authorized to give themselves the law of their lives. [...] This attitude is ever more decisively used to make the human person absolute."[26]

Guardini wrote his analysis only a few years after the end of the Second World War. He added: "The original sin was that man did not want to be just an image anymore, but to be himself the archetype; knowing and being as powerful as God. Thus, he fell from his relationship with God. The bridge just led into emptiness."[27] Christopher Dawson describes this process, and he states that the modern man—who owes his capacities to the Christian heritage—"does not identify the great central tradition of human civilization with Christian civilization or even with the tradition of Christendom."[28]

The roots were cut off and this fact creates a vacuum that will be replaced with something else. This attitude of modern man radically changes everything. The Second Vatican Council warned about this in *Gaudium et Spes* #36, affirming: "For without the Creator the creature would disappear."[29] The original sin of modern times consisted in substituting the Creator with the creature, and therefore with often arbitrary criteria. If the roots are cut off, the plant may be sustained artificially for a certain period, but it will

---

26 In German: "In der Neuzeit zeigt sich etwas Eigentümliches, das Jeden betroffen machen muss, der fähig ist, Wesentliches zu sehen. Der Mensch—richtiger gesagt, viele Menschen; jene, die geistig Maß und Ton bestimmen—lösen sich von Gott ab. Sie erklären sich für autonom, das heißt für fähig und befugt, sich selbst das Gesetz ihres Lebens zu geben. [...] Diese Haltung geht immer entschiedener darauf zu, den Menschen absolut zu setzen." Romano Guardini, *Die Annahme seiner selbst. Den Menschen erkennt nur, wer von Gott weiß* (Kevelaer: C. H. Beck Verlag, 2010), 53. For a more detailed analysis, see Ralph Weimann, "Das Jahr des Glaubens zur Überwindung der Glaubenskrise: Der Glaube verdunstet in den Seelen," in *Die Neue Ordnung* 66 (2012): 417-28.

27 "Die Ursünde bestand darin, dass der Mensch nicht mehr Ebenbild sein wollte, sondern selbst Urbild; wissend und mächtig wie Gott. Damit fiel er aus der Beziehung zu Gott heraus. Die Brücke ging ins Leere." R. Guardini, *Die Annahme seiner selbst*, 54.

28 Russello (ed.), *Christianity and European Culture*, 89.

29 GS, 36.

not stay alive. The emphasis put on the concept "quality of life" corresponds to what Guardini had foreseen already in the 50s, man himself wants to be the archetype.

When man becomes the measure of everything, society will become inhuman. The *homo faber* arises, the self-made person, the constructed man. The human person is no longer considered to be a likeness of God, which implied his intrinsic dignity, independent of his functions, qualities, race, or social status. The self-made person does not recognize and accept anymore this innate dignity, because it is submitted to the criteria of the feasible. At the same time governments, science, and society need to find new criteria, in order to assure the most basic ethical principles. Since a clear reference point is missing, due to the abandonment of a metaphysic and intrinsic dimension, they proceed according to arbitrary principles. A "self-constructing mentality" inspired by relativism is increasing, and this mentality produces a problematic vision of man. Whenever a new archetype is created, everything will depend on it. A new starting point will automatically lead to a new concept of man.

As shown above, a culture depends on its roots and has to do with a religious foundation. If the roots are substituted by others—in this case even by a new archetype—it will have a great impact on all the other elements of the culture. Today, political and social leaders present new definitions of what man is. This is a compelling consequence of changing the roots. They replace God and as a consequence, a metaphysical foundation, necessary to justify the intrinsic value of man, is lost. Therefore, the intrinsic value of man cannot be guaranteed anymore, and this affects especially the handicapped, the unborn, the suffering, and the elderly. Often, the new principles are based on ideologies, on economic premises, or simply on convenience. This mentality is widespread; the created order, as well as the creator, are rejected and a new reality is created.

Therefore, everything depends upon the starting point. If the starting point is able to guarantee intrinsic values directed towards the ultimate good, the culture will be valuable and, therefore, it will be a culture of life. If the starting point is not able to guarantee the intrinsic dignity of *all* men, it will turn into a culture of death. Then any ethical orientation will be difficult and arbitrary.

Today, it seems that the Marxist axiom, according to which it is necessary to change the world, is widely accepted. This form of thinking is based on a reductionistic view, which is gaining more and more influence today. Most scientists do not reflect any more on the foundations of ethical issues and values, they simply look on a practical level for solutions. Technological progress is widely accepted and promoted, but not the ethical criteria necessary to control the advance of technology. Sometimes it is even a taboo to address the difficulties of an ever-bigger gap between technical possibilities and ethical orientation. The Marxist axiom is growing stronger.

This new way of thinking does not spare bioethics. Most specialists are somehow forced to submit to these new criteria. According to Romano Guardini, the spirit had sold itself to technology, and it became a means in order to fulfill the purpose of technology.[30] The *homo faber* has become reality; according to which man himself is submitted to this process and reduced to an object. The progress of science and technology makes it possible. However, technology without ethics becomes blind. It is comparable to driving a fast car without a steering wheel. Whenever technology becomes autonomous, separated from its roots, and does not recognize any criteria but its own, there will be no place left for ethics.

It must be underlined that any ethical approach, proposing an ethics of life, would fail when the basic paradigm of modernity is accepted. The roots of the current culture must be put to the test; only then may a real analysis start. Unfortunately, this wasn't always respected due to the dominant relativism. The encyclical *Laudato Si'* states:

> A misguided anthropocentrism leads to a misguided lifestyle. In the Apostolic Exhortation *Evangelii Gaudium*, I noted that the practical relativism typical of our age is "even more dangerous than doctrinal relativism." When human beings place themselves at the center, they give absolute priority to immediate convenience and all else becomes relative. Hence we should not be surprised to find, in conjunction with the omnipresent technocratic paradigm and the cult of unlimited human power, the rise

---

30 Cf. Romano Guardini, *Die religiöse Offenheit der Gegenwart* (Ostfildern: Matthias-Grünewald/Schöningh, 2008), 40; 43.

of a relativism which sees everything as irrelevant unless it serves one's own immediate interests.[31]

The paradigm of an almost unlimited technological advance has achieved a breakthrough without moral limits. This might lead to a total dominion of technology. Whoever raises his voice to address the dangerous consequences is labeled as "medieval," "backward orientated," or even as "anti-scientific." However, any type of stereotypical thinking is against reason, because it would be a limitation of reason. That is why Pope Benedict XVI promoted an enlargement of reason, an opening up of horizons extending beyond the sphere of technology and positivistic science.[32] A culture has to have solid roots and ethical principles because they will guarantee real and responsible progress. If reason would limit itself to the standards of technology then there would be growing discrimination against those who think and articulate themselves in a different way.

The German philosopher Robert Spaemann († 2018) pointed out that the "preciousness of human life is not primarily a function of some *quality of life* but first and foremost the preciousness of life itself. Thus it is a perversion if allowing a human being to live or not is made dependent upon certain states, especially upon the state of being without pain."[33] The limitation of a merely "science-based ethics" consists in reducing human life to certain functions, which science can observe and—to a certain degree—change or improve. Nevertheless, human life has to be considered within a broader perspective. This has to be kept in mind for most of the bioethical discussions taking place today. They often presuppose a reduction of the human person to certain functions and to the quality of life.

THE CULTURE OF DEATH

The previous general considerations are helpful to understand what it means to talk about a "culture of death." The term first entered common usage after Pope John Paul II had mentioned it several times in the 1995 encyclical letter *Evangelium Vitae*. Even

---

[31] Francis, LS, 122.
[32] Benedict XVI, DCE, 28.
[33] Robert Spaemann, "On the anthropology of the Encyclical *Evangelium Vitae*," in Correa and Sgreccia, *Evangelium Vitae: Five Years of Confrontation*. Proceedings of the Sixth Assembly of the Pontifical Academy for Life (Vatican City: Libreria Editrice Vaticana, 2001), 437-51, here 442.

though the term is somewhat new, the reality already existed long before. The culture of death describes a secular culture opposed to life and to God. John Paul II says in #12 of the encyclical:

> In fact, while the climate of widespread moral uncertainty can in some way be explained by the multiplicity and gravity of today's social problems, and these can sometimes mitigate the subjective responsibility of individuals, it is no less true that we are confronted by an even larger reality, which can be described as a veritable structure of sin. This reality is characterized by the emergence of a culture which denies solidarity and in many cases takes the form of a veritable "culture of death." This culture is actively fostered by powerful cultural, economic and political currents which encourage an idea of society excessively concerned with efficiency.[34]

It is important to consider that the Pope relates a culture of death to a veritable structure of sin. Sin is a religious category and refers to the category "root." In order to understand this affirmation, it is necessary to recall what sin is. According to the *Catechism of the Catholic Church*, "Sin is an offense against reason, truth, and right conscience; it is a failure in genuine love for God and neighbor caused by a perverse attachment to certain goods. It wounds the nature of man and injures human solidarity. It has been defined as 'an utterance, a deed, or a desire contrary to the eternal law.'"[35] In other words, sin is opposed to God and to his commandments. Whenever a culture accepts and even promotes sin, it cuts off its own roots because it is in opposition to God. The consequences will be reflected in each of the "flower petals," which means in its values and in their practical application. What is at stake are not just some changes in the practical application or behavior of a culture, but the loss of intrinsic values innate to man, who is created in the image of God.

Therefore, the culture of death is a culture opposed to God, since only God is life and the giver of life. Pope John Paul II called this a real tragedy of modern man. Those who allow themselves to be influenced by this climate easily fall into a sad vicious circle: when

---

34 John Paul II, EV, 12.
35 CCC, 1849.

the sense of God is lost, there is also a tendency to lose the sense of man, of his dignity and his life; in turn, the systematic violation of the moral law, especially in the serious matter of respect for human life and its dignity, produces a kind of progressive darkening of the capacity to discern God's living and saving presence.[36] Whenever the sense of God is lost, man is no longer seen as a creature, and he is not capable of recognizing that every man has innate rights anymore. Wolfgang Waldstein refers to the natural law, addressing this problem. Whenever the humility is lost to consider the human person as a creature, it will become difficult to affirm that there are innate rights, with an unchangeable objective validity. "This capability has in general been lost progressively by the development of scientific positivism, relativism and scientism." He concludes that one "of the lethal effects of this loss is exactly the *culture of death*."[37] If the human person is enclosed in the narrow horizon of positivistic science, he is reduced to being a "thing." Then human life is no longer considered a gift of God and as something "sacred," but merely as a "thing." It is therefore subjected to arbitrary principles and manipulation. This changes the understanding and dealing with the beginning and the end of life.

Within this context, the human body is no longer considered a "temple of the Holy Spirit" (cf. 1 Cor 3:16) and the only goal to achieve is the well-being and an ever higher "quality of life." According to such a perspective suffering becomes a burden to human existence. It is rejected as useless and considered an evil, which must be avoided in every way. This is one of the main reasons euthanasia is considered more and more acceptable today. Pope John Paul II wrote in his encyclical letter *Evangelium Vitae*: "When it cannot be avoided and the prospect of even some future well-being vanishes, then life appears to have lost all meaning and the temptation grows in man to claim the right to suppress it."[38]

A materialistic positivistic view of the human person reduces man and promotes a mentality in which life is considered only according to immanent principles. It is reduced to certain functions,

---

36 John Paul II, EV, 21.
37 Wolfgang Waldstein, "Natural Law and the Defence of Life in *Evangelium Vitae*," in Correa and Sgreccia, *Evangelium Vitae: Five Years of Confrontation*, 223-42, here 230.
38 John Paul II, EV, 23.

to well-being and life quality, and everything else is submitted to the criteria of pleasure and efficiency. This is true not only for the beginning and end of life but also one's sexuality can be depersonalized and exploited. Love becomes irrelevant and in consequence, people feel abandoned and alone. It is quite striking that the U. K. appointed a minister for loneliness in January 2018, which is—according to the former British Prime Minister Theresa May—the sad reality of modern life. In 2017:

> a British commission found that nearly nine million people in the country either often, or always, feel loneliness—a condition that can have harmful health repercussions. [...] Physicians have long warned that social isolation is a growing epidemic that can have physical, mental and emotional consequences. It's been associated with higher risk of heart disease, diabetes, cancer and more, according to researchers. "It's proven to be worse for health than smoking 15 cigarettes a day," Mark Robinson, head of Age UK, Britain's largest non-profit working with older people, told the *Times*. According to the government's research, about 200,000 elderly people in the country have not had a conversation with a friend or a relative in over a month.[39]

This is all part of a culture of death, a culture that has cut itself off from its roots and which has lost its orientation. Even though television and the internet provide much information and entertainment, people are lonely and they feel abandoned. A materialistic perspective is not sufficient for an ethical evaluation since it does not do justice to the human person. The human person is from his constitution a man in relation, open to the supernatural; he needs God to find fulfillment and salvation.

The rise of a culture of death is very problematic and is linked to certain "structures of sin," as Pope John Paul II called it. Sin obscures and weakens the intelligence;[40] the concept of subjectivity is carried to an extreme. As a result, the moral conscience

---

39 Laignee Barron, "British People Are So Lonely That They Now Have a Minister for Loneliness," *Time*, 18.1.2018, in time.com/5107252/minister-for-loneliness-uk [15.1.2022].
40 Cf. GS, 15. See also John Paul II, FR, 82.

becomes autonomous and in the end leaves no place for solidarity, but leads to a distortion of life in society.[41] Such a mentality is often promoted by the media, based on materialistic-positivistic considerations. The culture of death becomes increasingly acceptable. In this context, it might be sufficient to mention just one example related to the social media *Facebook*, which claims to be neutral regarding ethical standards and decisions. In January 2018, *Facebook* blocked access to a crowd-funding site, hindering efforts to finance the production of a movie that aimed to tell the real story of *Roe v Wade*, through which abortion was widely legalized in the US. *Facebook* even blocked the promotion of the movie in 2019.[42] The movie's producers were looking for sponsors in order to make the true story known to the people. They wanted to show how many lies were told, how the main actors according to their own testimony were betrayed, how the media lied, and how the courts were manipulated in order to permit abortion. Since the law was passed, over 60 million unborn Americans have been killed.

SPIRITUAL COMBAT AGAINST THE CULTURE OF DEATH

The culture of death is spreading tremendously and gravely affects bioethical decisions. Whenever someone talks about the beginning or the end of life the result will depend on the underlying culture. A culture of death is grounded on foundational structures of sin. At this point, it becomes obvious that bioethical issues always have a spiritual dimension, which should not be neglected. Rightly understood, they imply a fight against sin. Pope John Paul II was aware of this dimension and he did not simply condemn a culture of death, but he encouraged all Catholics and people of good will to join in spiritual combat and to rediscover the spiritual dimension to life. He wrote:

> The words and deeds of Jesus and those of his Church are not meant only for those who are sick or suffering or in some way neglected by society. On a deeper level

---

41 Cf. William E. May, *Catholic Bioethics and the Gift of Human Life*, 3rd ed. (Huntington, IN: Our Sunday Visitor, 2013), 20–22.
42 Cf. Doug Mainwaring, "Facebook blocks ad for pro-life movie telling the true story about *Roe v Wade*," LifeSiteNews, 14.1.2019, in www.lifesitenews.com/news/facebook-blocks-ad-for-pro-life-movie-telling-the-true-story-about-roe-v-wa [15.1.2022].

they affect the very meaning of every person's life in its moral and spiritual dimensions. Only those who recognize that their life is marked by the evil of sin can discover in an encounter with Jesus the Savior the truth and the authenticity of their own existence.[43]

John Paul II used to call the prevalent culture a "culture of death"; Pope Francis calls it a "use and throw away" culture.[44] It seems that there is a tremendous battle going on between life and death, between God and the devil. On January 18th, 2018, Cardinal Timothy Dolan spoke about this issue during the "March for Life" in Washington, D.C. He mentioned the "powers of darkness" and the importance of being prepared for spiritual combat. He said: "The forces we face are not just those we can see, [which] are ominous enough. I'm afraid we battle, as well, an axis we cannot see, whose powers are stronger than any in creation, save one: our Lord and Savior Jesus Christ, who called himself 'the Way, the Truth, and the Life.'"[45] This aspect has to be taken into consideration while approaching bioethics. Death, for example, as we are going to see later on, also has a spiritual dimension. God is a God of life; meanwhile, the devil is "a murderer from the beginning and does not abide in the truth, because there is no truth in him. When he tells a lie, he speaks in character, because he is a liar and the father of lies" (Jn 8:44). This quotation helps to understand the spiritual dimension of the end of life, which everyone has to face and which can be reflected on all levels of bioethical issues at the same time. Within this battle, as John Paul II mentioned, our Lady has a special role.

> Mary is a living word of comfort for the Church in her struggle against death. Showing us the Son, the Church assures us that in him the forces of death have already been defeated: "Death with life contended: combat strangely ended! Life's own Champion, slain, yet lives to reign." The Lamb who was slain is alive, bearing the marks of

---

43 John Paul II, EV, 32.
44 Cf. Francis, LS, 123.
45 See Pete Baklinski, "Only prayer will defeat 'power of darkness' called abortion: Card. Dolan at March for Life vigil," *LifeSiteNews*, 18.1.2018, in www.lifesitenews.com/news/only-prayer-will-defeat-power-of-darkness-called-abortion-card.-dolan-at-ma [15.1.2022].

his Passion in the splendor of the Resurrection. He alone is master of all the events of history: he opens its "seals" (cf. Rev 5:110) and proclaims, in time and beyond, the power of life over death.[46]

To conclude this chapter it has to be reaffirmed that life includes a spiritual dimension, and life and death are linked to spiritual combat. Bioethics is supposed to offer guidelines, which should indicate the way to a life that is rooted in God and reflected in the vision of man, who is created in the image and likeness of God. Whenever the human person recognizes himself as creature, he will recognize the innate dignity that must always and in every circumstance be respected.

---

46 John Paul II, EV, 105.

III
Anthropological Foundation

THE ANTHROPOLOGICAL PROBLEM

After the introduction and considering the culture of death, which strongly affects the issues related to the end of life, one might have expected to begin by directly addressing the bioethical problems. However, this chapter is going to address the anthropological foundations and ethical principles, since all bioethical issues have to do with anthropology. The correct understanding of man is the basis for any reasonable ethical argumentation and evaluation. It will be important to see the big picture, to understand the broader context within an always more specialized world. It is, therefore, necessary to know who and what man is in order to be able to decide how to treat man at the end of his life.

The concept of man is *the* central aspect for all types of ethics and it belongs to the philosophical discipline anthropology. At the same time, it is intrinsically linked to questions that aim toward transcendence, since the human person cannot be limited to his functions, nor reduced to his material-physical dimension. Bioethics as an interdisciplinary subject includes various dimensions and they have to provide a reliable concept of man. This aspect is of fundamental importance and should always be present considering the end of life and all debates related to this topic. To be ignorant on this level or to hold a reductionist vision of man would automatically lead to serious consequences.

There is a tendency to delegate these questions to the so-called "specialists," who have to provide ethical evaluations based on a certain concept of man. However, this would be dangerous, since it would signify bowing to expert opinions. Everyone has the responsibility and duty to form his own conscience. William Kilpatrick comments on the Emperor's New Clothes, a famous story written by Hans Christian Anderson. It is a story about a total self-delusion of an emperor. According to the opinion of his counselors, he was wearing the most beautiful robes, but in reality, he was naked. In a public presentation, he was wearing his new clothes. Finally, a little boy exclaimed that the Emperor was naked. Something similar could happen when everything is simply delegated to experts. Kilpatrick connects this fact to psychological fashions, but his comment can easily be applied to bioethics:

> It has to do with vanity, and conformity, and foolishness in high places as well; but mainly it's about the folly of letting common sense take a back seat to expert knowledge. If you recall, the ploy used by the swindlers was to claim that the beautiful clothes could only be seen by those who were fit for the offices they held or who were very clever. They could not be seen by anyone who was unfit for the office he held or who was very stupid. Who can blame the Emperor and his court for being duped? Most of us would much rather be thought very bad than very stupid. The Emperor, despite his vanity, is really a bit unsure of his judgment; so he sends his faithful Minister to check on the progress of the weavers. The Minister, despite his position, is likewise unsure of himself. And so on down the line. Each one thinks, "I can't see anything in this, but who am I to say?" Moreover, by the time the contagion reaches the public, the new enlightened view of clothes-making has the added authority of state endorsement.[1]

This danger is very real regarding bioethical challenges, especially if common sense takes a back seat. This happens whenever the anthropological foundations are neglected. In other words, even the most complex bioethical issues and problems have ultimately to do with an anthropological foundation, and thus should not be delegated only to experts. One example might be enough to illustrate what was said so far.

The Italian law regarding the end of life was changed in December 2017, right before Christmas. The Italian Senate has approved a legislation that allows people to choose what medical intervention they wish to receive or refuse to receive at the end of their lives. The so-called "informed consent" receives a new quality, including

---

1 William Kilpatrick, *The Emperor's New Clothes: Psychological Fashions and Religious Faith*, 2nd ed. (Ridgefield, CT: Roger A. McCaffrey Publishing, 1998), 1–2.

that people can decide, once they can no longer eat or drink by themselves, whether or not to be fed and hydrated artificially. This could be understood as meaning "assisted suicide," and according to the new legislation this practice does not violate the right to life. 180 Senators voted in favor, 71 did not approve the proposal, and there were six abstentions. Politicians claimed that this new law would be more humane respecting the dignity of man.[2]

Without any doubt, it is a big change in the juridical situation regarding the end of life in Italy. It implies that no medical treatment can be continued or started without the patient's informed consent and the doctors will have to respect their "biological testament" (*biotestamento*), the so-called "living will." The former Italian Prime minister Paolo Gentiloni (2016–2018) wrote on Twitter that the Senate has cleared the way for a civilized choice to respect the dignity of the person.[3] He referred to the dignity of the person; meanwhile, the new legislation offers an option to end life. This type of argumentation is quite common today, and for that reason, it is important to observe what "clothes" politicians, doctors, and even a great part of society propose to wear. Often they do not even provide explanations. In this case, for example, they do not show how human dignity will be protected and preserved in the future. Often they rely simply on the opinions of some experts who, under a certain pressure by the mass media, recommend to do what pleases the public opinion. Nevertheless, in any case, the question about the anthropological foundation must be raised in order to guarantee the dignity of the person. It seems that everybody assumes they know what dignity means, even if what is at stake gets lost. Sometimes, while referring to the dignity of man, this very dignity is trampled on or even violated. In the case of the shift in the Italian legislation, assisted suicide is justified while referring to the dignity of the person and is even celebrated as an important step towards a more "civilized society."

---

2 Cf. Caterina Pasolini, "Biotestamento: da oggi i desideri dei malati sono legge," *La Repubblica*, 31.1.2018, in www.repubblica.it/cronaca/2018/01/31/news/bioestamento_da_oggi_i_desideri_dei_malati_sono_legge-187697062/ [15.1.2022].
3 Cf. Elena De Stabile, "Il biotestamento è legge dello Stato: via libera definitivo al Senato con 180 sì," *La Repubblica*, 14.12.2017, in www.repubblica.it/politica/2017/12/14/news/biotestamento_ok_definitivo_al_senato-184086928/ [15.1.2022].

This example shows that everything depends on the concept of man. What will happen to people in a society where the exercises of certain functions or certain qualities of life become the new criteria for ethics? Is man only the sum of his cells? Should man be defined according to a functional or materialistic concept? Is man autonomous? Does a deeper meaning to suffering and illness exist? Do the sick or disabled have an intrinsic right to live, do they even have an intrinsic dignity? These considerations are of great importance in order to understand the ethical problems related to the end of life and they are all related to the concept of man. Therefore, the most basic question is: Who is man? If this question is neglected, then the basics are overlooked and most people will welcome the new clothes, even though they might lead towards a culture of death.

LOOKING FOR A REFERENCE POINT

There are numerous different anthropological models and approaches,[4] but which of them can serve as a reference point, as a valid approach? An answer to this question becomes easier by considering briefly the recent development in this regard.

After the collapse of the Soviet Union and the German reunification, people dreamed that there would be peace and prosperity. The danger of a possible third world war was overcome. In any case, science continued to develop as before. Ethical restrictions, which were important for the whole society, were not enforced. Well-being and the quality of life were becoming the measures for "ethical evaluations." The German chancellor Helmut Kohl (1982–1998) mentioned on several occasions the importance of a spiritual-moral turn,[5] necessary for Germany and Europe in order to grow together, but even though he proposed it, he and his party weren't able to realize it.

Ethical principles and values cannot proceed from well-being or economic prosperity. These principles—which are intrinsically linked to a culture's roots—were more and more neglected; an abyss was created between what is technically possible and what is ethically

---

4 The following work, consisting of two volumes, describes different ethical models: Annemarie Pieper (ed.), *Geschichte der neueren Ethik* (Tübingen: A. Francke Verlag, 1992).

5 Cf. Helmut Kohl, *Erinnerungen 1990–1994* (München: Droemer Verlag, 2007), 658–64.

Anthropological Foundation

acceptable. Science becomes progressively independent from ethics and is usually guided by the paradigm of feasibility. Romano Guardini had already foreseen in the 50s that a process had started, which he related to the creation of a new prototype and which goes hand in hand with the abandoning the Christian heritage.[6]

Joseph Weiler, a South-Africa-born legal scholar, son of a Latvian rabbi and one of the leading experts on European constitutional law, has shown that today many academics neglect the Christian heritage. Europe especially is becoming increasingly post-Christian and therefore their values, based on the Christian heritage, are beginning to disappear. Weiler published the best-selling book *A Christian Europe*,[7] pleading for the European Union to embrace its Christian heritage. He said in an interview with John L. Allen:

> When they [Christians] go into the public space, they've internalized the secular sentiment that religion is a private affair. That's much more important than whether or not to have the cross in the classroom. To be clear, I'm against militancy. I'm not asking Christians to march in the streets. I always cite Micah's famous reference to "walk humbly with your God." My message is, "Walk humbly, but don't hide him."[8]

Instead of promoting and reinforcing Christian values, which are intrinsically linked to the Christian faith, there was and is an increasing secularization.[9] Even political parties who bear in their name the word "Christian" have lost their most basic Christian foundations, which affects also the concept of man and includes man's intrinsic dignity and value. A new form of nominalism is

---

6 Cf. Romano Guardini, *The End of the Modern World*, trans. Joseph Theman and Herbert Burke (Wilmington, DE: ISI Books, 2001), 95-113. See also chapter II.

7 For now only published in Italian and in German: see Joseph Weiler, *Ein christliches Europa: Erkundungsgänge* (Salzburg-München: Anton Pustet Verlag, 2004).

8 John L. Allen, "Tackling taboos on Jews and Christians, the cross and deicide," *National Catholic Reporter*, 21.1.2011, in www.ncronline.org/blogs/all-things-catholic/tackling-taboos-jews-and-christians-cross-and-deicide [15.1.2022].

9 Cf. Martin Rhonheimer, *Christentum und säkularer Staat: Geschichte-Gegenwart-Zukunft* (Freiburg im Breisgau: Herder, 2012).

spreading. There is still a reference to freedom, solidarity, and justice as basic pillars of society, but these concepts have lost their (Christian) meaning. They are subjected to the changing opinions of the majority. The power of relativism and pluralism have taken their place and submitted these important values to the influence of subjectivism and change. This is the reason why Europe is engaging in one of the biggest challenges in its history, because whenever the roots are cut off then the ethical principles will change as well.

The Basic Law of the Federal Republic of Germany, for example, was written from the point of view of a Christian concept of man; it defines human dignity as sacrosanct/inviolable. This was due to the experience of the Second World War and to the fathers of the Constitution. The founders of post-war Europe were Catholics, practicing Catholics.[10] They wanted to avoid that something similar could reoccur and they thus realized that they would need to firmly anchor the dignity of man in the Constitution. In consequence, they wrote in the preamble of the German Basic Law: "Conscious of their responsibility before God and man, inspired by the determination to promote world peace as an equal partner in a united Europe, the German people, in the exercise of their constituent power, have adopted this Basic Law."[11] The fathers of the German Basic Law considered human dignity as sacrosanct (Art. 1) and therefore as a perpetuity clause, a fundamental right of every human being, as well as freedom (Art. 2), the equality of all people (Art. 3), the freedom of religion (Art. 4), and the freedom of expression (Art. 5); marriage and family got the special protection of the state (Art. 6) and the care and upbringing of children was declared a natural right of the parents (Art. 6§2).

In a secularized society there is no longer an awareness of responsibility before God. How can politicians, scientists, and researchers be responsible before man, if they are not responsible before God? How can crucial concepts such as "human dignity" be defined and guaranteed, if the majority becomes the only criterion for an ethical evaluation? The national-socialists, like the communists, based their legislation—to a certain point—on the

---

10   Cf. Mary Anne Perkins, *Christendom and European Identity: The Legacy of a Grand Narrative since 1789* (Berlin: Walter de Gruyter, 2004), 72–76.
11   Cf. Deutscher Bundestag, *Basic Law*, 13.

majority, manipulated and controlled through the mass media. They were atheistic systems, which excluded the reference to God. As a consequence, they redefined the "dignity of man" according to arbitrary principles, corresponding to their ideologies. Now the new "ethics" depended on the position of the political party with devastating consequences.

The fundamental question is: How to define man, and how can his inviolable dignity be guaranteed? Is it unworthy for a human being to be conceived in a test tube? Does it correspond to man's dignity, when an old or sick person commits suicide, because he doesn't want to be a burden to anyone? Who and which ethical system can guarantee that the concept of the "dignity of the human person" does not become empty chatter? In order to answer this question, a choice has to be made in favor of an approach, which is able to explain who the human person is. The problem consists in the fact that politicians and scientists are not willing or able to give an answer, even though this is *the* central question for any ethical evaluation. This is due to different reasons, one being the fact that relativism has become the new "state philosophy."

However, *the* human person needs to be defined and a clear anthropological vision is necessary, even though there may be a minority that would feel disadvantaged or even discriminated against. The broken relationship of Western society with its own history and identity is one of the consequences of the Second World War. People were traumatized by the violence and barbarism, and sometime after the war, they started to look for something new, something totally different even, in contraposition towards their own history. This is a strange fact, even though the war was a consequence of having cut off the Christian roots and of having replaced God by ideologies.[12] Joseph Weiler concludes that Europe denies its own heritage and identity, calling this a worrying process with devastating consequences. The *telos* was lost, that is the identity and orientation of Europe, together with the foundational principles.[13] Sometimes this process even turns into self-hatred towards their heritage. Crosses are removed under the claim of tolerance; a reference to Christianity is refused in the preamble of

---

12 Cf. Alexandre del Valle, *Il complesso occidentale: Piccolo trattato di de colpevolizzazione* (Isola del Liri: Paesi Edizioni, 2019).
13 Cf. Weiler, *Ein christliches Europa*, 18-19.

the European Constitution, etc. The situation is a paradox. On one side the progress of technology increases continuously and makes it necessary to take decisions concerning human dignity. On the other side, there is no clarity on how to justify and guarantee this, since the Christian heritage is neglected and abandoned.

Within this confusing situation, different anthropological models and approaches arose. It is not the purpose of this book to explain them. However, a fundamental option in favor of a certain anthropological and ethical approach has to be taken. Joseph Weiler suggests using the encyclical letter *Redemptoris Missio* written by John Paul II as a starting point to provide an ethical orientation[14] since this papal document develops basic concepts such as truth, diversity, and tolerance.[15] Indeed, the subsequent explanations will rely also on some of the ethical principles offered by Karol Wojtyła / John Paul II and they will serve as a reference point. The reasons for this choice are the following. First, Karol Wojtyła was a professor of ethics, presenting a solid concept of man.[16] Throughout his whole life, he was an advocate for the dignity of man based on a Christian understanding of man. Secondly, after he was elected as a successor of St. Peter he developed in his catechesis the so-called "Theology of the Body,"[17] which is meant to renew moral theology by offering ethical principles and reference points. John Paul II also issued significant magisterial documents, which are part of the authentic Magisterium of the Church. If understood correctly they can become an important tool to recover the richness of the Christian heritage.

---

14 John Paul II, Encyclical Letter *Redemptoris Missio*, 7.12.1990, in www.vatican.va/content/john-paul-ii/en/encyclicals/documents/hf_jp-ii_enc_07121990_redemptoris-missio.html [15.1.2022].

15 Cf. Weiler, *Ein christliches Europa*, 95-113.

16 Karol Wojtyła, *The Acting Person*, trans. by Andrzej Potocki, in *Analecta Husserliana. The Yearbook of Phenomenological Research*, vol. X (Dordrecht et al.: D. Reidel Publishing Company, 1969). Another important work concerning the human person: Karol Wojtyła, *Metafisica della Persona: Tutte le opera filosofiche e saggi integrativi*, Giovanni Reale and Tadeusz Styczeń (eds.) (Milano: Bompiani, 2003). As a secondary literature, see also Pontificia Universitas a Sancto Thoma Aquinate in Urbe, "Studia in Honorem Caroli Wojtyla," *Angelicum* 56 (1979), fasc. 2-3.

17 John Paul II, *Man and Woman He Created Them: A Theology of the Body*, trans. Michael Waldstein (Boston: Pauline Books & Media, 2006).

In his encyclical letter *Evangelium Vitae*, he offers some guidelines describing the concept "dignity of the person":

> The Second Vatican Council, in a passage which retains all its relevance today, forcefully condemned a number of crimes and attacks against human life. Thirty years later, taking up the words of the Council and with the same forcefulness I repeat that condemnation in the name of the whole Church, certain that I am interpreting the genuine sentiment of every upright conscience: "Whatever is opposed to life itself, such as any type of murder, genocide, abortion, euthanasia, or willful self-destruction, whatever violates the integrity of the human person, such as mutilation, torments inflicted on body or mind, attempts to coerce the will itself; whatever insults human dignity, such as subhuman living conditions, arbitrary imprisonment, deportation, slavery, prostitution, the selling of women and children; as well as disgraceful working conditions, where people are treated as mere instruments of gain rather than as free and responsible persons; all these things and others like them are infamies indeed. They poison human society, and they do more harm to those who practice them than to those who suffer from the injury. Moreover, they are a supreme dishonor to the Creator."[18]

Since all bioethical decisions have to do with the concept of man, the question needs to be raised; which concept of man is relevant for our society and for an ethical discernment? Are there any reference points; is there any irrefutable norm or foundation? This is where the real problem of bioethics begins.

SOME BASIC CONSIDERATIONS REGARDING THE CONCEPT OF MAN

Considering the human person will always include a twofold approach, which accentuates an objective and subjective dimension. Both together provide a balanced view of man.[19] The person is a whole and must be seen in its concrete totality. For that reason,

---

18 John Paul II, EV, 3, citing GS, 27.
19 Cf. Avery Dulles, "John Paul II and the Mystery of the Human Person," *America* 190 (2004): 414-29.

the metaphysical dimension is important, "which addresses the human being in his entity. The ontological approach to the person seeks a substantial and not merely functional definition of him, although it does not underestimate the *signa personae*, all those elements or indications that can signal the presence thereof."[20] Bioethics is at the service of man and thus presupposes that one knows who the human person is. Some basic points will be taken into consideration and they justify further reasoning. They provide the foundations for any further discussion of bioethical issues.

Some Basic Distinctions

There is a fundamental difference between things and persons. Things, such as a car or a bicycle, are objects, while humans are personal subjects. This difference is important, not just on a linguistic level, but on a metaphysical level. The question "what is man?" would be inadequate; one needs to ask rightly "who is man?" For man is not an object, like any other thing, which is produced, rather man is unique. This is affirmed in Psalm 8, which states: "Yet you have made him little less than a god, crowned him with glory and honor" (Ps 8:5). The book of Genesis provides one of the most profound descriptions of man, which is related to his creation: "God created man in his image; in the divine image he created him; male and female he created them" (Gen 1:27). Scripture affirms that man is created by God, he is not manufactured, nor the result of an accidental development, but willed and loved by God. He himself generates, meanwhile his spiritual form (soul) is directly created by God. Pope John Paul II explains: "God himself is present in human fatherhood and motherhood quite differently than he is present in all other instances of begetting on earth. Indeed, God alone is the source of that image and likeness which is proper to the human being, as it was received at Creation. Begetting is the continuation of Creation."[21] Even though this is a beautiful description of man, which shaped Western society and the concept "dignity of man,"

---

20 Sgreccia, PB, 136.
21 John Paul II, EV, 43. An explanation of the human person as *imago dei* with helpful distinctions regarding natural and supernatural dimensions of this crucial concept is presented by Romanus Cessario, *Introduction to Moral Theology* (Washington, D. C.: Catholic University of America Press, 2001), 22–38.

it is not anymore recognized in a secularized society. This definition is part of the Judeo-Christian Tradition and has lost its significance at least among big parts of the so-called "scientific community." This theological approach does not contradict a more rational approach since "faith and reason are like two wings on which the human spirit rises to the contemplation of truth,"[22] which includes an answer to the question who man is.

From a biological point of view, it must be said that man is a living organism, which—like any organic creature—consists of an organized (formed) matter, composed of atoms and molecules. The organism is part of what can be perceived, it is visible and perceptible and develops within a certain time. An organism can be measured and weighed. The cells and organs can be microscopically analyzed. Like every living organism, it comes to existence and develops from the embryo to the adult; it does so without changing its identity, which is constitutive to man, during its lifetime.[23] Some scientists prefer to create a system of classification, according to which the identity of man is not present from the very beginning of life, but develops. These classifications are not the result of scientific data, but of philosophical preconceptions necessary to justify research and certain (often) immoral conclusions, such as euthanasia, abortion, and—up to a certain degree—also organ transplantation. However, it must be affirmed that a cat is not first a dog and then develops into a cat but is always a cat, even though not fully developed. The same has to be applied to the human person.

Karol Wojtyła / John Paul II approaches the same topic from a different perspective. He understands the human person not as consciousness but life, even though a potentially conscious life. Human beings are not potential persons, but potentially conscious of themselves. As soon as they exist, they are real and "a new human being with his own growth. It would never be made human if it were not human already."[24] The different expressions of life are *a posteriori* to the fact of being. Everything develops according to one's nature and the development is only possible because of

---

22 John Paul II, FR.
23 Cf. Ramón Lucas Lucas, *Antropología y problemas bioéticos* (Madrid: Biblioteca de Autores Cristianos, 2005), 75.
24 John Paul II, EV, 60.

being. Elio Sgreccia affirms: "The person is an *in se existens* (being existing in itself) and a *per se existens* (being existing for itself). [...] The person is set as an end, not a means."[25]

Therefore it is correct to affirm that identity does not change during time and through development, even though there is—without any doubt—physical development and process The human person is a human being from the beginning until natural death. This is a fact proven by science; it is not a religious discovery. Each person has the same identity from the first until the last moment of life.[26] This identity, however, is subjected to the laws of organic matter and is submitted to disease and death. The "material organism" of man is the "human body" and the body is the first comprehensible fact, regarding identity and diversity; man is a "material being."[27]

In this context another distinction has to be made, crucial for any consideration of man. The human person consists of a substantial unity between the spiritual form and the physical body, which constitutes the human identity. This was expressed in the classical Latin axiom *corpore et anima unus*. Both elements form an inseparable unity. This unity is so essential that one element does not exist without the other. The body would not be a human body without the spiritual form, and the spiritual form would not be human without the body.[28] It is thus not a functional unity, but a substantial unity. A computer and electricity are two things that need each other on a functional level. One can exist without the other. Regarding human beings, this is not the case. In the body the spiritual soul is present; it is the principle of life within the body. Robert Spaemann comments that life "is neither pure subjectivity nor is it pure objectivity. It is an inseparable

---

25   Sgreccia, PB, 137.
26   Cf. Weimann, BSG, 78-85.
27   Cf. Ramón Lucas Lucas, *Bioética para todos* (México: Ediciones Trillas, 2003), 14-15.
28   Thomas Aquinas justified the immortality of the soul, separated from the body: "the human soul has the privilege of surviving the dissolution of the body: besides being the substantial form, the soul is the subsisting form because it has an autonomous being, as is evident from the fact that it performs operations independently of the body. These operations can be identified in the consciousness that the soul has of all bodies, in its knowledge of what is universal, and self-consciousness." See Sgreccia, PB, 138.

unity of inside and outside, of interiority and exteriority; it is an inseparable unity of being for itself and being for others."[29] This substantial unity is no type of dualism, but a substantial duality; the soul gives form to the matter and so the body is formed, it is its principle of life. The separation of the soul from the body is rightly called death. Karol Wojtyła calls the soul the "principle of transcendence and integration."[30] He says that the soul can be compared to a boundary in man, "which sets a limit to the scope of the dynamism and thus also of the reach of the body, or of what is also called 'matter'. They also reveal a capacity of a spiritual nature that seems to lie at the root of the person's transcendence, but also indirectly of the integration of the person in the action."[31] These explanations are important since they lead to a twofold affirmation regarding issues related to human life.

a. There is a spiritual principle of transcendence and integration, which is not the brain, nor the heart, nor any other organ. Even from a scientific point of view, this is simple to prove, referring to the development of the human person. At the very beginning of human life neither the brain nor the heart is fully developed, but both develop in an organized way. Therefore, there *must* be a form-giving principle, which John Paul II called *the* principle of integration, which corresponds to the soul.[32]
b. Man cannot be reduced to physical or even psychological processes since he is able to perform acts that transcend the sphere of the physical-material. This aspect indicates an important distinction from any other creature on earth and needs to be explained further.

Spiritual actions realized by man are reflected in the human body—for example, when someone studies, prays, speaks, etc. All this

---

29 Robert Spaemann, "On the anthropology," 444.
30 Wojtyła, *Acting Person*, 257.
31 Ibid., 258.
32 A precise and complete overview regarding this topic is offered by Richard A. Spinello, "Bioethics and the Human Soul. Pope St. John Paul II's Reflections on Ensoulment," in *NCBQ* 18 (2018): 291–316. See also, in general, David Albert Jones, *The Soul of the Embryo: An Enquiry into the Status of the Human Embryo in the Christian Tradition* (London: Continuum Books, 2006).

finds an echo in the body and underlines the substantial unity between spirit (soul) and body. Human knowledge starts with the senses but surpasses them. However, man cannot be reduced to his senses, qualities, or functions. He has the capacity to form abstract, universal, and non-material concepts. Whoever tries to deny this, affirms it at the same time.

One might think that the reading of this book is either quite boring or interesting; it is possible to be distracted and to think even about other things while reading it. One might observe a house and relate it to his own house, or a tree and associate it with a forest. Man has the capacity to form abstract concepts and therefore, he can transform concepts into universal ideas. These ideas are not located in physical space; they are timeless and therefore intellectual. Judgments are formed with abstract concepts, such as: "The book is interesting" or: "The building is beautiful." General laws can be formulated from the perception of reality, such as the law of gravitation. The capacity to form concepts (ideas), the capacity of reasoning, is the precondition for having a language. Man is capable of speaking, which is a typical human characteristic. Even though human language differs from nation to nation, language is formed by words that presuppose a universal recognition by men, proven by any translation. The language also differs from time to time, but principally it is possible that—to mean the same thing—different words are used throughout the ages. The ancient Romans called a house "domus," the Spaniards "casa," the Germans "Haus."[33] Meanwhile, there are words that have several meanings and can be interpreted differently. It must be said that human language is fundamentally different from what is known as the "language" of animals. In contrast to human beings, animals communicate by signs or gestures, but they do not speak. The dog barks, the lion roars, the pig squeals, but always in the same way, in all parts of the world and at all times. Human language differs significantly. In this context, another aspect must be mentioned.

Man has the capacity to love. One can love his friends, his parents, God, brothers, sisters, etc. Love is not a physically measurable dimension, nevertheless, love is real. The ability to love is unlimited. Since it is a spiritual capacity, it would degrade love

---

33   Cf. Lucas, *Bioética para todos*, 16-17.

if it would be reduced to material things, such as "loving" money, cars, etc. The highest form of love can be experienced towards God, who is Spirit, and "those who worship him must worship in Spirit and truth" (Jn 4:24). This spiritual faculty will reach its highest degree of perfection within the realm of Him who is Spirit: God. In this sense, the ability to love is not limited, even though "many who are first will be last, and the last will be first" (Mt 19:30). In a time when the concept of love is trivialized,[34] it is important to take this dimension into consideration, since it reflects an important dimension of man.

One last aspect should be mentioned in this context. Man has the ability to make free decisions, he can decide to do something and omit something else. This capacity is denied by some ethical approaches today, but whoever denies this capacity will affirm it at the same time. In practice, this capacity can only theoretically be denied. For example, one can decide whether he wants a coffee or a cappuccino, whether he reads this or that book, whether he ends his life or not, etc. For that reason, man is responsible for his actions. Free actions have a moral-ethical value; they are "good" or "bad," since man is "capable of truth" and, according to Robert Spaemann, this

> constitutes the dignity of the human person. Only truth liberates man from being trapped in himself, from the inverted centeredness in oneself characteristic of all non-personal living beings. By their actions, human beings are able to do justice to the things as they are; i.e. they are able to transcend themselves. Self-surrender, self-transcendence, and that is to say: love, is the highest form of life. In this, human beings realize themselves as persons.[35]

All these aspects show that man has an ability that is clearly distinct from matter, even different from all other living beings. The capacity for abstraction presupposes a spiritual faculty since it cannot simply be reduced to space-time, or even to matter. This is what John Paul II called the "principle of integration."

---

34 Pope Francis develops the concept of love in marriage quite extensively. Cf. Francis, AL, 89-123.
35 Spaemann, "On the anthropology," 445.

The Church calls this faculty a spiritual soul. The doctrine of the soul was ultimately defined in 1336 by Pope Benedict XII through the papal bull *Benedictus Deus*. In this dogma, the Pope explains the Church's belief regarding the souls of the departed. The souls do not remain in a state of an unconscious existence after death. The Pope declared that the souls of the faithful departed, who are not in need of any purification when they die, enjoy eternal life. Meanwhile the souls of those who die in mortal sin go down into hell immediately (*mox*) after death and suffer the pains of hell.[36] This was and is, the timeless teaching of the Church, confirmed in many other magisterial documents and in the *Catechism of the Catholic Church*.[37] It affirms and concretizes the essence of man's spiritual faculty.

Contrarily to the bodily dimension, the existence of a spiritual soul cannot be "scientifically"—considering science as a positivistic method—demonstrated, because it is a spiritual faculty. At the same time, its existence cannot be denied scientifically, for otherwise, science would not respect its own limits. Each effect has a cause. If a human person is capable of acting in a spiritual-rational way—clearly reflected in the capacity of reasoning, reflection, love, etc.—then it is only because of the existence of a spiritual faculty, which the Church calls soul. Elio Sgreccia therefore concludes, "understanding and will express two faculties of the soul, whereby it is not formally bound up with the body."[38] The phenomenological school is particularly helpful in overcoming an anthropological dualism between soul and body. Edmund Husserl introduced the distinction between *Körper*—understood in a purely material sense—and *Leib*—understood as the living body. The *Leib* participates "in the functions of consciousness and in the relation that a human being has with the world."[39]

The Human Person

Basic considerations and distinctions are helpful for the right understanding of man. However, the concept "person" needs further

---

36 Cf. Benedict XII, Constitution *Benedictus Deus*, 29.1.1336, in DH, 1000–1002.
37 CCC, 366.
38 Sgreccia, PB, 139.
39 Ibid., 141.

clarification. It will be helpful to rely on some already existing definitions as a starting point.

The Roman senator and philosopher Boethius, who composed several books and translated important works of Aristotle, defined man as follows: "Persona est rationalis naturae individua substantia."[40] According to Boethius a human person is an individual ("indivisible") substance of rational nature. For centuries this definition was of great importance and even St. Thomas Aquinas relied on it. Nevertheless, he presented his own, modified definition: "persona significat id quod est perfectissimum in tota natura, scilicet subsistens in rationali natura."[41] Person signifies what is most perfect in all nature, that is, a subsistent individual of a rational nature. Commenting on Thomas Aquinas the German philosopher Robert Spaemann affirms that person is not a genre, but a *nomen dignitatis*, a name of dignity. To call someone a person means to grant him a certain status, namely the status of a self-purpose.[42] These definitions describe quite well some of the most important elements of the concept "person" and will be briefly explained.

The Person is an Individual

The word individual derives from the Latin word *individuum* and signifies "indivisible." A person cannot be divided into two, otherwise, it would die. Individual also means that the person is a moral subject, bearer of rights, responsibilities, and duties. The person has an inner unity in himself but is different from others. Because of this difference every person is irreplaceable, which can be reflected best in the relation between a mother and her child. As an individual, the person differs numerically from others, but also regarding qualities. Each person is unique and unrepeatable. The intrinsic value of the person thus derives from the fact that the person is unique.

Therefore, the person has an intrinsic (Latin *intrinsecus* = "inside" or "internally") value, the person belongs to itself. It exists for

---

40 Boethius, *De persona et duabus naturis*, PL 64:1343. Regarding the development of the concept of the person, see Weimann, BSG, 123-40.
41 Thomas Aquinas, STh, I, q. 29, a. 3.
42 Robert Spaemann, "Wann beginnt der Mensch Person zu sein?," in Spieker, *Biopolitik*, 39-50, here 39.

itself, even if there are certain dependencies, as in the case of a baby, a handicapped person, or a person at the last stage of his life. To be an individual signifies having an indwelling dignity, which does not depend on any function or exercise of a function. This dignity can be trampled on and violated, but no one can ever take it away. In contrast to objects, a human person should not be used since it would always be abuse. It would contradict the intrinsic dignity of the person.

Dictatorships are usually characterized by not respecting, denying or even annulling the intrinsic dignity of *all* men and their rights. In Communism and National Socialism, for example, only the mass, the proletariat, the race, and above all members of the political party were granted a certain dignity, but it was not granted to all individuals. Today there is a radical individualism, which, presumably, is based on the uniqueness of the person. In reality, however, the exact opposite is true. If individualism becomes absolute, it absorbs the individual by promoting a "one-dimensional view," which leads to a new kind of collectivism,[43] which again would limit the most basic rights.[44]

The Person is a Rational Being

The person is a rational being. "Rational" does not mean that the person must be able to exercise this rationality at all times; otherwise, Peter Singer would be right. He promoted the idea that a person who is asleep or unconscious loses his personhood.[45] A "rational being" does not have to carry out rational actions, such as thinking, speaking, etc., at all times. A rational being *is* a rational being, it refers to the very nature. Otherwise many human beings would not be considered persons, such as embryos, babies, anyone asleep, people suffering from Alzheimer's disease, etc. Even if rational actions are not accomplished, that does not

---

43 See Dale O'Leary, *The Gender Agenda: Redefining Equality* (Lafayette: Vital Issues Press, 1997).
44 Cf. John Paul II, EV, 23.
45 Peter Singer wrote: "There are many beings who are sentient and capable of experiencing pleasure and pain, but are not rational and self-conscious and so not persons. I shall refer to these beings as conscious beings. Many non-human animals almost certainly fall into this category; so must newborn infants and some intellectually disabled humans." *Practical Ethics*, 2nd ed. (Cambridge: University Press, 1999), 101.

change the rational nature of man, which even includes certain dependencies and mutual reciprocity, which is the source of many bioethical discussions.

Rationality points to higher qualities of man, including intelligence, love, emotions, moral behavior, religiosity, etc. Therefore, it is not necessary that rationality is *in actu*, it refers to a potential capacity of man. Consequently, a functional understanding of man, widespread today, must be rejected because it does not do justice to the nature of man. Indeed, he would be recognized as a person only if he performs a certain function and therefore, he would be exposed not only to arbitrary criteria regarding the definition of these functions but also regarding his dignity.

The concept of rational nature is therefore significant. A cat, for example, belongs to the species "cat," her nature is that of a cat. This would be the case even if her nature has not yet been fully developed when the cat is not capable of exercising her own "functions" and even after a serious accident. Every human being has a rational nature; whether he exercises it or not is unimportant. "Nature" has to be understood according to an ontological perspective. Karol Wojtyła writes: "The person as such possesses, however, its own ontological structure, though one very different from all the others that surround the human being in the visible world."[46] Part of this ontological structure is his rational nature and for that reason, a person is always a person, not in a state of becoming but being. The status as a person cannot be reduced or increased; it is not gradual but constitutional. Therefore no one is more or less person, a "sub-person" or "subhuman." In other words, either someone is a person with a constitutive rational nature, or is not. There is no intermediate status.

The Significance of the Concept of Man

In the world of science and politics today the concept of person is questioned. Its meaning and importance are unknown to many. Even some philosophers, theologians, and humanists reject this basic concept, meanwhile attempts to substitute it through others have failed.[47] This development creates a dangerous vacuum since

---

46 Wojtyła, *Acting Person*, 74.
47 See the German philosopher Dieter Birnbacher, "Hilft der Personenbegriff bei der Lösung bioethischer Fragestellungen?," in H.-J. Kaatsch and

human rights and the dignity of man rely on this concept. This becomes even more evident, when we consider that many national constitutions and universal declarations use it as a foundational reference point. Nevertheless, if the classical and valid explanation of this concept—achieved by outstanding experts such as Boethius or Thomas Aquinas—is no longer taken into consideration, this concept will lose its meaning. This problematic development—if it is not resolved—will inevitably lead to misunderstandings and false ideas of who man is.

It is indeed possible and necessary to defend the concept of personhood based on reason and enlightened by faith. This is all the more important because there is an ever-greater gap between technology and ethics. Hans Urs von Balthasar summed up the main difficulty when he said, "The power instruments of man to dominate the world overcome man's restraining power and enslave him: from person he is reduced to thing."[48] At this point one of the main difficulties regarding bioethics becomes evident. Without a solid anthropology, an objective ethical foundation will be lost.[49] Therefore, it will be necessary to acknowledge the basic elements regarding the human person, which are difficult to deny by reason, but which can be denied by ideology. The more a reasonable approach to the concept "person"—including openness to transcendence—is withdrawn, the more ideologies will spread. This is shown clearly in the "ideology of gender,"[50] which

---

H. Kreß (eds.), *Ethik interdisziplinär*, vol. 3 (London: LIT Verlag, 2003), 31–43, here 35–37; 43. According to Livio Melina, this is also the result of a general rejection of identity and history: cf. Livio Melina, *The Epiphany of Love: Toward a Theological Understanding of Christian Action* (Cambridge: William B. Eerdmans, 2010), 67ff.

48 Author's translation of Hans Urs von Balthasar, *Romano Guardini, Reform aus dem Ursprung* (Einsiedeln: Johannes Verlag, 1995), 16.

49 Cf. Melina, *The Epiphany of Love*, 67ff.

50 Francis, LS, 56. In a meeting with the Polish bishops, Pope Francis said: "In Europe, America, Latin America, Africa, and in some countries of Asia, there are genuine forms of ideological colonization taking place. And one of these—I will call it clearly by its name—is [the ideology of] 'gender.' Today children—children!—are taught in school that everyone can choose his or her sex. Why are they teaching this? Because the books are provided by the persons and institutions that give you money. These forms of ideological colonization are also supported by influential countries. And this terrible!" Francis, Meeting with the Polish Bishops, 28.7.2016, in w2.vatican.va/content/

leads to a destruction of freedom eliminating the anthropological basis.[51] Instead, it would be necessary to recognize the Christian heritage and its vision of man in the twofold dimension of *fides et ratio*. According to such a perspective, a reference to God would not limit reason but enlarge it, and would reveal and justify the most exalted concept of man, that of being created in the image of God. Romano Guardini affirmed that "I only understand who I am, when I understand who is above me."[52]

ANTHROPOLOGY IN OUR TIME

Nowadays, anthropology has a difficult stand. Even what is evident is questioned or contradicted. However, there is no other way to explain anthropology to people than by accepting reality and by using faith and reason. When an approach through reason is chosen, it must be guaranteed that reason does not remain immanent but is enlarged, as Pope Benedict affirmed on several occasions. In 2012, addressing the Roman Curia, he said:

> The Church represents the memory of what it means to be human in the face of a civilization of forgetfulness, which knows only itself and its own criteria. Yet just as an individual without memory has lost his identity, so too a human race without memory would lose its identity. What the Church has learned from the encounter between revelation and human experience does indeed extend beyond the realm of pure reason, but it is not a separate world that has nothing to say to unbelievers. By entering into the thinking and understanding of mankind, this knowledge broadens the horizon of reason and thus it speaks also to those who are unable to share the faith of the Church. In her dialogue with the state and with society, the Church does not, of course, have ready answers for individual questions. Along with other forces in society, she will wrestle for the answers that best correspond to the truth of the human condition. The values that she recognizes as fundamental and non-negotiable for the human condition

---

francesco/en/speeches/2016/july/documents/papa-francesco_20160727_polonia-vescovi.html [15.1.2022].
51   Cf. Kuby, *Global Sexual Revolution*, 7–14.
52   Cf. Guardini, *Die Annahme seiner selbst*, 30.

she must propose with all clarity. She must do all she can to convince, and this can then stimulate political action.[53]

It is indeed a fundamental problem regarding bioethical issues that many experts focus on individual cases and scientific development; meanwhile, non-negotiable criteria are less and less recognized. This is due to the fact that a metaphysical approach was replaced by self-centered perceptions of man, taking into account above all existential and experiential conditions. In this way, objectivity and non-negotiable foundations are eliminated and the realities of life become the new decisive factor. Anthropology threatens to become immanent and thus loses the ability to promote and defend what is most important: the unconditional and intrinsic dignity of man. The encyclical letter *Laudato Si'* states:

> Modernity has been marked by an excessive anthropocentrism which today, under another guise, continues to stand in the way of shared understanding and of any effort to strengthen social bonds. The time has come to pay renewed attention to reality and the limits it imposes; this in turn is the condition for a more sound and fruitful development of individuals and society. An inadequate presentation of Christian anthropology gave rise to a wrong understanding of the relationship between human beings and the world.[54]

Reason, and therefore also anthropology, is more and more closed in an immanent perspective. There is a strong tendency to make ethical evaluations based on excessive individualism. In these cases the intrinsic dignity of a person cannot be guaranteed, everything becomes negotiable according to arbitrary criteria.

However, the anthropological question is essential for each bioethical debate, because without anthropology no reliable statement can be made about man. Therefore, fundamental and non-negotiable values have to be recognized, a task that can be solved only if the metaphysical dimension of creation is respected. Each person, because of being human, has intrinsic dignity. This approach implies an enlarged reason, which does not reduce the

---

53 Benedict XVI, Christmas Greetings to the Roman Curia, 21.12.2012, in w2.vatican.va/content/benedict-xvi/en/speeches/2012/december/documents/hf_ben-xvi_spe_20121221_auguri-curia.html [15.1.2022]. Francis, LS, 116.
54 Ibid.

human person to a mere material being, but recognizes his spiritual capacity, even though it might not be *in actu*. This is where reason and faith meet; this is where faith enlarges reason revealing the full meaning of the concept "dignity," which is essentially linked to the concept of person. With a new self-confidence—to mention once again Joseph Weiler—Christians need to leave their ghetto mentality, offering orientation based on the common heritage. "The dignity of the human person is rooted in his creation in the image and likeness of God."[55] And for that reason:

> Respect for the human person entails respect for the rights that flow from his dignity as a creature. These rights are prior to society and must be recognized by it. They are the basis of the moral legitimacy of every authority: by flouting them, or refusing to recognize them in its positive legislation, a society undermines its own moral legitimacy. If it does not respect them, authority can rely only on force or violence to obtain obedience from its subjects. It is the Church's role to remind men of good will of these rights and to distinguish them from unwarranted or false claims.[56]

---

[55] CCC, 1700.
[56] Ibid., 1930.

IV
Some Aspects About the End of Life

SOME INTRODUCTORY CONSIDERATIONS

Pope John Paul II spoke of a spreading "culture of death" in his Encyclical *Evangelium Vitae* and he received criticism from many sides for doing this. His vision was considered as "too negative," since it didn't correspond to the idea of a modern society dominated by individualism and autonomy. In 1995, the encyclical letter was discussed in *The New York Times* with the title "The Pope vs. the Culture of Death."[1] John Paul II had great moral authority, and he gave the Church a strong voice in questions regarding ethics. Besides his encyclical letters and his numerous speeches related to this topic, in society and politics there was no fundamental debate or real discussion of this theme. Even though the rise and existence of the culture of death was becoming more evident, it was and still is not commonplace to talk about it. For various reasons, the topic is simply ignored.

If the existence of such a culture would be recognized by politicians and scientists, then they would need to face up to it and they would need to deal with it, being forced to take a clear ethical position. Since relativism is the dominant state philosophy in many countries, politicians mostly avoid clear ethical standards, since this would contradict the dominating culture of relativism promoted by the mass media. As most politicians want to be re-elected they avoid this type of debate. However, this leads to tragic consequences since in some cases even the right to life is denied.

A look at the current developments in society, politics, and science gives new relevance to the papal document *Evangelium Vitae* and reveals its prophetic character. Not only is the beginning of human life increasingly subjected to the premises of a mentality dominated by technique and feasibility, but also the end of life. John Paul II mentioned that the culture of death is actively

---

1 Cf. Paul Baumann, "The Truth has a Voice. The Pope vs. the Culture of Death," *New York Times*, 8.10.1995, in www.nytimes.com/1995/10/08/opinion/the-pope-vs-the-culture-of-death.html [15.1.2022].

promoted by "powerful cultural, economic and political currents which encourage an idea of society excessively concerned with efficiency."[2] The economy is dominated by efficiency and profit; society by autonomy based on an individualistic and excessive conception of freedom.

This creates several contradictions. On the one hand, human rights are in theory solemnly affirmed and personal freedom is exalted. On the other hand, they are denied in practice. This is related to a false idea of freedom that elevates the individual as an "absolute." This is stated in the encyclical letter *Evangelium Vitae*:

> While it is true that the taking of life not yet born or in its final stages is sometimes marked by a mistaken sense of altruism and human compassion, it cannot be denied that such a culture of death, taken as a whole, betrays a completely individualistic concept of freedom, which ends up by becoming the freedom of "the strong" against the weak who have no choice but to submit.[3]

Freedom becomes self-destructive when the fundamental connection between truth and freedom is no longer respected.[4] In a society strongly influenced by relativism, it is problematic to speak of truth, above all of the revealed truth. In some countries, this already falls under the category of what they call "hate-speech." On February 5th, 2017, just to mention one example, a Christian

---

2 John Paul II, EV, 12.
3 Ibid., 19.
4 Pope John Paul II explained the intrinsic connection between freedom and truth in his encyclical letter *Veritatis Splendor*. He writes: "The truth about moral good, as that truth is declared in the law of reason, is practically and concretely recognized by the judgment of conscience, which leads one to take responsibility for the good or the evil one has done. [...] Consequently *in the practical judgment of conscience*, which imposes on the person the obligation to perform a given act, *the link between freedom and truth is made manifest*. Precisely for this reason conscience expresses itself in acts of 'judgment' which reflect the truth about the good, and not in arbitrary 'decisions'. The maturity and responsibility of these judgments—and, when all is said and done, of the individual who is their subject—are not measured by the liberation of the conscience from objective truth, in favor of an alleged autonomy in personal decisions, but, on the contrary, by an insistent search for truth and by allowing oneself to be guided by that truth in one's actions." John Paul II, VS, 61.

evangelist was accused of hate crime in Scotland and locked up in a cell after he told a gay teenager what the Bible says about homosexuality. The *Telegraph* describes this with the following words:

> Gordon Larmour, 42, was charged by police after telling the story of Adam and Eve to a 19-year-old who asked him about God's views on homosexuality. The street preacher referred to the Book of Genesis and stated that God created Adam and Eve to produce children. Within minutes he was frog marched to a police van, accused of threatening or abusive behavior "aggravated by prejudice relating to sexual orientation"—despite not swearing or using any form of offensive language. The father-of-one spent a night in custody and faced a six-month ordeal before a sheriff cleared him of any blame. The incident, which occurred in his home town of Irvine in Ayrshire, has become a rallying point for Christian campaigners who are concerned that freedom of speech is being stifled by political correctness.[5]

Moral relativism is spreading and transforming itself into a dictatorship. Revealed truth related to Christianity is no longer accepted and tolerated in some countries. Pope John Paul II attributed this to a "perverse and evil significance" of human freedom, which consists of "an absolute power over others and against others. This is the death of true freedom."[6] Whenever the view of God is darkened, the moral law will lose its meaning and consequently, freedom is set as the absolute.[7] The same mentality of a falsely understood autonomy affects bioethical challenges at the end of life. The "person ends up by no longer taking as the sole and indisputable point of reference for his own choices the truth about good and evil, but only his subjective and changeable opinion, or, indeed, his selfish interest and whim."[8]

---

[5] "Preacher locked up for hate crime after quoting the Bible to gay teenager," *The Telegraph*, 5.2.2017, in www.telegraph.co.uk/news/2017/02/05/preacher-locked-hate-crime-quoting-bible-gay-teenager/ [15.1.2022].
[6] John Paul II, EV, 20.
[7] This is described in a broader context by Hans Gleixner, *"Wenn Gott nicht existiert...": Zur Beziehung zwischen Religion und Ethik* (Paderborn: Verlag Ferdinand Schöningh, 2005).
[8] John Paul II, EV, 19.

Also for that reason, Saint John Paul II considered the current situation as a dramatic struggle between good and evil, between a "culture of life" and a "culture of death." From a theological point of view it can be said that 'life' is related to the God of life (cf. Ps 139:14), meanwhile the devil is called the father of lies (Jn 8:44). John Paul II was aware of this situation and opposed to the darkness of the evil the splendor of the cross, in which he shared particularly.

The dominant culture is particularly relevant and influential in society. The intrinsic value of the person, as well as the meaning of suffering, has been lost. Old and weak people, the sick and suffering are mostly perceived as a burden in a threefold sense: a) they limit the autonomy of other persons; b) they are a burden to the efficiency of society; c) they perceive themselves as a burden.

DEFINITION OF "EUTHANASIA"

The word euthanasia originates from the Greek εὖ (eús), meaning "good" or "beautiful," and θάνατος (thánatos), meaning "death."[9] The etymological meaning is, therefore, a good/beautiful death, it means to die in a "good way." The understanding of euthanasia has changed over the course of history. The Greeks and Romans had a certain idea of a "good death," but through Christianity, the meaning of death was profoundly changed. Modern times adopted a new understanding of death and of euthanasia, which was soon related to terrible crimes committed during the reign of totalitarianism of the National-Socialist dictatorship.

The Christian vision of death marked a big difference from other concepts. Today, it is often substituted by a secularist understanding, which also changes the meaning of euthanasia. However, the word euthanasia is necessarily related to the meaning of death. Whoever wants to define euthanasia must define death. This becomes evident by taking a look at the historical development, which will be helpful for understanding the present situation.

Antiquity

In antiquity, the term euthanasia was not related to a technical understanding of death, but rather to the manner of one's dying.

---

9 A more detailed description can be found in Udo Benzenhöfer, *Der gute Tod? Euthanasie und Sterbehilfe in Geschichte und Gegenwart* (München: C. H. Beck Verlag, 1999).

It was important to meet death in a balanced state of mind, thus being in peace and with minimal pain. "To ensure such a death, it was permissible to arrange the circumstances surrounding one's death, including measures that would shorten one's life."[10] Even though this was more or less the basic concept, there were significant differences between certain approaches. Plato (428-348/347 BC) argued, for example, that medical treatment should be discontinued if the patient lacked the strength for life. In these cases, the help would be of no use, and it would even do damage to the state.[11] According to his vision, the understanding of euthanasia is ordered to the welfare of the state. Plato was opposed to suicide, but generally sympathetic to euthanasia.

Socrates (circa 470-399 BC) understood euthanasia in the context of a "rational lifestyle," which was to be directed towards a good preparation for death. Infanticide and assisted dying were not considered euthanasia. It was commonly accepted that a physician could end the life of one of his patients if the patient's consent was respected. Socrates was not opposed to such a practice since people feared a painful death and it was already common that physicians administered poison on the patient's request.[12]

The basic norm for ethical evaluations in antiquity was the Hippocratic Oath, even though some authors hold the position that most of the physicians at that time weren't even aware of the oath's existence.[13] However, it dates back to the physician Hippocrates of Kos (circa 460-370 BC). He formulated a medical ethic that has had a major impact on medicine, as well as on the understanding of what can be described as "euthanasia." The following part of the oath is relevant for our consideration: "I will neither give a deadly drug to anybody who asked for it, nor will I make a suggestion to this effect. Similarly, I will not give to a woman an abortive remedy. In purity and holiness, I will guard my life and my art."[14] The oath and its development will be addressed later on.

---

10   Michael Manning, *Euthanasia and Physician-Assisted Suicide: Killing or Caring?* (New York: Paulist Press, 1998), 6.
11   Plato, *Republic*, Book 15, trans. Paul Shorey (Cambridge: Harvard University Press, 1930), 407e.
12   Cf. Manning, *Euthanasia*, 8.
13   Cf. ibid.
14   So quoted in William C. Shiel, "Medical Definition of Hippocratic Oath," in www.medicinenet.com/script/main/art.asp?articlekey=20909 [15.1.2022].

Aristotle (384–323 BC) developed a detailed ethic. His two works of reference are the *Eudemian Ethics* and the *Nicomachean Ethics*. He examines the meaning of euthanasia discussing the problem of suicide. In the *Nicomachean Ethics*, he considers suicide as an act of injustice against the state and oneself. If a physician were to assist a person to kill oneself, he would violate the sanctity of human life. Therefore, Aristotle considered active and passive euthanasia as blameworthy and not justifiable.[15]

The probably best-known definition of euthanasia from Antiquity goes back to the historian Suetonius and referred to the death of Augustus. The Emperor had always desired to have a "good death," which he did indeed have. Suetonius reports: "He was fortunate to have an easy death, as he had always wished. Almost always, when he heard of someone who had been able to die quickly and without suffering, he asked the gods to grant a 'euthanasia' for himself and for his family, that was the word he used to describe an easy death."[16] In this context, euthanasia signifies a pleasant and, if possible, painless death accompanied by family and good friends. It has nothing to do with ending life by artificial means; instead, it was about "dying well." At the time of Augustus different types of eugenic selection and infanticide were practiced, especially in Sparta, but also in Rome. Weak or sick children were sorted out in antiquity for "racial reasons," but the term "euthanasia" was not used for these practices. Euthanasia had a positive connotation.

Seneca, who was considered a Stoic, explained his view of ending one's life in Letter 70 on *Ethics to Lucilius*. As a general guideline, he confirms: "Non enim vivere bonum est, sed bene vivere" (For mere living is not a good, but living well).[17] The wise man will not live as long as he can, but as long as he ought. Dying well means to escape from the danger of living ill. For Seneca autonomy has a special meaning, but an orientated autonomy even though he does not use this word explicitly. He writes to Lucilius: "Reason, too, advises us to die, if we may, according to our taste; if this

---

15 Cf. Aristotle, *Nicomachean Ethics*, trans. David Ross (Oxford: Oxford University Press, 2009), vol. 5, 1138a, 11–15.
16 So quoted in Gaius Suetonius Tranquillus, *Leben der Caesaren (Meisterwerke der Antike)*, trans. and ed. André Lambert (München: Bertelsmann, 1972), 118.
17 Cf. Seneca, *Ad Lucilium Epistulae Morales*, vol. 2, trans. Richard M. Gummere (Cambridge: Harvard University Press, 1962), LXX, 4.

cannot be, she advises us to die according to our ability and to seize upon whatever means shall offer itself for doing violence to ourselves."[18] For him, a good death (*bene mori*) means a "decent dying," which he related to the ancient meaning of euthanasia.

Christian Influence

The understanding of the end of life was given a new direction and a deeper meaning through Christianity. According to the biblical view, only God is the Lord of life. He created man from the dust with an immortal soul (cf. Gen 2:7). The story of Cain and Abel makes clear that man should not end life, as it is supposed to be in God's hands. The fifth commandment expresses this with the words: "You shall not kill" (Ex 20:13). The coming of Jesus Christ revealed the full meaning of this commandment, as the Gospel of St. Matthew says: "But I say to you, love your enemies, and pray for those who persecute you, that you may be children of your heavenly Father, for he makes his sun rise on the bad and the good, and causes rain to fall on the just and the unjust" (Mt 5:44f). Death is the end of earthly life, and—as Sacred Scripture says (cf. Gen 2:17; Rom 5:12)—it entered the world because of sin.

Christianity offers the most profound explanation regarding the end of life since it gives an answer to the meaning of life and therefore to the meaning of death. Jesus Christ is risen from the dead and by dying has conquered death. The resurrection marks the big difference since whoever "believes in the Son has eternal life" (Jn 3:36). Jesus Christ provided a new meaning to life and death. For Christians, death "is the end of man's earthly pilgrimage, of the time of grace and mercy which God offers him so as to work out his earthly life in keeping with the divine plan, and to decide his ultimate destiny. When 'the single course of earthly life' is completed, we shall not return to other earthly lives: 'It is appointed for men to die once.'"[19] Life is therefore not in man's hands, but as a creature, he is dependent on the Creator. St. Paul said that we "hold this treasure in earthen vessels" (2 Cor 4:7). The human person receives life as a gift from God and will have to give it back to God. Therefore, it is not in his hands to decide, since this gift is *gratis data*, it is freely given by God. This affects

---

18   Ibid., LXX, 28.
19   CCC, 1013.

especially the understanding of death, in which man gives his life back into God's hands. God is the Master of life, but the person is responsible for his own life. In other words, life has to be administered like a talent (cf. Mt 18:23-35) since it is a participation in what man has received from God. For that very reason, suicide has always been rejected by the Church, because it contradicts this very condition of life.[20]

The more Christianity prevailed, the more the Christian understanding of death was accepted. Human life was considered a trust from God and the Hippocratic Oath was reinforced. However, the concept of "euthanasia" is not known in Scriptures. On the contrary, the focus is on solidarity with one's neighbor, as the Gospel of St. Mark says: "You shall love your neighbor as yourself" (Mk 12:31). The parable of the good Samaritan elevates charity—after the love of God—to the most important category; God revealed himself as love (cf. 1 John 4:8). In Judaism, the expulsion of lepers was practiced, but in Christianity, this was overcome by charity, as many saints impressively testify. The new ideal was sympathy with the needy and the poor.

The Middle Ages did not know the concept of euthanasia, in this regard they weren't "dark" at all. From the twelfth through the fifteenth century the unanimity of medical opinions was opposed to euthanasia. Instead, the so-called *ars moriendi* was practiced, which included a special accompaniment during the hour of death.[21] The "art of dying" was of great importance and it is widely described in the Christian literature.[22] Manuals explained the meaning of death and what the faithful would have to expect after death. They prescribed certain prayers, above all the sacraments, and other actions that would lead to a "good death" and therefore to salvation. A dying accompanied by the family, by prayer, and strengthened by the anointing of the sick and the *Viaticum* was suggested. It was part

---

20 Cf. ibid., 2280-2283.
21 Saint Robert Bellarmine explained with much detail the *ars moriendi*: cf. "The Art of Dying Well," in John Patrick Donnelly and Roland J. Teske (eds.), *Robert Bellarmine: Spiritual Writings* (New York: Paulist Press, 1989), 231-386.
22 Cf. Franz Falk, *Die deutschen Sterbebüchlein von der ältesten Zeit des Buchdrucks bis zum Jahre 1520: Nachdruck der Ausgabe Köln 1890* (Heidelberg: Tenner, 1969); also Adolph Franz, *Die kirchlichen Benediktionen im Mittelalter*, vol. 2 (Bonn: nova & vetera, 2006), 399-513.

of everyday life to pray that one would be prevented from sudden death in order to enter well prepared into eternal life. This ideal of a "good death" excluded the idea of self-killing or suicide, especially as people were aware of their responsibility, which would have an everlasting impact in Heaven, Hell, or Purgatory.

Saint Thomas Aquinas does not address euthanasia, but suicide, which violates self-love, the love of one's neighbors (society), and God. Thus, he laid the foundation from which the theological and philosophical discussions of the next centuries were decisively influenced, and he succeeded in integrating in his work the explanations provided by Augustine, Aristotle, and the early Christian theologians. In the *Summa Theologiae*, Thomas Aquinas provides an answer to the question, whether it is lawful to kill oneself? He says:

> It is altogether unlawful to kill oneself, for three reasons. First, because everything naturally loves itself, the result being that everything naturally keeps itself in being, and resists corruptions so far as it can. Wherefore suicide is contrary to the inclination of nature, and to charity whereby every man should love himself. Hence suicide is always a mortal sin, as being contrary to the natural law and to charity. Secondly, because every part, as such, belongs to the whole. Now every man is part of the community, and so, as such, he belongs to the community. Hence by killing himself he injures the community, as the Philosopher declares (Ethic. v, 11). Thirdly, because life is God's gift to man, and is subject to His power, who kills and makes to live. Hence whoever takes his own life, sins against God, even as he who kills another's slave, sins against that slave's master, and as he who usurps to himself judgment of a matter not entrusted to him. For it belongs to God alone to pronounce sentence of death and life, according to Deuteronomy 32:39, "I will kill and I will make to live."[23]

The *Ars moriendi* was a preparation for a good death, which was considered a door that leads to eternal life. It included not only a preparation for death but also a way to deal with suffering and pain, as well as with the grief of the dying person and their families. It wasn't limited to medical treatment but it included the whole

---

23   Thomas Aquinas, STh II-II, q. 64, a. 5.

person. These convictions are no longer universally shared. Step by step society has turned again to the pagan concept of euthanasia, providing new meaning to an ancient concept.

Renaissance and Enlightenment

In the Renaissance, the concept of "euthanasia" was reintroduced with a changed understanding. It was first Sir Thomas More who started an early discussion, described in his book *Utopia* in 1516.[24] However, it was due to Sir Francis Bacon (1561-1626), an English philosopher, statesman, scientist, jurist, and author, that this concept had its comeback. He referred this concept to the understanding of Emperor Augustus where it signified a pleasant and painless death, but Bacon added a new dimension based on the progress of medicine. He suggested that medicine should include skills that enable doctors to help patients to die easily; looking to reduce pain and to extend the life-span. Bacon called this dimension a *"Euthanasia exteriori"* (outward euthanasia), which he distinguished from a consoling, calm dying. The latter was a type of mental preparation (*animae praeparatio*), meanwhile, the "outward euthanasia" was related to a physical and agreeable termination of life.[25] This demand was soon accepted by doctors since medicine was able to provide more and more palliative medical care for healing and pain relief.

In the so-called period of Enlightenment, a new understanding of euthanasia as "easy dying" started to prevail. This concept is more than ambiguous since death is never something "easy" to go through. At the root of this new understanding is a new

---

24 Regarding people suffering with fixed and incurable diseases, More suggests the classical *ars moriendi*: "They visit them often and take great pains to make their time pass off easily: but when any is taken with a torturing and lingering pain, so that there is no hope either of recovery or ease, the priests and magistrates come and exhort them, that, since they are now unable to go on with the business of life, are become a burden to themselves and to all about them, and they have really out-lived themselves, they should no longer nourish such a rooted distemper, but choose rather to die since they cannot live but in much misery; being assured that if they thus deliver themselves from torture, or are willing that others should do it, they shall be happy after death." Thomas More, *Utopia* (Los Angeles: Norton, 2017), 62.
25 Cf. Francis Bacon, *The Works of Francis Bacon*, in ten volumes (London: W. Baynes, 1824), 4:223-33.

anthropology that emerged through English empiricism and continental rationalism. This made it possible for David Hume to break away from a metaphysical and religious-based ethics. The criterion of utility came into force and became the highest maxim.[26] From this perspective, it was possible to consider even suicide as an option, whenever it corresponded to the new criteria.

Probably the greatest change regarding the concept of euthanasia was made in the second half of the 19th century. At that time the foundations for today's dominant understanding of euthanasia were developed. This happened due to a changed concept of man and due to the technical progress of medicine. New medical options were available, such as anesthesia and other types of painkillers. In this situation, the understanding of medicine was changed, as well as the self-understanding of doctors, and led to a reorganization and re-weighting of the hospital system. As medical and scientific possibilities increased, technical premises took over; the patient was considered and treated according to this new perspective. And yet, there was still a spiritual and medical accompaniment of dying.

Modernity

Even regarding euthanasia, the influence of Charles Darwin (1809-1882) is not to be underestimated, especially since he introduced the evolutionary theory.[27] This hypothesis, widely accepted even though there is no scientific proof, has had a great impact on the concept of man. If man is a result of chance it would inevitably lead to a different anthropology. The dignity of each human being would no longer be guaranteed, given that man has no inherent dignity since he is only a product of accidental circumstances. This has consequences for the treatment of human beings, especially for the sick and handicapped.

A social Darwinist-inspired understanding of death spread from England and the United States to other parts in the world.[28]

---

26 Cf. Martin Rhonheimer, *Die Perspektive der Moral: Philosophische Grundlagen der Tugendethik* (Berlin: Walter de Gruyter, 2001), 13-18.
27 The Jewish philosopher Jonas describes the consequences of "evolution" as the final triumph of materialism; the conception of being is changed to one of becoming. Cf. Hans Jonas, *The Phenomenon of Life: Toward a Philosophical Biology* (Evanston: Northwestern University Press, 2001), 58.
28 Cf. Neil M. Gorsuch, *The Future of Assisted Suicide and Euthanasia* (Princeton, NJ: Princeton University Press, 2006), 33-36.

Social Darwinism emerged in the second half of the 19th century; it was based on the hypothesis of evolution and the concept of natural selection.[29] These principles were transferred to human society. As early as 1870, the demand for "killing on request" was presented,[30] based on the influential Darwinist ideology. Eugenics were a logical result of social Darwinism. At the same time and due to the progress of medicine, life expectancy extended, which moved some to put the topic of "euthanasia" on the agenda.

The Nobel laureate prize winner and zoologist Ernst Haeckel (1834-1940), who based his research on the principles of social Darwinism, is considered the pioneer of German racial hygiene, even though its founder is Alfred Ploetz (1860-1940). Haeckel recommended the killing of the weak and sick, he recalled the customary infanticide in Sparta as an example of conscious care for the hereditary. This was only appropriate for National Socialism,[31] where it found rigorous application in the T4 program.[32] The central office for that program was in No. 4 Tiergarten Street in Berlin. It designed and coordinated the systematic elimination of the mentally and physically handicapped. This program was carried out from 1940 to 1941 and killed more than 70,000 people.[33] The national socialist ideology no longer required consideration for the sick and the disabled, only the strongest would merit living.

---

29 Cf. the following compilations: Roberto de Mattei (ed.), *Evoluzionismo: il tramonto di una ipotesi* (Siena: Cantagalli, 2009); Albrecht von Brandenstein Zeppelin, Alma von Stockhausen (eds.), *Naturphilosophische Gegenüberstellung von Evolutionstheorie und Schöpfungstheologie—Evolutionstheorie im Lichte heutiger Wissenschaften*, vol. I (Weilheim-Bierbronnen: Gustav-Siewerth-Akademie, 2009); Albrecht von Brandenstein Zeppelin, Alma von Stockhausen (eds.), *Naturphilosophische Gegenüberstellung von Evolutionstheorie und Schöpfungstheologie—„Im Anfang war das Wort": Naturphilosophische Reflexion auf die Schöpfungstheologie*, vol. II (Weilheim-Bierbronnen: Gustav-Siewerth-Akademie, 2009).

30 Cf. W. Bruce Fye, "Active Euthanasia: An Historical Survey on its Conceptional Origins and Introduction into Medical Thought," in *Bulletin of History of Medicine* 52 (1972): 492-503, here 495.

31 The whole process is well described by Richard Weikart, *Hitler's Ethic: The Nazi Pursuit of Evolutionary Progress* (New York: Cambridge University Press, 2009).

32 Cf. Kurt Gerstein and Stephen R. Pastore (eds.), *The Nazi Slaughter of the Disabled: The Euthanasia Program T4* (New York: American Bibliographical Press, 2017).

33 Cf. Ernst Klee (ed.), *Dokumente zur „Euthanasie"* (Frankfurt am Main: Fischer-Taschenbuch-Verlag, 1985), 232.

The Nazi propaganda exploited this for itself and pointed to the costs associated with the care of the disabled. At that time of darkness, man was measured according to his function, his utility, and race. For that reason, even mentally ill war veterans from the First World War were murdered.

It is noteworthy to mention a movie produced for the cinema in 1941, during the Third Reich, by Wolfgang Liebeneiner. The title of the film is: "I accuse" (*Ich klage an*). Today the film is considered a "restricted film." It is a pro-euthanasia propaganda film with a clear objective. The film tells the story of an incurably multiple sclerosis-afflicted beautiful young woman who, at her explicit request, asked to end her life. Her husband is a successful physician. Finally, the woman is killed by him through the administration of an overdose of drugs. Her family doctor had previously rejected her request. The last part of the film is about the court case against the husband for murder, leaving open the decision of the judges, but it is suggested that they may acquit him. The film is about no more and no less than assisted suicide, then called euthanasia. The death assistant is stylized to a hero, it is him who accuses the judges: "I accuse."

It is interesting to focus briefly on the reasons provided in favor of the T4 program, as presented in the film. The most common argument supportive of euthanasia is compassion. The following arguments were added: emphasis on the right to autonomy, the suffering woman requested it explicitly and deliberately; utilitarian reference to the consequences for the common good, the society would need to cover the costs for care; the questioning of the direct-indirect distinction regarding euthanasia, the murder is camouflaged; worse consequences were denied, since—according to this atheistic ideology—there is supposed to be nothing after death.

In the 1930s euthanasia grew popular, not only in Germany. British physicians had already performed euthanasia on patients and the *Euthanasia Society of America* was founded in 1938 in New York. In 1939, the first attempts were made to legalize euthanasia in the United States. The outbreak of World War II and the subsequent discovery of the crimes committed by the national socialists "quelled but did not eliminate the discussion of the euthanasia question."[34]

---

34   Manning, *Euthanasia*, 13.

In the post-war period, the concept of euthanasia was in strong discredit. Pope Pius XII repeatedly commented on the concept of euthanasia and understood euthanasia as an active, deliberate killing of a human being. Already in 1943, during the Second World War, the Pope published his encyclical letter *Mystici Corporis*, in which he stated:

> We deem it necessary to reiterate this grave statement today, when to Our profound grief We see at times the deformed, the insane, and those suffering from hereditary disease deprived of their lives, as though they were a useless burden to Society; and this procedure is hailed by some as a manifestation of human progress, and as something that is entirely in accordance with the common good. Yet who that is possessed of sound judgment does not recognize that this not only violates the natural and the divine law written in the heart of every man, but that it outrages the noblest instincts of humanity? The blood of these unfortunate victims who are all the dearer to our Redeemer because they are deserving of greater pity, "cries to God from the earth."[35]

Only after 1945 was the distinction between "active" and "passive" killing made, which is going to be explained in the next chapter, and for a certain period the discussions regarding euthanasia were stopped in the West. In the Soviet Union and under Stalinism things developed quite differently.

Post-Modernity

In the 1960s there were proposals in the United States for a so-called "living will" and a movement was revived, promoting a "death with dignity." In the 1970s, the Netherlands became the pioneer of euthanasia, followed by the United States in the late 1980s. Certain groups emerged, who campaigned for euthanasia and assisted dying.[36] *The World Federation of Right to Die Societies*,

---

35 Pius XII, Encyclical Letter *Mystici Corporis*, 29.6.1943, in w2.vatican.va/content/pius-xii/en/encyclicals/documents/hf_p-xii_enc_29061943_mystici-corporis-christi.html [15.1.2022], 94.
36 The first Voluntary Euthanasia Society was founded in London, and in 1938 a Euthanasia Society was established in the United States. In 1975, the latter was reactivated and changed its name into "Society for the Right

founded in 1980, became very influential. "Since its founding, the World Federation has come to include (2013) 51 right to die organizations from 28 countries around the world."[37] They promote a co-operation between voluntary euthanasia and the right to die issues. They also provide professional assistance where requested regarding legislation and court judgments. Their mission states that all people:

> 1. have the right to die with dignity, peacefully and without suffering;
> 2. are able to make their own choices about death while taking into account the reasonable interests of others; and
> 3. are able to make their well-considered end of life decisions in a safe and peaceful environment supported by the law.[38]

In order to achieve these goals they propose "activities including civil disobedience in the countries of the member societies."[39] This society claims to promote a "death with dignity" and dignity is related to the "right to die." In their "manifesto" they declare:

> We strongly believe that the manner and time of dying should be left to the decision of the individual, assuming such demands do not result in harm to society other than the sadness associated with death. The voluntarily expressed will of individuals, once they are fully informed of their diagnosis, prognosis and available means of relief, should be respected by all concerned as an expression of intrinsic human rights.[40]

The federation proposes a secular approach, in which God as a supreme reference point is excluded; therefore, the human

---

to Die." These groups gained influence in the English-speaking world and supported euthanasia. Public opinion had slowly changed to favor euthanasia. Cf. May, *Catholic Bioethics*, 235.
37   "The World Federation of Right to Die Societies: Our History," in wfrtds.org/history-of-the-world-federation-of-right-to-die-societies [15.1.2022].
38   "The World Federation of Right to Die Societies: Our Beliefs," in wfrtds.org/beliefs/ [15.1.2022].
39   Ibid.
40   "The World Federation of Right to Die Societies: Manifesto," in www.worldrtd.net/manifesto [15.1.2022].

being takes his place and is set up as absolute. According to this perspective, the individual has become the new "Lord over life," since his dependence on the Creator is ignored. The argumentation is quite similar to what was presented in the 1930s. Institutions such as *Planned Parenthood* are active promoters of a "right to die." They promote a culture of death, and in this way they are successful. According to the *Gallup poll* from May 2018, 72% of Americans support euthanasia.[41] There is much controversy and some resistance, but their agenda finds more and more consent in society. Euthanasia is considered a "pro-choice issue" and a manifestation of "compassion." One example helps us to better understand how these cases are presented:

> On November 1, 2014, twenty-nine-year-old Brittany Maynard ended her life surrounded by close friends and family. Her decision to end her life on her own terms has brought the issue to national attention and galvanized the right-to-die movement (also called "death with dignity") in the United States. Diagnosed last January with brain cancer, Maynard went through surgery only to find out the cancer had progressed to stage four and that she had only months to live. Knowing that the progression of the disease would cause untold pain and suffering to herself and to her loved ones witnessing it, Maynard and her husband made the decision to move to Oregon to take advantage of its Death with Dignity Act. Her controversial decision to end her life with lethal drugs prescribed by her physician, and to speak publicly about it, has catapulted the right-to-die movement into the collective consciousness and could lead to a watershed moment on the issue.[42]

As can be seen in this example, individual cases are brought up as part of their lobby-work in order to promote euthanasia and

---

41 Megan Brenan, "Americans' Strong Support for Euthanasia Persists," *Gallup*, 31.5.2018, in news.gallup.com/poll/235145/americans-strong-support-euthanasia-persists.aspx [15.1.2022].
42 Tone Stockenström, "Is Dying a Pro-Choice Issue? The Right to Die Movement Gains National Attention," *The Humanist*, 22.12.2014, in thehumanist.com/magazine/january-february-2015/features/is-dying-a-pro-choice-issue [15.1.2022].

to change legislation according to a spirit of "compassion" and "autonomy."[43] In contrast to the 12th century, the majority of the physicians today are inclined to favor euthanasia, which has led to changing the Hippocratic Oath. On October 14th, 2017 the *World Medical Association* approved a "modern successor to the Hippocratic Oath" for the first time after almost 2,500 years.[44] This is a drastic shift and it gives, as expected, more weight to the patient's autonomy. The *World Medical Association* wanted to update the existing oath; indeed, they changed it in its essence. The argumentation is quite simple: "The life of physicians today is completely different."[45] The argumentation is common: it is said that the life of physicians today is *completely* different, but what about the value and dignity of the human person? Do they change as well? The new oath will change the way in which people are treated. The new pledge says right at the beginning: "I SOLEMNLY PLEDGE to dedicate my life to the service of humanity; THE HEALTH AND WELL-BEING OF MY PATIENT will be my first consideration; I WILL RESPECT the autonomy and dignity of my patient; I WILL MAINTAIN the utmost respect for human life."[46]

The new oath exalts the autonomy of the person, which the physician must respect. This is a remarkable change; it can signify that the physician will be obliged to apply euthanasia if this corresponds to the autonomy of the person. It could even signify that he needs to procure an abortion if this corresponds to the "autonomy" of the person. Autonomy became the new criteria, an

---

43 The Letter *Samaritanus Bonus* points out that today, there is a false understanding of compassion. "In the face of seemingly 'unbearable' suffering, the termination of a patient's life is justified in the name of 'compassion'. This so-called 'compassionate' euthanasia holds that it is better to die than to suffer, and that it would be compassionate to help a patient to die by means of euthanasia or assisted suicide. In reality, human compassion consists not in causing death, but in embracing the sick, in supporting them in their difficulties, in offering them affection, attention, and the means to alleviate the suffering." CDF, SB, IV.

44 World Medical Association, "Modern Physicians' Pledge Approved by World Medical Association," 14.10.2017, in www.wma.net/news-post/modern-physicians-pledge-approved-by-world-medical-association/ [15.1.2022].

45 Ibid.

46 World Medical Association, "WMA Declaration of Geneva, The Physician's Pledge," 6.11.2017, in www.wma.net/policies-post/wma-declaration-of-geneva/ [15.1.2022].

autonomy based on the ambiguous concept "quality of life." John DiBaise comments that it is wrong to use this standard to justify euthanasia because it is an act of injustice against the patient. Furthermore, quality of life is an arbitrary and subjective criterion. He suggests that "decisions made on the basis of quality of life should focus on the burdens and utility of specific treatments rather than the perceived value of a person's life."[47]

Indeed, the human person is not autonomous, but will always depend on others and—as a creature—on God. If this is denied, his intrinsic dignity will not be guaranteed. Then a false understanding of human freedom and autonomy will spread together with a reduction of man according to a utilitarian perspective.[48] The social pressure in favor of euthanasia is increasing due to demographic development, but especially because a Christian understanding is steadily disappearing.

A LOOK AT THE CURRENT SITUATION IN SOME COUNTRIES

In many countries assisted suicide/euthanasia has already been legalized. The pressure is increasing and the majority of societies are inclined towards this option. If permission is granted in one country, it will soon cause a domino effect in other countries. This can be seen when considering the situation in the Netherlands.

For many years, starting in 1971, the Netherlands were the world's laboratory for open-euthanasia. The Dutch physician Geertruda Postma ended the life of her seventy-eight-year-old mother by administering a deadly dose of morphine. Even though many physicians had done this already long before, this case became famous, since the Dutch physician reported the deed and her public report opened the doors for a public discussion. Her mother was partially paralyzed, being bound to a wheelchair, deaf, and pleaded with her daughter to end her suffering by ending her life.

During the court case, the physician received considerable support and sympathy. Nevertheless, she was found guilty in 1973 and sentenced to a suspended "sentence of one week imprisonment and

---

47 John K. DiBaise, "Euthanasia and Quality of Life: Critique of a Subjective Standard," in *NCBQ* 17 (2017): 417-24, here 424.
48 The CDF addressed the danger of a growing individualism, which would lead to the claim of a radical autonomy with devastating consequences. Cf. SB, IV.

a year's probation."⁴⁹ By imposing a light sentence the court made known that the action was somehow justified. The court decision included the attempt to describe "criteria on which such a justification should be made. In this case, the court cited that the request for euthanasia was made by a suffering patient with no alternative for relief but her own death."⁵⁰ Debates started throughout the whole country and lobby groups were established to promote the legal right to voluntary euthanasia. In 1984, a similar case was brought to the court by Dr. Schoonheim, who had given a lethal injection to an 85-year-old patient. The case went to the Supreme Court, but even before a decision was taken, the *Royal Dutch Medical Association* clarified the criteria for euthanasia—at this time already widely accepted among physicians—providing the following guidelines:

1. Voluntary, competent, explicit, and persistent requests on the part of the patient;
2. Requests based on full information;
3. The patient is in a situation of intolerable and hopeless suffering (either physical or mental);
4. No further acceptable alternatives to euthanasia. All alternatives acceptable to the patient for relief of suffering having been tried;
5. Consultation with at least one other physician whose judgment can be expected to be independent.⁵¹

These criteria had a great impact on the Supreme Court decision, which only confirmed a conflict of duties between the doctor's professional ethical obligations to respect the patient's request to "die with dignity" and the Penal Code. In 1993, the Dutch Senate passed a bill creating a legal basis for guidelines and procedures. The most frequently cited reason for requesting euthanasia was the "loss of dignity"; fewer than five percent of cases indicate intolerable pain as the only reason.⁵² "The most important considerations by the physicians to perform a life-terminating act included no

---

49 David C. Thomasma et al. (eds.), "Introduction: Reexamining 'Thou Shalt Not Kill,'" *Asking to Die: Inside the Dutch Debate about Euthanasia* (Dordrecht: Springer, 1998), 7–16, here 7.
50 Ibid.
51 So described in ibid., 9.
52 Ibid., 12.

chance of improvement, low quality of life, all medical therapy had become futile, the suffering of the patient and their relatives, and therapy had been withdrawn but the patient did not die."[53]

After three decades of the debate, a new law was implemented in 2002. The Netherlands became the first country to legalize euthanasia as a legitimized medical intervention in April 2002. Even though the Dutch government has insisted that the new law does not legalize euthanasia, guidelines for euthanasia were established, similar to those cited above.[54] The new law does not set stricter or more precise requirements regarding the practice of euthanasia. Key concepts such as "suffering without the prospect of relief" weren't defined or limited. Does someone suffering from depression or who is tired of living fulfill these criteria? What about elderly people? As the *DutchNews.nl* revealed in April 2017, the number of "official cases of euthanasia rose 10% in the Netherlands." The monitoring

> committee chairman Jacob Kohnstamm said it is not easy to determine why there has been a rise in overall cases. The demographic make-up of the Netherlands could be one reason for the increase, as could a change of opinion among doctors, he said. Some 85% of euthanasia requests are carried out by the patient's own doctor, usually at home. Euthanasia is legal in the Netherlands under strict conditions. [...] There have been a number of controversial cases, including a woman suffering severe tinnitus and a serious alcoholic.[55]

---

53 Ibid., 13-14.
54 Henk ten Have summarized them as follows: "The physician must (1) hold the conviction that the request by the patient is voluntary, well-considered, and lasting, and that the patient's suffering is without prospect of relief and unbearable; (2) inform the patient about his or her situation as well as about the prognosis; (3) believe, together with the patient, that there is no reasonable alternative solution for the patient's situation; (4) consult at least one other independent physician who has seen the patient and formed an opinion about these requirements of due care; and (5) terminate the patient's life with due medical care." Henk ten Have, "End-of-Life Decision Making in the Netherlands," in Robert H. Blank and Janna C. Merrick (eds.), *End-of-Life Decision Making* (Cambridge: The MIT Press, 2005), 147-68, here 149.
55 "Number of official cases of euthanasia rise 10% in the Netherlands," DutchNews.nl, 12.04.2017, in www.dutchnews.nl/news/archives/2017/04/number-of-official-cases-of-euthanasia-rise-10-in-the-netherlands/ [15.1.2022].

The Netherlands was the first country to legalize euthanasia in Europe, followed by Belgium in the same year with an even more liberal legislation regarding euthanasia. The law, issued in May 2002 and signed by King Albert II, says in section 3 §1:

> The physician who performs euthanasia commits no criminal offense when he/she ensures that:
> 1. the patient has attained the age of majority or is an emancipated minor, and is legally competent and conscious at the moment of making the request;
> 2. the request is voluntary, well-considered and repeated, and is not the result of any external pressure;
> 3. the patient is in a medically futile condition of constant and unbearable physical or mental suffering that cannot be alleviated, resulting from a serious and incurable disorder caused by illness or accident;
> 4. and when he/she has respected the conditions and procedures as provided in this Act.[56]

The law in Belgium allows euthanasia even for minors and offers explicitly the option to apply euthanasia due to mental suffering.[57] There is a growing number of people who take advantage of this law and end their life, for example, a 44-year-old transsexual woman who after a sex-change operation felt like a "monster" and therefore applied for euthanasia.[58] In August 2018, it was made public that two children, aged nine and eleven, had become the world's youngest persons to be euthanized. *The Telegraph* reported these cases with the following words:

> The unnamed minors were administered lethal injections in Belgium, which has the world's only law allowing terminally ill children in "unbearable suffering" to choose to die.

---

56 Albert II, "The Belgian Act on Euthanasia of May 28, 2002," trans. Dale Kidd, Centre for Biomedical Ethics and Law, Leuven, in *Ethical Perspectives* 9 (2002): 182–88, here 182.
57 Cf. Stefaan van Gool and Jan de Lepeleire, "Euthanasia in Children: Keep Asking the Right Question," in David Albert Jones et al. (eds.), *Euthanasia and Assisted Suicide. Lessons from Belgium* (Cambridge, Cambridge University Press, 2017), 173–87.
58 Cf. Leo Cendrowicz, "Euthanasia and assisted suicide laws around the world," *The Guardian*, 17.7.2014, in www.theguardian.com/society/2014/jul/17/euthanasia-assisted-suicide-laws-world [15.1.2022].

[...] The nine-year-old, who had a brain tumor, and the 11-year-old, who was suffering from cystic fibrosis, were the first children under 12 to be euthanized anywhere, a member of the CFCEE told *The Washington Post*. [...] Once a child has expressed a wish for euthanasia in writing, child psychiatrists conduct examinations, including intelligence tests, to determine their level of discernment and ensure they were "not influenced by a third party." Parents can, however, overuse their request.[59]

In Germany, the legislation regarding euthanasia—even though for obvious reasons it is not called "euthanasia"—changed in 2017 and even more in 2020. This is an important fact, especially against the background of German history and the period of the national socialists, who tried to introduce it but failed because of widespread protests in the population, organized especially by the Catholic Church.[60] On March 2, 2017, Germany's Federal Administrative Court in Leipzig issued a law that allows a painless assisted death in limited cases, recognizing the "right to self-determination."[61] In February 2020, Germany's Federal Constitutional Court declared it a "right" to make decisions about one's death, including the right to professional assistance in doing so. It can also be called an unlimited right to suicide since it is allowed in all stages of a person's existence depending only on one's own quality of life.[62]

In the United States of America assisted suicide is legal in 10 states: District of Columbia, California, Colorado, Hawaii, Oregon,

---

59   Henry Samuel, "Belgium authorized euthanasia of a terminally ill nine and 11-year-old in youngest cases worldwide," *The Telegraph*, 7.8.2018, in www.telegraph.co.uk/news/2018/08/07/belgium-authorised-euthanasia-terminally-nine-11-year-old-youngest/ [15.1.2022].

60   The historian Aly Haydar Götz has proved that this fact is due especially to the protests of the bishop of Münster Clemens August Graf von Galen. Cf. Aly Haydar Götz (ed.), *Aktion T4 1929–1945: Die "Euthanasie"-Zentrale in der Tiergartenstraße 4*, 2nd ed. (Berlin: Edition Hentrich, 1989), 90. See also Henry Friedlander, *The Origins of Nazi Genocide: From Euthanasia to the Final Solution* (Chapel Hill, NC: University of North Carolina Press, 1995), 114–16.

61   Cf. Bundesverwaltungsgericht, Urteil vom 02.03.2017—BVerwG 3 C 19.15, in www.bverwg.de/020317U3C19.15.0 [15.1.2022].

62   Cf. Bundesverfassungsgericht, Verbot der geschäftsmäßigen Förderung der Selbsttötung verfassungswidrig, Pressemitteilung Nr. 12/2020 vom 26. February 2020, in www.bundesverfassungsgericht.de/SharedDocs/Pressemitteilungen/DE/2020/bvg20-012.html [15.1.2022].

Vermont, Washington, New Jersey, Montana, and—starting in January 2020—also Maine.[63] In 18 other states, it is discussed and expected to be changed soon. If life at the beginning is not respected, it will not be respected at the end of life. Assisted death becomes the new "pro-choice."

In India, a certain form of euthanasia has been legal since 2018. The withdrawal of life support to patients who are in a permanent vegetative state is permissible. The Supreme Court of India passed a new law, which places power over life in certain circumstances in the hands of others.[64]

In Italy, the situation regarding euthanasia changed at the end of 2017. On December 14, 2017, the Italian Senate approved by 180 votes to 71 a new law which allows people to decide which medical treatment to receive or not. According to the new law, the people are allowed to express their own will according to informed consent, which they call the "biological testament" (*biotestamento*).[65] This includes preferences about whether to receive artificial nutrition and hydration or not. Usually, both are not counted among medical treatments, rather they are considered a fundamental right.

When it comes to legalizing euthanasia, the procedure is always the same: singular cases are presented in order to change a universal law, pushed through by lobby-groups, and supported by the mass media. These "individual cases" are also called "exceptional cases," which are intended to change the legislation; they are a so-called breach in a dam. How does it work? Usually, there is a small leak, which—due to the water pressure—increases rapidly. Through the damage of the structure of the dam, the hydrostatic pressure (gravitational pressure) increases so much that the shearing stress leads to its destruction.

This image can be transferred to what has been said so far. An exceptional case in the area of euthanasia/assisted suicide is a breach in the dam which, under pressure—above all considering

---

63 Cf. Death with Dignity, current as of November 6, 2019, in www.deathwithdignity.org/take-action/ [15.1.2022].
64 Cf. Malini Menon and Suchitra Mohanty, "India's top court upholds passive euthanasia, allows living wills in landmark judgment," *Reuters*, 9.3.2018, in www.reuters.com/article/us-india-court-euthanasia/indias-top-court-upholds-passive-euthanasia-allows-living-wills-in-landmark-judgment-idUSKCN1GL0MF [15.1.2022].
65 See also chapter III.

the demographic, economic, and social situation—causes the dam to collapse. The legally permitted euthanasia/assisted suicide is such a leak that undermines and threatens to undermine the inviolable dignity of man. Whenever exceptional or singular cases are presented there is not much protest against it, due to the assurance that it is only about "very limited exceptions." But the question needs to be raised: do these exceptions concern the dignity of the human person? How could such an exception be justified, and how could they be limited?

In other words: in almost all areas of bioethics, there have been big changes, and the consequences can hardly be overestimated. Society and politics have become secular, failing to define and recognize the intrinsic dignity of all men. As a consequence, ethical and moral values and norms are increasingly disappearing while people refer to their freedom and autonomy. This is a contradiction in itself since freedom needs orientation; it needs ethical norms and values. Without them, freedom and autonomy will dissolve themselves. Since the debate on euthanasia is forcefully increasing, it is important to know its historical background.

V
Euthanasia

IN ENGLISH, FRENCH, AND ITALIAN, ASSISTED dying is used as a synonym for euthanasia. However, because of the painful experience with the Nazi ideology, this synonym is not used in German-speaking countries.[1] Euthanasia involves many different aspects and according to Elio Sgreccia, the most common arguments in favor of it are above all: the principle of autonomy and the assumption that suffering is unbearable and useless.[2] The social and economic pressure[3] due to the demographic situation of elderly societies must be added. This pressure is increasing in part because clear demarcations and definitions are missing.

National Councils of Ethics exist in many parts of the world and are implemented by governments and institutions. They are granted a special role and become something like a "public conscience of the country/institution." Politicians and scientists delegate ethical evaluations to them. It is a matter of fact that most of these ethical councils or committees are composed by a majority of experts from the fields of medicine and technological process.[4] Only in rare cases are philosophers and theologians forming part of these committees. However, a specialist in the fields of technological procedures and medicine usually has no competence on ethical issues, which always presupposes anthropology. In consequence, economic advantages, scientific development, and a purely medical-based assessment become the new criteria for "ethical" evaluations. Therefore, the

---

1   Cf. Deutsches Referenzzentrum für Ethik in den Biowissenschaften, Sterbehilfe und Euthanasie, in www.drze.de/im-blickpunkt/sterbehilfe/module/sterbehilfe-und-euthanasie [15.1.2022].
2   Cf. Sgreccia, PB, 667-74.
3   Jessica Berg shows that social media pervades many areas of life, it increases the pressure presenting decisions for "incompetent patients." Cf. Jessica Berg, "The Effect of Social Media on End-of-Life Decision Making," in Stuart J. Youngner and Robert M. Arnold (eds.), *The Oxford Handbook of Ethics at the End of Life* (Oxford: Oxford University Press, 2016), 279-90.
4   Cf. World Health Organization, *Research Ethics Committees: Basic Concepts for Capacity-building* (Geneva: WHO Document Production Services, 2009), 11-15.

results are often ambiguous; ethics is subordinated to progress, technology, and economy. Especially in the field of bioethics, any ambiguity will lead to devastating consequences, since it is about life or death. It must be underlined that ambiguity kills any ethics.

For example, most ethical councils or committees have abandoned the distinction between direct and indirect euthanasia and they have replaced it with concepts such as "care for the dying," "assisted dying," "assisted suicide," "killing on-demand," etc.[5] However, the lack of clarity opens the door towards these practices, since nobody knows exactly what they mean. If the concept is unclear, then so too is its application. Any ambiguity regarding the concept of dignity will lead to serious problems at the beginning or at the end of life. Frequently it occurs that a classical definition, such as the distinctions between direct and indirect euthanasia, is rejected or considered inappropriate, but a better distinction or definition is not provided. Often the impression is created that one's own tradition is thrown overboard, but without finding an adequate substitute. This provokes serious problems and needs to be taken into consideration.

In 1980, the CDF issued a *Declaration on Euthanasia*.[6] This document offers basic principles and presents a definition of euthanasia. The declaration summarizes what has been shown so far: etymologically euthanasia meant in ancient times an "easy death." This meaning changed to a "merciful killing" for the purpose of ending suffering, or for abnormal babies, the mentally ill, or the incurably sick. After further explanations the declaration offers a proper definition: "By euthanasia is understood as an action or an omission which of itself or by intention causes death, so that all suffering may in this way be eliminated. Euthanasia's terms of reference, therefore, are to be found in the intention of the will and in the methods used."[7] The document mentions that this definition has to be applied to humans at every stage: the embryo, the fetus, the infant, the adult, "an old person, or one suffering from an incurable disease, or a person who is dying."[8]

---

5 Cf. Nationaler Ethikrat, *Selbstbestimmung und Fürsorge am Lebensende: Stellungnahme* (Berlin: Druckhaus Berlin-Mitte, 2006), 96–97.
6 Cf. CDF, DE. In 2020 an updated version was published with the Latin title *Samaritanus Bonus*. Cf. CDF, SB.
7 CDF, DE, II.
8 Ibid.

The norms and principles offered in this declaration are important. The central definition is also resumed in the *Catechism of the Catholic Church*, which provides a further helpful distinction in number 2277: "Direct euthanasia consists in putting an end to the lives of handicapped, sick, or dying persons."[9] The *Catechism* distinguishes between direct and indirect euthanasia, which is most appropriate for an ethical evaluation and which will be taken into consideration.

DIRECT (ACTIVE) EUTHANASIA (KILLING ON REQUEST)

Direct and active euthanasia are synonyms for the same concept. They can be defined as a directly willed inducement of death. Direct/active euthanasia is about ending life with the intention to cause the patient's death in a single act. Based on the concept of man as image of God the Catholic Church has always had a clear position on this type of euthanasia. Especially Pope Pius XII had witnessed the eugenics and euthanasia programs of the Nazis and he condemned them.[10] In these historical circumstances, the Church became not only the advocate for life but offered clear guidelines, based on a healthy and not reductive concept of man, which leads to recognizing the dignity and sanctity of life. Therefore, the constitution *Gaudium et Spes* condemned whatever is opposed to life itself, "such as any type of murder, genocide, abortion, euthanasia or willful self-destruction, whatever violates the integrity of the human person, such as mutilation, torments inflicted on body or mind, attempts to coerce the will itself; whatever insults human dignity."[11]

As surveys show, the teaching of the Church is not accepted anymore. According to a survey published in 2019, 67 percent of the Germans could imagine putting an end to their lives, if they were seriously ill, elderly, in need of long-term care, or suffering from dementia. According to the survey around two-thirds of the Germans would opt in these cases for active euthanasia.[12] A similar development can be seen in many other countries and societies.

---

9   CCC, 2277.
10 Cf. Pius XII, Encyclical Letter *Mystici Corporis*, 94.
11 GS, 27.
12 Cf. *Deutsches Ärzteblatt*, 67 Prozent der Bundesbürger für aktive Sterbehilfe, 5.7.2019, in www.aerzteblatt.de/nachrichten/104419/67-Prozent-der-Bundesbuerger-fuer-aktive-Sterbehilfe [15.1.2022].

The arguments in favor are always the same: a) self-determination and dignity; b) prevention of suffering—quality of life; c) no burden for others.

In Switzerland, there are various organizations promoting direct euthanasia, such as *Exit*. This Swiss society claims to enforce the right to refuse treatment in the event of illness, and it is dedicated "to the cause of human self-determination."[13] The group *Dignitas*—already the name implies a contradiction—promotes death/dying with dignity and they offer a service in order to guarantee this "dignity."[14] Whoever becomes a member of this group is obliged to promote militant self-determination, autonomy of the individual, including the "right-to-die." They declare:

> it is especially important to ask why it is ethically commendable to put a severely suffering animal to death, but it is impossible to allow a severely suffering human to end his or her own life, without having to accept the inconceivable risks of failure and additional self-mutilation. What abstruse ideas could lead someone to declare that what is humane for a person to do to a suffering animal is unethical if done to a suffering human, especially since an animal *cannot* express itself in human speech, yet a human can clearly state his or her will?[15]

They offer explicitly, as they call it, "accompanied suicide." "In case of an illness which will lead inevitably to death, unendurable pain or an unendurable disability, DIGNITAS can arrange, on reasoned request and medical proof, for its members the possibility of an accompanied suicide."[16] The association actively promotes cases of people who end their life, as in the case of the French lesbian and author, Michèle Causse.

She had wished that her death be filmed and through this filming she wanted to protest against her native country for not legally

---

13   "Exit, Our Society," in exit.ch/en/englisch/who-is-exit/ [15.1.2022].
14   Cf. *Dignitas*, "Objectives and Purpose," in www.dignitas.ch/index.php?option=com_content&view=article&id=9&Itemid=45&lang=en [15.1.2022].
15   *Dignitas*, "Principles/Philosophy," in www.dignitas.ch/index.php?option=com_content&view=article&id=10&Itemid=46&lang=en [15.1.2022].
16   *Dignitas*, "Our Service," in www.dignitas.ch/index.php?option=com_content&view=article&id=6&Itemid=47&lang=en [15.1.2022].

allowing euthanasia.[17] As put into evidence in the film, she insisted on her autonomy and self-determination. She did not talk about the meaning of death or the sense of life, but she instrumentalized even her own death to promote direct euthanasia. The culture of death becomes evident, which eliminates God while making the person absolute. Regarding the presented argumentation it is important to notice a huge contradiction. On one side, Causse was fighting for her dignity as a lesbian, on the other side, she denied her dignity as a human person and her right to life. She considered her life worthless and placed it on the same level as an object. She desired her own death and applied for it willingly.

Since euthanasia is legal in some countries and since certain lobbies are pushing for more liberal legislation, this affects also the Church and religious communities. In August 2017 it became public that the "Brothers of Charity" allowed doctors working in their hospitals to perform euthanasia. The religious community holds 15 psychiatric hospitals in Belgium. If a person suffered unbearable pain and if three experts (three doctors, including one psychiatrist) were consulted, they permitted euthanasia, since there were—as they said—no reasonable treatment alternatives and since the decision of conscience of the doctors to carry out euthanasia or not, was guaranteed.[18] Pope Francis ordered the Belgian "Brothers of Charity" to sign a letter declaring that they

> "fully support the vision of the Magisterium of the Catholic Church, which has always confirmed that human life must be respected and protected in absolute terms, from the moment of conception till its natural end." Brothers who refuse to sign the joint letter renouncing the practice of euthanasia will face sanctions under canon law, while the Catholic charity group can expect to face legal action and even expulsion from the Church if it fails to change its policy.[19]

---

17 See Assisted Suicide of Michèle Causse, 30.5.2014, in www.youtube.com/watch?v=JfyxUO4ZsDo [10.3.2019].
18 Cf. Raf De Rycke, "Belgian Catholic group explains switch on euthanasia," *Mercatornet*, 6.5.2017, in www.mercatornet.com/careful/view/belgian-catholic-group-explains-switch-on-euthanasia/19757 [15.1.2022].
19 So quoted in Vatican Radio, "Pope orders Belgian Brothers of Charity to stop offering euthanasia," 11.8.2017, in en.radiovaticana.va/news/2017/08/11/pope_orders_belgian_brothers_to_stop_offering_euthanasia/1330120 [15.1.2022].

In September, the Belgian Brothers of Charity declared that they had defied the Pope. They announced their will to continue offering euthanasia at their hospitals. "The group said in a statement that it 'continues to stand by its vision statement on euthanasia for mental suffering in a non-terminal situation' and that they 'emphatically believe' the practice is compatible with Catholic teaching." The group also claimed the decision had come about starting from the Christian frame of thought and that "their position always takes into account the shifts and evolutions within society."[20] Even though the superior general of the community, René Stockman, was opposed to the practices of the hospitals under the guidance of his religious community, he was not able to correct these serious violations. A decision from the Vatican was taken in 2020. It was stated that "noting the lack of willingness to accept the Catholic Doctrine on euthanasia, it is announced, albeit with deep sadness, that the psychiatric hospitals run by the Association *Provincialat des Frères de la Charité asbl* in Belgium, henceforth, can no longer be considered Catholic institutions."[21]

As can be seen especially in Belgium, Switzerland, and the Netherlands, whenever the legislation permits such a practice it will be almost impossible to find clear rules and to offer limits. The Royal Dutch Medical Association declares that euthanasia is possible only under strictly specified circumstances and only physicians are allowed to perform euthanasia. The direction in which the association moves is clear:

> Most patients who receive euthanasia are in the final stages of a malignant disease. However, some patients with dementia or with a mental illness also suffer unbearably from their condition and might therefore fall within the scope of the law. In these cases, the physician must take

---

20   So quoted in Catholic News Agency, "Defying Vatican, Belgian religious brothers will continue to offer euthanasia," 12.9.2017, in www.catholicnewsagency.com/news/defying-vatican-belgian-religious-brothers-will-continue-to-offer-euthanasia-97406 [15.1.2022].
21   CDF, "Letter to the Superior General of the Congregation of the 'Brothers of Charity,' regarding the Accompaniment of Patients in Psychiatric Hospitals of the Congregation's Belgian Branch," 30.3.2020, in www.vatican.va/roman_curia/congregations/cfaith/documents/rc_con_cfaith_doc_20200330_lettera-fratellidellacarita-belgio_en.html [15.1.2022].

extra care to ascertain the voluntary nature of the request and the lack of a reasonable alternative.[22]

Legislation that could follow from this assertion pushes towards a wide application of euthanasia and it might be applied even against the declared will of the people. This tendency will surely increase since the demographic development and the economic pressure point towards the same direction.

This process is speeding up. In September 2004 the so-called "Groningen Protocol" was created at the University Medical Center Groningen (Netherlands), which offers directives with criteria under which physicians can perform "active ending of life on infants," which is also considered as "child euthanasia."[23] The regulation was created for the physicians involved, that they might not have to fear legal prosecution. This topic is very controversial because child euthanasia was not only practiced in Sparta; it corresponds to a eugenic mentality. In short, it follows consequently the same logic as applied in abortion and it can be compared to infanticide.[24] The protocol considers actively ending the life of a new-born infant a real option. The termination of a child's life (under the age of 1) is acceptable if the following requirements are properly fulfilled:

> a) The diagnosis and prognosis must be certain; b) Hopeless and unbearable suffering must be present; c) The diagnosis, prognosis, and unbearable suffering must be confirmed by at least one independent doctor; d) Both parents must give informed consent; e) The procedure must be performed in accordance with the accepted medical standard.[25]

This regulation came into effect in late 2006. It was developed by Dutch authorities, which incorporated into the Groningen

---

[22] The Royal Dutch Medical Association (RDMA), "Euthanasia in the Netherlands," 16.8.2017, in www.knmg.nl/actualiteit-opinie/nieuws/nieuwsbericht/euthanasia-in-the-netherlands.htm [15.1.2022].

[23] Cf. Eduard Verhagen, et al., "The Groningen Protocol—Euthanasia in Severely Ill Newborns," in *New England Journal of Medicine* 325 (2005): 959–62.

[24] Cf. Daniel A. Beals, "The Groningen Protocol: Making Infanticide Legal Does Not Make It Moral," 23.3.2005, in cbhd.org/content/groningen-protocol-making-infanticide-legal-does-not-make-it-moral [15.1.2022].

[25] Eduard Verhagen, et al., "The Groningen Protocol," 962.

Protocol regulations considering cases of late-term abortion. In 2016, a revised regulation took over which is presented in article 7 as follows:

> In the event of termination of life of a newborn, the doctor has carefully acted if: a) the doctor is convinced there is enduring and unbearable suffering of the newborn, which among other things means that the discontinuation of medical treatment is justified, that is, prevailing medical opinion has established that intervention is futile and there is no reasonable doubt about the diagnosis and resulting prognosis; b) the doctor fully informs the parents of the diagnosis and the resulting prognosis and that both the doctor and parents believe that there is no reasonable alternative solution to the newborn's situation; c) the parents have agreed to the termination of life; d) the doctor has consulted at least one other independent physician who provides a written judgement on the due diligence of the case, or, if an independent physician cannot reasonably be consulted, the doctor consults with the newborn's healthcare team, who provide a written judgement as to the due diligence of the case; e) the termination of life is conducted with due medical care.[26]

Generally, the Dutch euthanasia program requires people to ask for euthanasia (voluntary euthanasia) in order for the procedure to be legal. According to the Groningen Protocol, this requirement is already overcome since only the parents have to consent to the termination of the life of their child (non-voluntary euthanasia). This is a logical but dangerous development and it will affect also elderly people, especially those who suffer from dementia. If something is allowed and applied at the beginning of life, it will unavoidably be applied at the end of life. A culture of death is spreading. Before an ethical evaluation of direct euthanasia will be presented, a threefold distinction needs to be made.

---

26 English translation presented in Neil Francis, "Neonatal deaths under Dutch Groningen Protocol very rare despite misinformation contagion," in *Journal of Assisted Dying* 1 (2016): 7-19, here 8.

VOLUNTARY EUTHANASIA

In the case of voluntary euthanasia, the person wants to die and affirms it. The case of Michèle Causse is an emblematic example. Before she took the poison to end her life she explicitly requested the opportunity to kill herself. This is considered voluntary euthanasia. There are different methods of this euthanasia; in any case, voluntary euthanasia corresponds to the firm will of the patient to actively end life, for example by lethal injection. Whenever this type of euthanasia is legalized, it will be very difficult to set any limits and to avoid—for example—non-voluntary euthanasia. Whenever self-killing is permitted, this will inevitably open the way to a broader erosion.

NON-VOLUNTARY EUTHANASIA

Non-voluntary euthanasia means that a person cannot make a decision himself, or cannot make his wishes known. This can include cases such as a person who is in a coma, no longer capable of expressing his/her will; or a person with severe brain damage; or someone who is senile, or mentally ill or disturbed, unable to make decisions; or simply too young.

The affected person is not able to choose between life and death for himself. The Groningen protocol in the Netherlands permits this type of euthanasia and implies, for example, the active ending of the life of infants. Handicapped new-borns or ill people—for example after an accident through which the brain was severely damaged—are submitted to euthanasia, without that person previously indicating whether he/she would or would not ask for euthanasia in certain circumstances of their life.

INVOLUNTARY EUTHANASIA

There is still a further step: involuntary euthanasia. The path from non-voluntary to involuntary euthanasia is very small. Involuntary euthanasia refers to a person who wants to live but is killed anyway. The national socialists applied the T4-program on the basis of involuntary euthanasia, selecting and killing those people they considered not worthy to live. However, there are many other examples and one does not need to quote the national socialist if he wants to speak about these crimes.

During a war, for example, a soldier has his stomach blown open by a shell burst. He suffers great pain and is screaming in agony. He begs the medic to save his life. Since the medic has no painkilling drugs, he decides to spare the soldier further pain and shoots him. This would be a case of involuntary euthanasia. The British newspaper *Mail Online* listed cases of involuntary euthanasia in Belgium:

> Thousands of elderly people have been killed by their own GPs [General Practitioner = a doctor, who treats acute and chronic illnesses] without ever asking to die under Belgium's euthanasia laws, an academic report said yesterday [12.6.2015]. It said that around one in every 60 deaths of a patient under GP care involves someone who has not requested euthanasia. Half of the patients killed without giving their consent were over the age of 80, the study found, and two thirds of them were in hospital and were not suffering from a terminal disease such as cancer. In about four out of five of the cases, the death was not discussed with patients subjected to "involuntary euthanasia" because they were either in a coma, they were diagnosed with dementia, or because doctors decided it would not be in their best interests to discuss the matter with them. Very often doctors would not inform the families of plans to lethally inject a relation because they considered it a medical decision to be made by themselves alone, the report published by the *Journal of Medical Ethics* said. The report raised new questions over Belgium's increasingly controversial 13-year-old euthanasia law, which has won wide acceptance from the medical establishment, and which now allows even children to be killed by doctors. Report author Professor Raphael Cohen-Almagor of Hull University said: "The decision as to which life is no longer worth living is not in the hands of the patient but in the hands of the doctor."[27]

Something similar happens in countries where the law does not permit euthanasia. In March 2017 a report was published in Germany about the application of involuntary euthanasia in Germany.

---

27 Steve Doughty, "Belgian GPs 'killing patients who have not asked to die': Report says thousands have been killed despite not asking their doctor," *Daily Mail*, 12.6.2015, in www.dailymail.co.uk/news/article-3120835/Belgian-GPs-killing-patients-not-asked-die-Report-says-thousands-killed-despite-not-asking-doctor.html [15.1.2022].

Professor Karl Beine confirmed in a book, which was published in 2017, that in Germany every year about 21,000 people are killed by doctors or nurses. The atmosphere has changed; human life is valued according to a materialistic concept of man. The whole health system is somehow infected, as the author describes in his book *Crime-Scene Hospital* (*Tatort Krankenhaus*).[28]

ETHICAL EVALUATION OF DIRECT EUTHANASIA

The Roman Catholic Church has always strongly opposed direct euthanasia and condemned it. The *Catechism of the Catholic Church* says: "Intentional euthanasia, whatever its forms or motives, is murder. It is gravely contrary to the dignity of the human person and to the respect due to the living God, his Creator."[29] Euthanasia is considered a direct killing of a human being and is, therefore, an immoral act. Whatever reasons might be proposed, it does not change the fact that the act is evil: "Whatever its motives and means, direct euthanasia consists in putting an end to the lives of handicapped, sick, or dying persons. It is morally unacceptable."[30] For a Catholic it does not matter if politicians, social workers, physicians, or whosoever, agree to it; it is unacceptable to promote or to practice direct euthanasia. It seems that the same attitude which led to the legalization of abortion is now opening the doors to euthanasia.

The intrinsic dignity of human life, from the beginning (conception) until natural death, is replaced by other criteria, such as utility, autonomy, hedonism, eugenics, etc. The meaning of life and its sacredness has been abandoned, and any value in suffering has been lost. All this leads to a culture of death, it opens the doors to euthanasia. Even though the declaration of the CDF on euthanasia is almost forgotten, it still offers a safe guide and clear ethical orientation. It states in reference to St. Thomas Aquinas:

> Furthermore, no one is permitted to ask for this act of killing, either for himself or herself or for another person entrusted to his or her care, nor can he or she consent

---

28 Cf. Karl H. Beine, Jeanne Turczyknski, *Tatort Krankenhaus: Wie ein kaputtes System Misshandlungen und Morde an Kranken fördert* (München: Droemer Verlag, 2017), 17.
29 CCC, 2324.
30 CCC, 2277.

to it, either explicitly or implicitly, nor can any authority legitimately recommend or permit such an action. For it is a question of the violation of the divine law, an offense against the dignity of the human person, a crime against life, and an attack on humanity. It may happen that, by reason of prolonged and barely tolerable pain, for deeply personal or other reasons, people may be led to believe that they can legitimately ask for death or obtain it for others. Although in these cases the guilt of the individual may be reduced or completely absent, nevertheless the error of judgment into which the conscience falls, perhaps in good faith, does not change the nature of this act of killing, which will always be something to be rejected. The pleas of gravely ill people who sometimes ask for death are not to be understood as implying a true desire for euthanasia; in fact, it is almost always a case of an anguished plea for help and love.[31]

Pope John Paul II confirmed this, underlining the absolute inviolability of human life, which is a moral truth clearly taught by Sacred Scripture, Tradition, and the Magisterium of the Church. In his encyclical letter *Evangelium Vitae* he solemnly confirmed:

> Therefore, by the authority which Christ conferred upon Peter and his Successors, and in communion with the Bishops of the Catholic Church, I confirm that the direct and voluntary killing of an innocent human being is always gravely immoral. This doctrine, based upon that unwritten law which man, in the light of reason, finds in his own heart (cf. Rom 2:14-15), is reaffirmed by Sacred Scripture, transmitted by the Tradition of the Church and taught by the ordinary and universal Magisterium. The deliberate decision to deprive an innocent human being of his life is always morally evil and can never be licit either as an end in itself or as a means to a good end. It is in fact a grave act of disobedience to the moral law, and indeed to God himself, the author and guarantor of that law; it contradicts the fundamental virtues of justice and charity. "Nothing and no one can in any way permit the killing of an innocent human being, whether a fetus or an

---

[31] CDF, DE, II.

embryo, an infant or an adult, an old person, or one suffering from an incurable disease, or a person who is dying. Furthermore, no one is permitted to ask for this act of killing, either for himself or herself or for another person entrusted to his or her care, nor can he or she consent to it, either explicitly or implicitly. Nor can any authority legitimately recommend or permit such an action."[32]

Since some states legalized killing on a person's request in the name of autonomy and compassion, this statement needs to be well understood. Such legislation is always evil, for it decriminalizes killing on demand, which is always intrinsically evil no matter if it is voluntary, non-voluntary, or involuntary euthanasia. In his encyclical *Veritatis Splendor* John Paul II called these acts "*intrinsically evil.*" He wrote:

> Reason attests that there are objects of the human act which are by their nature "incapable of being ordered" to God, because they radically contradict the good of the person made in his image. These are the acts which, in the Church's moral tradition, have been termed "intrinsically evil" (*intrinsece malum*): they are such *always and per se,* in other words, on account of their very object, and quite apart from the ulterior intentions of the one acting and the circumstances.[33]

Euthanasia is a "grave violation of the Law of God," it is "an intrinsically evil act, in every situation or circumstance."[34] The Code of Canon Law also deals with this topic in Canon 1397, where it is placed under the category of homicide. It states:

> A person who commits a homicide or who kidnaps, detains, mutilates, or gravely wounds a person by force or fraud is to be punished with the privations and prohibitions mentioned in can. 1336 according to the gravity of the delict. Homicide against the persons mentioned in can. 1370, however is to be punished by the penalties established there.[35]

---

32 John Paul II, EV, 57. This is reaffirmed as definitive teaching of the Church in CDF, SB, V, 1.
33 John Paul II, VS, 80.
34 CDF, SB, V, 1.
35 CIC, c. 1397.

Most of what is called "mercy killing" can be considered homicide. Craig Paterson has shown that self-procured death has to be considered as a species of homicide according to a wider and more plausible interpretation.[36] Canon 1336 mentions among a list of penalties also the dismissal from the clerical state (cf. c. 1336 § 1/5). This aspect needs to be taken into consideration since even some religious—as the Brothers of Charity in Belgium—are sometimes involved in such practices.

The condemnation of euthanasia does not mean that any type of extraordinary medical procedure has to be applied; this is going to be treated later on. The ban on euthanasia signifies that the Church is the advocate for life and the defender of the dignity of man. For that reason, euthanasia is considered "a supreme dishonor to the Creator."[37]

The Eastern Orthodox Churches also oppose euthanasia and they condemn it as "murder." In their argumentation, they rely especially on the Church Fathers and Scripture. They define euthanasia as a "deliberate cessation of human life," which "must be condemned as murder."[38]

Some of the Protestant denominations oppose euthanasia, while others don't.[39] The Church of England, for example, accepts indirect euthanasia under certain circumstances, but it is opposed to direct euthanasia. The life-issues are somehow ambiguous in the Protestant communities. In 1949 there was already a petition signed by many leading Protestant and Jewish ministers to legalize euthanasia in New York, only 4 years after the end of World War II.[40]

According to Jewish ethics and law, taking another human life is forbidden. In 2005, there was a "new interpretation" of Jewish law. The law remains in vigor, but machines will perform euthanasia on terminally ill people, similar to the so-called "Sabbath clocks."

---

36 Craig Paterson, *Assisted Suicide and Euthanasia: A Natural Law Ethics Approach* (Cornwall: Taylor & Francis, 2008), 103-4.
37 GS, 27.
38 Victor Potapov, "Thou shalt not kill—Euthanasia," in stjohndc.org/en/orthodoxy-foundation/thou-shalt-not-kill-euthanasia [15.1.2022].
39 Cf. Miles S. Marsala, "Approval of Euthanasia: Differences Between Cohorts and Religion," in *SAGE Open* 9 (2019): 1-11.
40 Cf. Ian Dowbiggin, *A Merciful End: The Euthanasia Movement in Modern America* (New York: Oxford University Press, 2003), 63-96.

These are devices used in the homes of orthodox Jews so that electrical devices can be turned on during the Sabbath, without offending the norms. According to the parliamentarians and the new interpretation, a man would not be able to shorten human life, but a machine could.[41]

The Muslim's perspective is similar regarding the general norm. The Qur'an prohibits one's own destruction, which could be related to terminally ill persons. Islam teaches that Allah has absolute authority over life since he is the giver of life. For that reason, he alone is supposed to have control over death. Therefore, Muslim scholars have prohibited active euthanasia and physician-assisted suicide.[42] Regarding indirect euthanasia, there is no such agreement.[43]

However, on October 28th, 2019, a position paper was signed in the Vatican concerning the end of life in the so-called "Abrahamic Monotheistic Religions."[44] The document addresses the use of medical technology at the end of life and affirms:

> We oppose any form of euthanasia—that is the direct, deliberate and intentional act of taking life—as well as physician-assisted suicide—that is the direct, deliberate and intentional support of committing suicide—because they fundamentally contradict the inalienable value of human life, and therefore are inherently and consequentially morally and religiously wrong, and should be forbidden without exceptions.[45]

In conclusion, the document affirms once again: "Euthanasia and physician-assisted suicide are inherently and consequentially

---

41 Cf. Tim Butcher, "Israelis to be allowed euthanasia by machine," *The Telegraph*, 8.12.2005, in www.telegraph.co.uk/news/worldnews/middleeast/israel/1505018/Israelis-to-be-allowed-euthanasia-by-machine.html [15.1.2022].
42 Mahmud Adesina Ayuba, "Euthanasia: A Muslim Perspective," in *Scriptura* 115 (2016): 1-13, here 7.
43 Cf. Dariusch Atighetchi, *Islam e Bioetica* (Rome: Armando Curcio Editore, 2009), 247-55.
44 Cf. Position Paper of the Abrahamic Monotheistic Religions on Matters Concerning the End of Life (Casina Pio IV, 28 October 2019), in press. vatican.va/content/salastampa/en/bollettino/pubblico/2019/10/28/191028f.html [15.1.2022].
45 Ibid.

morally and religiously wrong and should be forbidden with no exceptions. Any pressure upon dying patients to end their lives by active and deliberate actions is categorically rejected."[46]

There is another argument that must be presented before concluding this chapter. Gonzalo Miranda wrote in an article about "The meaning of life and the acceptance of death" that there is a broad discussion about the meaning and the sense of euthanasia, but the question of the sense of life and death is often ignored. If the meaning of death is not understood, how can one take the right decision regarding euthanasia? Gonzalo Miranda states:

> The problem is that in favoring euthanasia as a right of the individual, one almost completely neglects the consideration of that which is involved on the most profound level of this type of human action. Prior to the question of the widely touted idea of "auto-determination," there is the question of why an individual would want to make use of it to end his own life, which at bottom coincides with the fact that this life no longer has any sense for him, and neither does his death, despite his apparent "will for death." Indeed, I would say that sometimes a person who favors euthanasia and avoids dealing with the question of the sense of life and death does so because at bottom he has a conception of human life as something that is devoid of "sense" or "meaning" in itself, beyond that which the individual wants to give it at that moment.[47]

Therefore, the main task should be transmitting to people the sense of life, which will work only if God is taken into consideration because he is "the way and the truth and the life" (John 14:6). God is the key to understanding the meaning of life. Only when the sense of life is understood will people rediscover the "sense of death," which will necessarily lead them to reject and condemn any form of active euthanasia, which is murder. Voluntary euthanasia is for Catholics a mortal sin, and it is not compassionate at all.[48]

---

46 Ibid.
47 Gonzalo Miranda, "The meaning of life and the acceptance of death," in Correa and Sgreccia, *Dignity of the Dying Person*, 297–312, here 298ff.
48 See the book written by Rita Marker, *Deadly Compassion: The Death of Ann Humphry and the Truth about Euthanasia* (New York: William Morrow &

INDIRECT (PASSIVE) EUTHANASIA

Today, mortality is mostly considered a technical process and therefore, loses its human dimension, which would usually give ground to morality. The sense and meaning of life is intrinsically related to mortality. Death has to be recognized as a human act and a perspective that goes beyond death is needed as the foundation for ethics. All religions and substantial philosophies have this in common. In other words, mortality gives ground to morality. Active euthanasia is a typical example of leaving behind morality, it is the non-acceptance of mortality. If death is only considered as a technical problem, it will lead physicians, nurses, advisers, social workers, and even friends to submit life to the standards of technology. Consequently, the dying person is overly medicalized and often reduced to a technical problem; he becomes an object.

According to this perspective, a (total) manipulation of the dying is possible. Also for that reason, euthanasia is often presented to the people under the perspective of "compassion," since the human person is exposed to manipulation, which is a result of reducing the human person to his functions and to the technical dimension. An immanent view of human life has led people to abandon the very foundations of anthropology; thus, many contemporary ethics claim an unlimited "right to choose" for the patient. Quality of life and autonomy are the new guiding principles.[49] The main problem is an insufficient and defective anthropology, which does not respect the intrinsic value of the person, with its duality of soul and body. In some cases this inseparable unity is separated, the patient's will becomes independent from the patient's body. The will is set as the absolute and the body is considered purely as an object, certainly not as the temple of the Holy Spirit.

Depending on the argument, it can also happen that this is turned upside down. According to a second approach, no importance is attributed to the soul (the spiritual dimension) and the body is viewed in the way in which a veterinarian views an animal's body, neglecting a spiritual dimension. This defective anthropology leads to dramatic consequences, including the impression that

---

Co, 1993).
49 Cf. Michael D. Bayles, "Euthanasia and the Quality of life," in James J. Walter and Thomas A. Shannon (eds.), *Quality of Life: The New Medical Dilemma* (Mahwah, NJ: Paulist Press, 1990), 265-81.

the patient gets what he wants since he lives immersed in an immanent perspective. Ethical relativism is a logical consequence, and the concept of compassion is changed.

Indirect euthanasia, also called passive or negative euthanasia,[50] is an indirect inducement of death by withholding medicine or stopping a procedure. It can also be an act of omission that causes death, even though the intention is to eliminate suffering. The withholding of life-sustaining treatments ends life. For example: if someone turned off a respirator so that the patient, whose lungs cannot work on their own, should die, it would be considered indirect euthanasia. This distinction is helpful for ethical evaluation.

Indirect euthanasia means death brought about by an act of omission. The three distinctions between voluntary, non-voluntary, and involuntary euthanasia can be applied also to indirect euthanasia. Usually, it refers to the withdrawal of treatments, such as not carrying out a surgery that might extend life for a short time; or to switching off a machine that is keeping the person alive.

Some examples are helpful for understanding. The case of the Italian Piergiorgio Welby is well known at least in Italy. This man was paralyzed and had muscular dystrophy. The BBC reported about his case on December 13th, 2006:

> Mr Welby is confined to bed, is fed through a tube and speaks through a computer that reads his eye movements. He appealed to President Giorgio Napolitano in October for euthanasia to be legalized so that he could then request it. He wants his artificial respirator turned off and to be given sedatives to ease his pain until he dies. The case hinges on whether Mr Welby is being forcibly administered life-sustaining medical treatment—which is against Italy's constitution. Prosecutors told the court on Monday that Mr Welby had the right to have the respirator turned off, but that doctors also had the right to turn the machine back on if he was suffering. "The problem in this case is

---

50 The adjective "passive" implies a broader meaning and could give rise to ambiguities. Elio Sgreccia commented: "Euthanasia is always passive in a certain sense, from the perspective of the sick person, and always active on the part of those who instigate it, whether by action or omission." Sgreccia, PB, 680.

to know if we are really faced with a case of prolonging life by artificial means," Javier Lozano Barragan, president of the Vatican's pontifical health council, told *La Repubblica* newspaper.[51]

The case of Welby was made public.[52] It was used as part of the lobby pushing to legalize euthanasia in Italy. The methodology applied is always the same. First, a singular case is chosen, with whom the broad majority can identify themselves. They give the impression that the ethically bad action is something good and the only way to deal with the painful situation. This happened in the case of Welby. In October 2006 he sent a video-letter to the Italian President Giorgio Napolitano describing his situation and explaining his desire to die. The campaign sparked a public debate on euthanasia. Some radical lobby groups supported Welby, organizing even a hunger-strike and demonstrations. At the end, the Italian court denied the request for euthanasia, urging the parliament to solve the problem. In December 2006, Mario Riccio acting in close collaboration with the lobby ensured that Welby's request was voluntary and he granted him what he was looking for. Under sedation, he ended his life on December 20th.[53] His death was made public the next day through radio and press. Even though the doctor committed a very immoral act not covered by the law, the Ethical Committees and the Criminal court judged Dr. Riccio's acting to be legitimate.[54] The Catholic Church offered a precise ethical orientation but was ignored at the end. She refused to allow a religious funeral affirming: "Welby had repeatedly and publicly affirmed his desire to end his own life, which is against Catholic doctrine."[55]

This case is of importance in order to understand the movement promoting a culture of death: 1) The case was made public from

---

51 BBC News, "Italian man sparks euthanasia row," *BBC*, 13.12.2006, in news.bbc.co.uk/2/hi/europe/6174603.stm [15.1.2022].
52 Even the medical diary was published, containing all details. Cf. Gianna Milano, *Mario Riccio, Storia di una morte opportuna. Il diario del medico che ha fatto la volontà di Welby* (Milano: Galápagos, 2008).
53 Mario Riccio describes this moment in his book: ibid., 89–109.
54 Cf. "Welby, prosciolto il medico Riccio," *La Repubblica*, 23.7.2007, in www.repubblica.it/2007/07/sezioni/cronaca/welby-medico/welby-medico/welby-medico.html [15.1.2022].
55 So quoted in "Church denies funeral for Italian," *BBC*, 22.12.2006, in news.bbc.co.uk/2/hi/europe/6204995.stm [15.1.2022].

the beginning on. In other words, Welby was used to promote euthanasia. Welby's suffering was presented in such a way that it appeared to be an act of compassion to help him end his life. His case had a profound impact on public opinion regarding euthanasia. 2) Welby desired voluntary indirect euthanasia; therefore, he rejected God, who is the Lord of life, and at the same time he rejected his intrinsic dignity as a human person. The act of omission was the switching off of the machine, which was sustaining Welby. 3) The argumentation in favor is linked to a false understanding of compassion and autonomy. 4) The doctor, who was involved, was not punished, even though this practice was against the law. From this moment on the public pressure in favor of euthanasia increased, since there were no negative consequences for this doctor. 5) Even though the law had not been changed immediately, it was just a question of time. Since this procedure was tolerated, it was only a small step to change the legislation.

In December 2017 these groups achieved their goal in Italy: the so-called *Biotestamento* was approved by the Italian Senate.[56] The new law puts an emphasis on what they call "dignity" and "self-determination." The legislation was changed. According to the new law, a patient who affirms the informed consensus is registered and may end his life. In other words, each adult now has the right to refuse artificial nutrition and hydration, completely or partially in each moment. Before nutrition and hydration were considered natural means, now they are considered "health treatments" and each person has—according to the bio-testament—the right to stop or refuse them. There are also some changes regarding the doctors involved. Now they have the right to stop treatment, even though it might provoke death; at the same time, their "freedom of conscience" is respected and therefore they are not obliged to take part in this suspension of treatment. In the case that a doctor refuses, the patient can ask someone else to take over. The wife of Piergiorgio Welby, Mina, was quite enthusiastic about this new law. She promised to take further steps. She wants to campaign in favor of "assisted dying," with the result that people can freely and voluntarily end their life whenever they want. Even if it is

---

56   Cf. Caterina Pasolini, "Biotestamento."

a contradiction per se, she said that she is willing to assist the dying, the ones who committed suicide.[57]

The *ars moriendi* is no longer accepted. Life is submitted more and more to the conditions offered by medicine and technique. People such as Mina Welby claim that they want to assist the dying in radical opposition to the classical *ars moriendi*.

Something similar happened in the United States. Terri (Theresa Marie) Schiavo was 27 years old when she suffered from a cardiac arrest. This occurred on February 25, 1990. Terri was resuscitated but had massive brain damage, and soon after (2.5 months later) her state was judged persistent vegetative. She was at home together with her husband Michael when she collapsed and never recovered.[58] This became one of the most important ethical legal test-cases for the following 15 years. Her case was sensationalized through the media and affected not only the medical field but also the juridical and political systems; ultimately, her case reached even the U. S. president, George W. Bush. Her husband argued that Terri did not want any prolonged artificial life support and opted for removing her feeding tube. Her parents were opposed to Michael and in favor of continuing artificial nutrition and hydration.[59] Finally, the Sixth Circuit Court of Florida determined that Schiavo would not have wished to continue life-prolonging measures in 2001. Her feeding tube was removed but several days later was reinserted. In a second process, the federal court system affirmed the decision to remove the feeding tube and it was disconnected on March 18, 2005. Terri died on March 31, 2005, due to starvation.

The allowance of euthanasia is often justified appealing to the concept of "quality of life." John Paul II affirmed that it is often used as an excuse to give in and to opt for euthanasia. The question must be asked, what is "quality of life"? Today, many people are physically healthy but have no quality of life, suffering for example from depression or psychological distresses. However, the quality of

---

57 Cf. Mauro Bazzucchi, "Biotestamento, Mina Welby: Anche chi ha votato contro nel profondo del cuore la approva. Ora legge sulla morte assistita," *Huffington Post*, 14.12.2017, in www.huffingtonpost.it/2017/12/14/biotestamento-mina-welby-anche-chi-ha-votato-contro-nel-profondo-del-cuore-la-approva-ora-legge-sulla-morte-assistita_a_23307140/ [15.1.2022].
58 Her case is described in detail by Arthur L. Caplan et al. (eds.), *The Case of Terri Schiavo: Ethics at the End of Life* (New York: Prometheus, 2006).
59 Cf. ibid., 123-71.

life is related to the sense of life. The loss of Christian faith and its meaning of life will lead to a culture dominated more and more by selfish economic measures and arbitrary subjective criteria, which will lead inevitably to the abandonment of solidarity. In other words, even if someone were to recognize a patient in a "vegetative state" as a human person with its intrinsic dignity, it would still require solidarity to take care of such a person. Without a deep Christian conviction, this will become very difficult. For that reason, John Paul II affirmed that a person being in the vegetative state is a big burden for the family; not only on a human or psychological level but also regarding the financial situation. He concludes that a society inspired by Christian solidarity needs to support those families. The Pope suggests creating a network of support for these people in different dimensions, including the spiritual and pastoral dimension.[60] One criterion in judging the moral standards of society is looking at how it treats the sick, handicapped, unborn, and elderly. If there is no sensitivity and solidarity shown toward them, society will become inhuman.

The position of the Catholic Church regarding vegetative state patients requires respect for the intrinsic dignity of the person. However, if a person is, for example, suffering from cancer in the terminal stage and it is impossible for him/her to drink and eat, then the process of dying should not be prolonged. In these cases the following principle needs to be applied: *impossibilia nemo tenetur*—nobody is committed to the impossible.[61]

ETHICAL EVALUATION OF INDIRECT EUTHANASIA

John Paul II wrote in his encyclical letter *Evangelium Vitae* that euthanasia "in the strict sense is understood to be an action or omission which of itself and by intention causes death, with the purpose of eliminating all suffering. 'Euthanasia's terms of reference, therefore, are to be found in the intention of the will and in

---

60 Cf. John Paul II, Address to the Participants in the International Congress of "Life-sustaining Treatments and Vegetative State scientific progress and ethical dilemmas," 20.3.2004, in w2.vatican.va/content/john-paul-ii/en/speeches/2004/march/documents/hf_jp-ii_spe_20040320_congress-fiamc.html [15.1.2022], 6.
61 This will be explained in chapter VII.

the methods used.'"⁶² The Church's position is clearly formulated and refers to direct and indirect euthanasia, with the intention to cause death: "Abortion and euthanasia are thus crimes which no human law can claim to legitimize. There is no obligation in conscience to obey such laws; instead, there is a grave and clear obligation to oppose them by conscientious objection."⁶³ The Church considers it a moral duty to refuse injustice. This becomes true whenever the action or omission has the intention to cause death. For that reason, another distinction will be helpful to clarify these concepts and to present an ethical evaluation.

> Indirect euthanasia with the intention to cause death: This type is considered ethically immoral; death is caused by the withdrawal of natural means, such as nutrition and hydration.
>
> Indirect euthanasia with the intention not to cause death: This procedure is sometimes referred to in different ways. To avoid ambiguity and to offer clear guidelines, it will be called indirect euthanasia, with the intention not to cause death. In this case, death isn't intended or directly caused, but a consequence of the process of dying and its accompaniment. Generally speaking, this type isn't considered ethically immoral.

As can be seen, much depends on the definition and understanding of euthanasia. There is a profound difference between killing and letting die. It must be affirmed that life does not need to be prolonged at any cost. Nonetheless, an omission of ordinary care should never be the "sufficient cause" for death. It is to be ensured, but discontinuation of special nutrition, another dialysis treatment, antibiotic treatments, or circulation-supporting measures, can be legitimate. This is reflected in the life of Pope John Paul II. At the end of his life, he refused to go to the Gemelli hospital for life-prolonging treatments. He did not want to lengthen his life at all costs; he was ready to enter into the "house of the Father." The case of an elderly woman might be similar, dying of cancer, and also suffering diabetes. At this point she could, for example, refuse insulin injections as long as she has already started the

---

62   John Paul II, EV, 65.
63   Ibid., 73.

process of dying. Nevertheless, it is important to make sure that the medicine or the treatments being withheld aren't the direct cause of death. The *Catechism* says in #2278:

> Discontinuing medical procedures that are burdensome, dangerous, extraordinary, or disproportionate to the expected outcome can be legitimate; it is the refusal of "over-zealous" treatment. Here one does not will to cause death; one's inability to impede it is merely accepted. The decisions should be made by the patient if he is competent and able or, if not, by those legally entitled to act for the patient, whose reasonable will and legitimate interests must always be respected.[64]

Indirect euthanasia, with the intention not to cause death, will be morally licit, if the following criteria are applied:

- Life does not need to be prolonged at all costs; the process of dying does not have to be artificially stayed.
- There will be the moment when a doctor must accept the dying process. It is important to look closely at the intention of the doctor.
- The intention shouldn't be death per se, but to permit the unstoppable process of dying.
- The death of the patient is in the range of the possible, it can be expected, but it is not intended, only allowed.

Sometimes it is not easy to distinguish what kind of treatment is morally licit. Suppose a man dying of acute leukemia. Must he participate in treatments to prolong his life? The answer is: no! But suppose this person is suffering tremendously and comes to a point in which not even morphine helps anymore. Can he be submitted to the administration of new drugs in the experimental phase, even though they might shorten his life? The *Declaration on Euthanasia*, issued by the CDF in 1980, provides some helpful clarifications:

> - If there are no other sufficient remedies, it is permitted, with the patient's consent, to have recourse to the means provided by the most advanced medical techniques, even if these means are still at the experimental stage and are

---

64 CCC, 2278.

not without a certain risk. By accepting them, the patient can even show generosity in the service of humanity.

- It is also permitted, with the patient's consent, to interrupt these means, where the results fall short of expectations. But for such a decision to be made, account will have to be taken of the reasonable wishes of the patient and the patient's family, as also of the advice of the doctors who are especially competent in the matter. The latter may in particular judge that the investment in instruments and personnel is disproportionate to the results foreseen; they may also judge that the techniques applied impose on the patient strain or suffering out of proportion with the benefits which he or she may gain from such techniques.

- It is also permissible to make do with the normal means that medicine can offer. Therefore, one cannot impose on anyone the obligation to have recourse to a technique which is already in use, but which carries a risk or is burdensome. Such a refusal is not the equivalent of suicide; on the contrary, it should be considered as an acceptance of the human condition, or a wish to avoid the application of a medical procedure disproportionate to the results that can be expected, or a desire not to impose excessive expense on the family or the community.

- When inevitable death is imminent in spite of the means used, it is permitted in conscience to take the decision to refuse forms of treatment that would only secure a precarious and burdensome prolongation of life, so long as the normal care due to the sick person in similar cases is not interrupted. In such circumstances the doctor has no reason to reproach himself with failing to help the person in danger.[65]

The explanations make clear that in the case of indirect euthanasia, with the intention not to cause death, is found an act with a double effect, which can be morally licit. There is an intended good, but also a negative effect involved.

---

65   CDF, DE, IV.

PRINCIPLE OF DOUBLE EFFECT

The progress of medical technology has created new challenges for bioethics. On one side medicine is able to prolong life through technological advancement; on the other side, it could mean that the often-painful moment of dying is prolonged. What are the limits? Are there any principles that can provide orientation? Sometimes the difference between killing and allowing to die is not very big, especially when using palliative sedation. For that reason, it will be helpful to mention the principle of double effect, which is a solid guide. It offers an orientation in highly complex circumstances if rightly applied since there are often acts that have both positive and negative effects, as described in the example above.[66]

A general affirmation must be made right at the beginning. Whenever this principle is applied, death isn't intended or directly caused, but is a consequence of the process of dying and its accompaniment. This can be the case regarding the application of medical treatment at the expense of the shortening of life. Let us say there is a patient suffering from unbearable pain because of cancer and he asks the doctor to prescribe pain killers. He knows that the use of these drugs (morphine) may affect the circulatory and renal functions; they may be so strongly affected that death may be more likely to occur through the medicine than through the main disease.

There is another important issue related to the principle of double effect. Normative ethics offers or should offer general principles of how to act in certain circumstances. It does not solve every situation, but it offers general guidelines. The principle of double effect in comparison is applied only in specific circumstances and singular instances. It is a general principle.

Even though this principle might have existed before, as some argue,[67] St. Thomas Aquinas was the first to formulate the principle of double effect, which had a great influence on traditional Catholic ethics. In the *Summa Theologiae*, Thomas Aquinas raises the question of whether it is lawful to kill a man in self-defense? As usual, Thomas presents various objections to this topic, quoting Scripture

---

66 Cf. Jordan Potter, "The Principle of Double Effect in End-of-Life Care," in *NCBQ* 15 (2015): 515–29.
67 Ibid., 516.

and Tradition. Finally, he responds: "I answer that nothing hinders one act from having two effects, only one of which is intended, while the other is beside the intention."[68] For any moral evaluation the intention, the object, and the circumstances are of crucial importance. When St. Thomas developed the principle of double effect, he referred to all three. Meanwhile, the side-effects are considered secondary for moral evaluation. The case of self-defense has usually two effects, "one is the saving of one's life, the other is the slaying of the aggressor." Thomas Aquinas comments: "Therefore, this act, since one's intention is to save one's own life, is not unlawful, seeing that it is natural to everything to keep itself in being, as far as possible."[69] The Dominican theologian focuses also on the other elements, including a certain proportion to the end, which corresponds to the object of the action. If the violence used in self-defense does not correspond to a certain proportion, it would be unlawful.[70] Thomas mentions this principle—which needs to be applied according to the circumstances—only in one *Questio* and it took some centuries for this principle to start gaining attention. Nevertheless, it was he who formulated it. In short, this principle consists of four different aspects, which have to be taken into consideration.

1. The action considered by itself and independently of its effects is morally good.

2. The intention of the acting person is good, evil effects are unavoidable. They must not be the means of producing the good effect.

3. The evil effect is not intended, only tolerated. The end does not justify the means.

4. There must be a proportion in spite of the evil consequences.

In order that an action can be considered morally good, all four conditions have to be fulfilled. This was summarized with the following words: "*Bonum ex integra causa, malum autem ex singularibus defectibus*," "good results from the entire cause, evil from each particular defect."[71]

---

68 Thomas Aquinas, STh, II-II, q. 64, a. 7.
69 Ibid.
70 Cf. ibid.
71 Thomas Aquinas, STh, I-II, q. 19, a. 6, ad 1.

BIOETHICAL CHALLENGES AT THE END OF LIFE

It will be helpful to consider in the light of this principle the case mentioned above. There is a person, suffering from cancer in the final stage. A pain killer or new experimental medicine that the person might take could shorten the life-span. Is it allowable? Applying the principle of the double effect it becomes quite clear that it is morally licit. The action—to use pain killers or even to use a new experimental medicine—is morally good. The intention is to reduce the pain and not to end life. The evil effects are unavoidable relative to the good intention. They are not intended but tolerated, and finally, there is a proportion regarding the methods used.

Due to the progress in medicine and technology, death does not always come in dramatic circumstances; often it is predictable. Sometimes it is accompanied by physical and psychological suffering. Today, medicine offers pain killers, which are able to exclude or to diminish physical suffering to a great extent. Some of these painkillers generate problems, because they may lead to a state of semi-consciousness and reduced lucidity. Considering this difficulty in the light of the principle of double effect it becomes clear that the crucial point is the proportion. How far can we go? Is it possible to limit or even to suppress the consciousness of man?

To provide an adequate answer, another aspect must be mentioned. According to a Christian understanding, the goal of life is reaching eternal life and the Church is supposed to be like an instrument in order to reach this goal.[72] All ethical orientations are meant to illuminate this path. This is supposed to be the guiding principle, and everything must be subordinated to it. Today this is often misunderstood, or not understood at all; people's lives are immersed in the material immanent world. However, the path to eternal life does not follow an automatism, but depends on the free decision of the person, since God does not force anyone. A free decision implies will and intellect and therefore also the capacity to take a responsible decision. This becomes even more evident in connection with the sacrament of the anointing of the sick. This sacrament is not meant only for the dying or those people who are about to die, but it is a sacrament that can unfold its sacramental grace only if the sick

---

[72] Cf. LG 1.

person collaborates and participates in it with the true desire to receive the graces God wants to grant. Until the Second Vatican Council, there was the prescription to administer this sacrament in the moment of death and it was called *Extreme Unction*. It was one of the reforms to change its application and to administer the sacrament to those "who, having reached the use of reason, begins to be in danger due to sickness or old age."[73] Therefore, the so-called "use of reason" is of great importance, because only through the use of this human capacity can the person freely decide to be for or against God. This becomes even clearer if Canon 1007 of the Code of Canon Law is taken into consideration: "The anointing of the sick is not to be conferred upon those who persevere obstinately in manifest grave sin."[74] Of course, the sacrament can be administered even when the patient is unable to make a confession and unable to react, but it will be received (more) fruitfully if received consciously. This needs to be kept in mind when considering palliative measures and their proportion, even within the principle of double effect.

There are intensive painkillers which will limit the capacity of reasoning. Pope Pius XII already considered this question in 1957. He addressed a group of doctors and affirmed that it was important that a patient could carry out his religious and moral duties. Painkillers that cause unconsciousness need special consideration regarding its proportion. The most important duty is to prepare oneself with full consciousness for the final encounter with Christ. Within this logic, Pius XII said that it is regrettable to deprive the dying person of consciousness without a serious reason.[75]

Regarding palliative sedation, the principle of double effect can serve as a normative tool to guide ethical decisions. Jordan Potter concludes: "Thus, for palliative sedation to be ethically justified by the principle of the double effect and distinguished from evil acts like euthanasia, the intent in its use must be the management of pain and not the death of the patient, and the goal should be to administer the minimal amount of effective

---

73   CIC, c. 1004§1.
74   CIC, c. 1007.
75   Cf. Pius XII, *Allocutio*, in AAS 49 (1957), 129–47, here 145.

sedation to achieve pain relief without inducing the undesirable state of full unconsciousness."[76]

In conclusion, the principle of double effect can be applied for all end-of-life options that are real options. Regarding the different types of euthanasia, such as direct and indirect, voluntary, non-voluntary, and involuntary, this principle can be applied only to indirect euthanasia, with the intention not to cause death.

---

[76] Jordan Potter, "Principle of Double Effect," 528.

VI
Suicide and Assisted Suicide

SUICIDE

According to the *American Foundation for Suicide Prevention*, suicide is the 10th leading cause of death in the U. S. In 2017, 47,173 Americans died by suicide. For every suicide, there are more than 25 attempts. In other words, there were an estimated 1.4 million people who attempted to commit suicide in 2018 in the U. S. The annual costs of suicide and self-injury amount to $69 billion. In 2018, 7 out 10 suicides were white males and the highest suicide rate was among adults between 45 and 54 years of age. It is an average of 132 suicides a day.[1] Many suicide attempts are unreported, as the foundation affirms that at least one million people in the U. S. engage in intentionally inflicted self-harm, for which approximately 575,000 people visited a hospital in 2015. Female attempted suicide is twice as frequent as male, but males are about 4 times more likely to die than females.

The data show that suicide is a serious problem in many countries, rich and poor. An international research team led by epidemiologist Mohsen Naghavi concluded that there were about 817,000 suicides worldwide each year between 1990 and 2016.[2] The reasons for committing suicide vary; often a combination of different factors pushes people to end their life. Usually, these people are given over to despair, they feel lonely, and thus depression becomes one of the major causes for suicide.[3] Depression and mental disorders are intrinsically linked to one's sense of the meaning of life and well-being. Wherever this deeper meaning of life is missing, people

---

1 American Foundation for Suicide Prevention, "Suicide Statistics," in afsp.org/suicide-statistics/ [15.1.2022].

2 Cf. Mohsen Naghavi, "Global, regional, and national burden of suicide mortality 1990 to 2016: systematic analysis for the Global Burden of Disease Study 2016," *The British Medical Journal*, 6.2.2019, in www.bmj.com/content/364/bmj.l94 [15.1.2022].

3 Cf. Aaron Kheriaty and John Clark, *The Catholic Guide to Depression* (Manchester: Sophia Institute Press, 2012), 89-111.

are more easily inclined towards suicidal thoughts.[4] Even though this connection can be made clear statistically, the problem as such has not been addressed. As a consequence, a rapidly increasing number of people suffer because of mental health problems. In the U. S. there are more than 577,000 mental health professionals practicing today (2016-2017), which reveals the dimension of this problem.[5] It seems that society is growing sick, also because of a "spiritual vacuum," which leaves people disorientated and exposed to despair. Within this situation, suicide becomes an increasing problem, especially in societies where people seem to have everything but a sense of life, which is related to the question of God.

Christianity and Suicide

Before considering suicide, it will be helpful to provide a definition and to explain the Christian position on suicide. Even though the *Catechism of the Catholic Church* describes suicide in the numbers 2280-2283, the document does not offer a proper definition. This difficulty might be due to the existence of various types of suicide. Emile Durkheim, for example, based on sociological factors distinguished between four types of suicide.[6] However, the Fathers of the Church had already made some helpful distinctions, considering this topic with regards to the Old and New Testaments and the challenge of the first persecutions, in which Christian women were especially threatened seriously. They preferred to die rather than sin; nevertheless, there are some cases where it is difficult to distinguish between giving one's life and suicide.

---

[4] Cf. Magdalena Błażek et al., "Sense of Purpose in Life and Escape from Self as the Predictors of Quality of Life in Clinical Samples," in *Journal of Religion and Health* 54 (2015): 517-23.

[5] John Grohol enlists the following categories: "Clinical and counseling psychologists—166,000 (8.4% increase from 2011); Mental health and substance abuse social workers—112,040 (23% decrease); Mental health counselors—139,820 (19% increase); Substance abuse counselors—91,040 (5% increase); Psychiatrists—25,250 (36% decrease); Marriage and family therapists—42,880 (37% increase)." John M. Grohol, "Mental Health Professionals: U. S. Statistics 2017," 9.4.2019, in psychcentral.com/blog/mental-health-professionals-us-statistics-2017/ [15.1.2022].

[6] Cf. Emile Durkheim, *Suicide, A Study in Sociology* [1951] (New York: Snowball, 2013).

The Old Testament makes reference to some cases which could be considered a type of "suicide." For example, when Samson was captured and tortured by the Philistines, he chose to die in the collapse of the temple of the god Dagon. After invoking God and asking for strength he grasped the two middle columns of the temple saying: "'Let me die with the Philistines!' He pushed hard, and the temple fell upon the lords and all the people who were in it. Those he killed at his death were more than those he had killed during his lifetime" (Judg 16:30). Two similar cases are exalted in the sacred texts as positive examples, mentioned in the books of the Maccabees (cf. 1 Mac 6:43-47; 2 Mac 14:37-46). However, in both events it is not suicide in the strict sense, "but rather an act of abandonment of self into the hands of God, offering their lives for the salvation of their brothers."[7] These cases already anticipate the new meaning of self-giving of one's life, as presented in the New Testament: "No one has greater love than this: to lay down one's life for one's friend" (Jn 15:13). The gift of self is a heroic act, which receives a new meaning through the self-giving sacrifice of Jesus Christ (cf. Tit 2:14; cf. 1 Tim 2:6). The suffering servant described by Isaiah becomes emblematic (cf. Is 53:12) of a new and salvific perspective. Within this perspective martyrdom becomes the supreme testimony of love; and as such, it is something totally different from suicide.[8]

Within the persecutions of the early Christians, the distinction between the giving of one's life and suicide was at times a challenge. For instance, the historian and bishop Eusebius describes with admiration the example of a mother who preferred to commit suicide together with her daughters, rather than to be dishonored. Instead of being sold as prostitutes, they preferred to "flee to the Lord" and threw themselves into a river.[9] Similar cases happened

---

7   Gianfranco Ravasi, "It is the Lord who gives life and death. Towards a theology of death," in Correa and Sgreccia, *Dignity of the Dying Person*, 287-96, here 295.
8   Cf. Ralph Weimann, "Il Martirio. Suprema testimonianza d'amore," in M. Graulich and ibid. (eds.), *Deus Caritas Est: Porta di Misericordia* (Vatican City: Libreria Editrice Vaticana, 2016), 123-41.
9   Eusebius describes it with the following words: "And a certain holy person, admirable for strength of soul yet in body a woman, and famed as well by all that were at Antioch for wealth, birth and sound judgement, had brought up in the precepts of piety her two unmarried daughters,

during the persecutions and some of the Fathers of the Church, such as Saint Ambrose, spoke with great admiration about these testimonies.[10]

Among the sect of the Donatists, there were some who believed that by killing themselves they could attain heaven by considering themselves as martyrs. St. Augustine reproached them—together with everyone committing suicide—clarifying these concepts in the *City of God*: "Not for nothing it is that in the holy canonical books no divinely inspired order or permission can be found authorizing us to inflict death upon ourselves, neither in order to acquire immortality nor in order to avert or divert some evil."[11] Augustine referred to the fifth commandment "Thou shalt not kill" when explaining and clarifying that no authority, in any case, gives Christians the right to die of their own will. Following this well-argued tradition Catholic theologians considered suicide as murder and as a mortal sin. According to St. Augustine the commandment "thou

---

distinguished for the full bloom of their youthful beauty. Much envy was stirred up on their account, and busied itself in tracing in every manner possible where they lay concealed; and when it discovered that they were staying in a foreign country, of set purpose it recalled them to Antioch. Thus they fell into the soldiers' toils. When, therefore, the woman saw that herself and her daughters were in desperate straits, she placed before them in conversation the terrible things that awaited them from human hands, and the most intolerable thing of all these terrors—the threat of fornication. She exhorted both herself and her girls that they ought not to submit to listen to even the least whisper of such a thing, and said that to surrender their souls to the slavery of demons was worse than all kinds of death and every form of destruction. So she submitted that to flee to the Lord was the only way of escape from it all. And when they had both agreed to her opinion, and had arranged their garments suitably around them, on coming to the middle of their journey they quietly requested the guards to allow them a little time for retirement, and threw themselves into the river that flowed by." Eusebius, *Ecclesiastical History, Books 6-10*, Jeffrey Henderson (ed.), trans. J. E. L. Oulton (Cambridge: Harvard University Press, 1932), Book VIII, XII, 3-5.

10 Cf. Ambrosius Mediolanensis, *Verginità e vedovanza*, Franco Gori (ed.) (Milano/Roma: Biblioteca Ambrosiana, 1989), 237. Saint Augustine made different distinctions explaining these cases and providing clarifications. Cf. Augustine, *The City of God Against the Pagans*, Books I-III, G. P. Goold (ed.), trans. George E. McCracken (Cambridge: Harvard University Press, 1995), Book I, XVI-XX.

11 Ibid., XX.

shall not kill" forbids suicide, but not the death penalty.[12] The gradual spreading of Christianity brought about a downward trend in the acceptance of suicide. The prohibition of suicide became common and was based on natural law and religious revelation. Only to God was attributed the power of life and death over human beings.[13] In later centuries a Christian burial was denied to those who had committed suicide. The *Catechism of Saint Pius X* affirmed this doctrine once again in no. 417. He emphasized that only God is the master of life, and the Church, therefore, punishes suicide by the deprivation of Christian burial.[14]

Definition and Ethical Evaluation of Suicide

At this point, it is necessary to provide a definition of suicide, which will be helpful in order to come to an ethical evaluation. Suicide can be defined as the act through which one causes his own death, either directly or indirectly, by inflicting on himself a mortal injury. At times it is not easy to distinguish between suicide and direct or indirect euthanasia. John Paul II described suicide by taking into consideration multiple dimensions. He did not focus primarily on the intention of the person committing suicide but on the act of suicide per se. He wrote in his encyclical letter *Evangelium Vitae*: "it involves the rejection of love of self and the renunciation of the obligation of justice and charity towards one's neighbor, towards the communities to which one belongs, and towards society as a whole. In its deepest reality, suicide represents a rejection of God's absolute sovereignty over life and death."[15]

For that very reason, suicide is as morally "objectionable as murder."[16] The *Catechism* provides a detailed explanation. It mentions that the sovereign Master of life is God; life is, therefore, a gift, which needs to be accepted. In other words, God has entrusted life to man and man is not its master but steward, and consequently, it is not for man to dispose of it. This becomes even more understandable when considering life as something sacred. However,

---

12   Cf. ibid., XXII.
13   Cf. Thomas Aquinas, STh, II-II, q. 64, a. 5.
14   Cf. Pius X, *Il Catechismo Maggiore di Pio X nel centenario della sua promulgazione*, 15.6.1905 (Vigodarzere: Ares, 2005), 417.
15   John Paul II, EV, 66.
16   Ibid.

this will work only if the Creator—the origin of sacredness—is at the same time recognized. According to the *Catechism*, suicide is "gravely contrary to the just love of self,"[17] to the neighbor and to the living God. The document mentions further that the voluntary "co-operation in suicide is contrary to the moral law."[18] From this perspective, it becomes understandable why the Church refused burial to people who committed suicide because they acted gravely against the living God in the last moment of their life.

Already St. Thomas Aquinas considered suicide as a mortal sin and he justifies his position with the enumeration of the following arguments:

> Suicide is contrary to the inclination of nature, and to charity whereby every man should love himself. [...] By killing himself he injures the community. [...] Whoever takes his own life, sins against God, even as he who kills another's slave, sins against that slave's master, and as he who usurps to himself judgment of a matter not entrusted to him.[19]

Pope John Paul II adopted much of the teaching of St. Thomas, due to the fact that St. Thomas offers an objective theology, which is helpful in providing clear orientation. The question which arises is, whether people who have committed suicide can still be saved? This is a very delicate topic, especially when planning funerals. Since suicide is also an offense against the family, the neighbors, and society, the mourning community is often very hurt and close to despair. If a priest then says that the soul of the departed most probably could not reach heaven, it would likely cause scandal. People need to be comforted, but without renouncing the truth. Once again, suicide is objectively a mortal sin, which "destroys charity in the heart of man by a grave violation of God's law; it turns man away from God."[20] In other words, a mortal sin separates from God. In this context it will be helpful calling to mind the three conditions that must be fulfilled for a sin to be mortal:

---

17   CCC, 2281.
18   CCC, 2282. This aspect will be considered when dealing with assisted suicide.
19   Thomas Aquinas, STh, II-II, q. 64, a. 5.
20   CCC, 1855.

Suicide and Assisted Suicide

a. Object as grave matter: The *Catechism* and the encyclical letter *Evangelium Vitae* confirm, suicide is a grave matter, because of the reasons presented above.

b. Deliberate consent: Suicide usually implies deliberate consent; the person voluntarily decides to end his life.

c. Full knowledge: Today some experts in moral theology claim that it is almost impossible to have full knowledge, and by consequence, they deny that a person is capable of committing a mortal sin. Such a position implies a false understanding of the human nature since human beings are not angels. An angel has a "full knowledge" in the perfect sense of the word and knows exactly what he is doing. It is due to the human condition that full knowledge does not imply an angelical understanding of the concept, but a human. In this sense full knowledge "presupposes knowledge of the sinful character of the act, of its opposition to God's law."[21]

In the case of suicide, it might indeed happen that a person is lacking full knowledge but in a different sense. A person may not have given full consent of will and intellect while committing suicide. Especially in the case of a person who is suffering depression, his mind and will might be obscured. The *Catechism* is aware of this difficulty, affirming: "Grave psychological disturbances, anguish, or grave fear of hardship, suffering, or torture can diminish the responsibility of the one committing suicide."[22] Suicide is never an option or a right action, but the Church does recognize that persons may not be totally culpable for their actions. Therefore, the *Catechism* adds: "We should not despair of the eternal salvation of persons who have taken their own lives. By ways known to him alone, God can provide the opportunity for salutary repentance. The Church prays for persons who have taken their own lives."[23]

On one occasion it was said that a woman was devastated because her husband had committed suicide, and so she approached the holy Curé of Ars († 1859). She knew that suicide is a grave sin, and she was troubled because she had lost her beloved spouse in this way. Having heard of St. John Vianney's mystical insights, she approached him in her despair. She couldn't reach him for hours and was about

---

21 CCC, 1859.
22 CCC, 2282.
23 CCC, 2283.

to give up and to leave still quite desperate. Suddenly, as the story is told, the priest exclaimed through the crowd: "He is saved!" The woman was incredulous, so the saint repeated, stressing each word: "I tell you he is saved. He is in Purgatory, and you must pray for him. Between the parapet of the bridge and the water he had time to make an act of contrition."[24] This is a powerful example that reminds us not to judge (cf. Lk 6:37) since we often do not know—as opposed to assisted suicide—why people commit suicide and if they were able to repent. If someone is suffering psychological disturbances, anguish, or is in grave fear of hardship, etc., his guilt might be reduced, his mind obscured. However, hope is a theological virtue, and suicide is opposed to hope.

The Code of Canon Law, where it regards those to whom ecclesiastical funerals must be denied, has to be taken into consideration. Canon 1184 §1 says: "Unless they gave some signs of repentance before death, the following must be deprived of ecclesiastical funerals: 1/ notorious apostates, heretics and schismatics; 2/ those who chose the cremation of their bodies for reasons contrary to Christian faith; 3/ other manifest sinners who cannot be granted ecclesiastical funerals without public scandal of the faithful."[25] No. 3 especially refers to cases of suicide, since through it the person has caused public scandal. If one were to celebrate the funeral of a notorious sinner, one would send the message to society that the sinful act is licit for Catholics. For that very reason, the Church is supposed to refuse funerals in certain circumstances, even though it is always a delicate matter. This does not mean, however, that the Church judges the souls of the departed, but rather she wants to avoid sending the wrong moral message. The social acceptance of suicide would lead to disastrous consequences. The philosopher Ludwig Wittgenstein was very much aware of this danger and wrote: "If suicide is allowed, then everything is allowed. If anything is not allowed, then suicide is not allowed."[26] Writing his considerations in the context of the First World War, Wittgenstein called suicide the "elementary sin."

---

24   Cf. Francis Trochu, *Le curé d'Ars Saint Jean-Marie Baptiste Vianney* (Montsûrs: Résiac, 1987), 209–10.
25   CIC, c. 1184 §1.
26   Ludwig Wittgenstein, *Notebooks 1914–1916*, trans. Gertrude E. M. Anscombe (New York: Blackwell, 1961), 91.

ASSISTED SUICIDE

In public opinion assisted suicide is more and more presented as a real "choice" at the end of life. To promote this "pro-choice mentality," even the language is often manipulated. Lobbies demanding euthanasia and assisted suicide use synonyms such as "helping to die," "assisting in dying," "pro-choice," or even concepts such as "death with dignity." This language makes something intrinsically evil appear as good. Nonetheless, expressions such as "assisted dying" or "accompaniment" miss the core of the issue. The accent is placed on the process or the circumstances rather than on the person.

Assisted suicide is related to the lived experience of the dying, who often find themselves in difficult situations because of the illness and pain, as well as faced with substantial burdens and expenses. People have difficulty enduring the suffering and/or the costs associated with a prolonged death. Physician-assisted suicide seems to be the answer. For others, it conjures fear that someone other than themselves will determine "what is to be considered excessive suffering or costs, and that others might seek to eliminate the suffering or the costs by eliminating those persons."[27]

A brief look at the situation in Switzerland is helpful to understand why assisted suicide is becoming increasingly popular there. First of all, Switzerland is the only country that accepts foreign nationals for legal medically assisted suicide. End of life "tourism" is a possibility. All that is needed is membership in one of the Swiss "self-determination" organizations such as "Dignitas" or "EXIT." The latter presents itself (since 2020) as a "democratically organized society under Swiss law" with "currently over 120,000" members.[28] Their work "is dedicated to the cause of human self-determination. Options offered by EXIT include living wills, legal counsel, and—if need be—safe and dignified end-of-life care."[29]

According to a survey carried out in January 2020 in the Netherlands, an increasing number of people over 55 years of age are

---

27   Felicia Cohn, Joanne Lynn, "Vulnerable People: Practical Rejoinders to Claim in Favor of Assisted Suicide," in Kathleen Foley and Herbert Hendin (eds.), *The Case against Assisted Suicide* (Baltimore and London: Johns Hopkins University Press, 2002), 238–60, here 238.
28   "Exit, Our Society," in exit.ch/en/englisch/who-is-exit/ [15.1.2022].
29   Ibid.

willing to end their life, despite being in good physical health. The indicated reasons in favor of assisted suicide are loneliness, not wanting to be a burden for others, and financial problems. The Dutch Minister of Health noted that the government has to do more to combat this crisis; they need to provide a meaning to life.[30]

This topic has gained much political relevance. An aging population in many countries is a challenge and an "economical solution" is desirable at least from a cost-effective perspective. The justifications are similar to the arguments presented in favor of euthanasia, based especially on a false understanding of autonomy. Even the "catholic" theologian and priest Hans Küng promoted such a vision in favor of a self-determined death.[31] Although an increasing majority of society is in favor of granting the right to undergo assisted suicide, studies have shown that only 10% of terminally ill patients (in the USA) would consider it for themselves.[32]

In any case, it must be said that a government has to protect and defend the life of its citizens, which is the most basic of all rights. The United States Conference of Catholic Bishops published in 1998 the statement *Living the Gospel of Life: A Challenge to American Catholics as a Response to the Challenges Against Life*. In this document the bishops, encouraged by Pope John Paul II after their *ad limina* visit, say in number 4:

---

[30] Cf. "Resultaten Perspectief—onderzoek naar ouderen met een doodswens aangeboden," 30.1.2020, in www.zonmw.nl/nl/actueel/nieuws/detail/item/resultaten-perspectief-onderzoek-naar-ouderen-met-een-doodswens-aangeboden/ [15.1.2022].

[31] Cf. Alexander Foitzik, "Korrektiv," in *Herder Korrespondenz* 68 (2014): 491–92.

[32] Cf. David Jeffrey, *Against Physician-Assisted Suicide: A Palliative Care Perspective* (Oxford: CRC Press, 2009), 78–87. The author reveals an interesting fact regarding the situation in Oregon (USA). "Studies of dying patients have shown that about half would like the option of PAS [Physician Assisted Suicide] to be available for possible future use. However, only 10% of these patients seriously consider PAS, only 1% specifically request it, and only 0.1% actually take a lethal prescription. [...] The data from Oregon for the period 1997-2005, during which 246 patients died by ingesting a lethal dose of medication, show that the most important concerns were loss of autonomy, inability to participate in enjoyable activities, and loss of dignity. Inadequate pain control and self-perceived burden on others were less common concerns." Ibid., 79–80.

The losers in this ethical sea change will be those who are elderly, poor, disabled and politically marginalized. None of these pass the utility test; and yet, they at least have a presence. They at least have the possibility of organizing to be heard. *Those who are unborn, infirm and terminally ill have no such advantage.* They have no "utility," and worse, they have no voice. As we tinker with the beginning, the end and even the intimate cell structure of life, we tinker with our own identity as a free nation dedicated to the dignity of the human person. When American political life becomes an experiment on people rather than for and by them, it will no longer be worth conducting. We are arguably moving closer to that day. Today, when the inviolable rights of the human person are proclaimed, and the value of life publicly affirmed, the most basic human right, "the right to life, is being denied or trampled upon, especially at the more significant moments of existence: the moment of birth and the moment of death" (Pope John Paul II, *The Gospel of Life [Evangelium Vitae]*, 18).[33]

Beginning and end of life are topics with vast political implications and politics are often moved by certain pressure groups and guided by economic interests. Besides the political dimension the question must be raised: How are we to define assisted suicide, and how are we to distinguish it from euthanasia? According to Richard Fenigsen the "two acts, stopping life-support and assisting a suicide, are profoundly different as to the grounds for their justification, the intentions of the acting persons, and the factual consequences." Fenigsen adds: "In assisted suicide, the intention of the patient and of the doctor is to end the patient's life."[34] Even though this distinction is right, it does not bring us closer to a definition, especially if one would refer to direct and voluntary euthanasia. Pope John Paul II offers an explanation in his encyclical letter *Evangelium Vitae* regarding assisted suicide, which is helpful for a classification:

---

33   USCCB, "Living the Gospel of Life: A Challenge to American Catholics," in www.usccb.org/issues-and-action/human-life-and-dignity/abortion/living-the-gospel-of-life.cfm [15.1.2022], 4.
34   Richard Fenigsen, "Euthanasia and moral reflection," in Correa and Sgreccia, *Dignity of the Dying Person*, 212–18, here 212.

To concur with the intention of another person to commit suicide and to help in carrying it out through so-called 'assisted suicide' means to cooperate in, and at times to be the actual perpetrator of, an injustice which can never be excused, even if it is requested. In a remarkably relevant passage Saint Augustine writes that "it is never licit to kill another: even if he should wish it, indeed if he request it because, hanging between life and death, he begs for help in freeing the soul struggling against the bonds of the body and longing to be released; nor is it licit even when a sick person is no longer able to live." Even when not motivated by a selfish refusal to be burdened with the life of someone who is suffering, euthanasia must be called a false mercy, and indeed a disturbing "perversion" of mercy. True "compassion" leads to sharing another's pain; it does not kill the person whose suffering we cannot bear. Moreover, the act of euthanasia appears all the more perverse if it is carried out by those, like relatives, who are supposed to treat a family member with patience and love, or by those, such as doctors, who by virtue of their specific profession are supposed to care for the sick person even in the most painful terminal stages.[35]

The explanation provided by John Paul II indicates the way. Within the same number, he speaks first about assisted suicide and—after offering an example referred to St. Augustine—about euthanasia. Therefore, it can be said that he considers assisted suicide as a synonym for euthanasia and vice versa. The person—with the aid of a physician—has the intention to bring about one's own death.[36] This becomes even more evident in the second part of the same number of *Evangelium Vitae*, which states:

> The choice of euthanasia becomes more serious when it takes the form of a murder committed by others on a person who has in no way requested it and who has never consented to it. The height of arbitrariness and injustice is reached when certain people, such as physicians or

---

35   John Paul II, EV, 66.
36   Cf. Stefan Buchs, *Ärzteethos und Suizidhilfe: Theologisch-ethische Untersuchung zur Praxis der ärztlichen Suizidhilfe in der Schweiz* (Basel: Echter Verlag, 2018), 54.

legislators, arrogate to themselves the power to decide who ought to live and who ought to die. [...] When man usurps this power, being enslaved by a foolish and selfish way of thinking, he inevitably uses it for injustice and death. Thus, the life of the person who is weak is put into the hands of the one who is strong; in society the sense of justice is lost, and mutual trust, the basis of every authentic interpersonal relationship, is undermined at its root.[37]

Pope John Paul II always defended the sanctity of life, especially the lives of the weak, the needy, and dying. Since life is a gift from the life-giver, it has to be safeguarded. Despite his efforts, the culture of death continues to spread promoting the so-called "right-to-die."[38] In reality, this is a clear sign that democracy contradicts its own principles when it moves, as John Paul II said, towards "the oppressive totalitarianism of public authority."[39] Freedom detached from objective truth makes it impossible to establish personal rights on a firm rational basis. The American Bishops wrote in their statement *Living the Gospel of Life*:

> *All direct attacks on innocent human life, such as abortion and euthanasia, strike at the house's foundation.* These directly and immediately violate the human person's most fundamental right—the right to life. Neglect of these issues is the equivalent of building our house on sand. Such attacks cannot help but lull the social conscience in ways ultimately destructive of other human rights. [...] Democracy is not served by silence. Most Americans would recognize the contradiction in the statement, "While I am personally opposed to slavery or racism or sexism I cannot force my personal view on the rest of society." *Real pluralism*

---

37 Ibid.
38 Cf. Derek Humphry and Mary Clement, *Freedom to Die: People, Politics and the Right-To-Die Movement* (New York: St. Martin's Griffin, 1998), 339-45. The authors present a chronology of voluntary euthanasia and physician-assisted suicide, which confirms the existence of certain pressure groups promoting it. At the same time it becomes evident that there is no step back, once the door is open.
39 John Paul II, EV, 96.

depends on people of conviction struggling vigorously to advance their beliefs by every ethical and legal means at their disposal.[40]

When promoting the culture of death, some of its advocates claim assisted suicide and euthanasia pertain only to a few people. If that is the case, why would they spend so much time, money, and other means, for the benefit of only a few exceptional cases? The facts uncover their true motive. The *National Review* revealed on January 22, 2018 that advocates for assisted suicide/euthanasia promote a broad application of euthanasia, even though they talk about a few exceptions. In Delaware, the people running the state's assisted suicide legalization bill have included in their proposal the terminally ill and intellectually disabled. Amendment 2 of House Bill 160 says:

> "'Intellectual disability' means a disability that originated before the age of 18, characterized by significant limitations in both intellectual functioning and in adaptive behavior, which covers many everyday social and practical skills." This means disabled people with significant intellectual impairments. They could be eligible for assisted suicide if a social worker says they understand.[41]

This is a disturbing course of action, which seems to spread more and more. However, as Frederick White affirms, it seems that the support of the population for physician-assisted suicide is not nearly as strong as has been reported in the press. He adds: "Even where physician-assisted suicide is legal, it is rarely requested by terminally ill cancer patients. In the course of discussion on physician-assisted suicide, the proposition that should be placed before the public is simply this: it is never morally acceptable for a physician to hasten the death or take the life of a patient as a primary end."[42] It will be almost impossible to restrict assisted suicide, whenever and wherever it is permitted. It was a wise judgment from Ludwig Wittgenstein to consider suicide an "elementary sin."

---

[40] USCCB, "Living the Gospel of Life," 22f.
[41] So quoted in Wesley J. Smith, "Delaware Push for Intellectually Disabled Assisted Suicide," *National Review*, 22.1.2018, in www.nationalreview.com/corner/455665/delaware-push-intellectually-disabled-assisted-suicide [15.1.2022].
[42] Frederick J. White, "Lessons from Recent Polls on Physician-Assisted Suicide," in *NCBQ* 17 (2017): 247-57, here 257.

FINAL MORAL EVALUATION

The moral evaluation of assisted suicide is very similar to what has been said regarding euthanasia. The encyclical letter *Evangelium Vitae* states: "'assisted suicide' means to cooperate in, and at times to be the actual perpetrator of, an injustice which can never be excused, even if it is requested."[43] The encyclical letter *Veritatis Splendor* calls such actions intrinsically evil (*intrinsece malum*)[44] and adds that these actions are always and per se evil on account of their object and apart from the intention and circumstances. The Letter *Samaritanus Bonus* affirms that any "formal or immediate material cooperation in such an act is a grave sin against human life."[45] In consequence, the CDF affirms in 2020: "Those who approve laws of euthanasia and assisted suicide, therefore, become accomplices of a grave sin that others will execute. They are also guilty of scandal because by such laws they contribute to the distortion of conscience, even among the faithful."[46] Even assisting in a suicide is "an unjustified collaboration."[47] Healthcare institutions must resist the economic pressure to accept euthanasia and even more Catholic institutions, otherwise they would endanger "the identification of the institution itself as 'Catholic.'"[48]

Life is sacred, inviolable, and unique. Therefore, assisted suicide is always the wrong choice and the circumstances can never make an action that is intrinsically evil good. As the pastoral constitution *Gaudium et Spes* says, all of this poisons human society, but they "do more harm to those who practice them than those who suffer from the injury. Moreover, they are a supreme dishonor to the Creator."[49]

---

43   John Paul II, EV, 66.
44   John Paul II, VS, 80.
45   CDF, SB, V, 1. Andrew McLean Cummings provides an excellent overview about this topic in *The Servant and the Ladder: Cooperation with Evil in the Twenty-First Century* (Herefordshire: Gracewing, 2014).
46   CDF, SB, V, 1.
47   Cf. John Paul II, EV, 74.
48   CDF, SB, V, 9.
49   GS, 27.

SUMMARY

Direct (active) euthanasia	The deliberate decision to deprive an innocent human being of his life.
Voluntary euthanasia	The person wants to die and affirms it.
Non-voluntary euthanasia	A person that cannot decide or simply cannot make known his wishes.
Involuntary euthanasia	A person who wants to live but is killed anyway.
Indirect (passive) euthanasia	Death brought about by an indirect inducement of death, by withholding medicine or stopping a procedure.
—**Indirect euthanasia with the intention to cause death**	Death is caused by the withdrawal of natural means.
—**Indirect euthanasia with the intention not to cause death**	Death isn't intended or directly caused, but a consequence of the process of dying.
Suicide	Act, through which one causes his own death, either directly or indirectly, by inflicting on himself a mortal injury.
Assisted suicide	A synonym for euthanasia.

VII
Ordinary (Proportionate) and Extraordinary (Disproportionate) Means

THE DEVELOPMENT OF TECHNOLOGY AND MEDicine offers many new options and means that can be applied at the end of life. The question arises of what types are well-proportioned and which methods are ill-proportioned. In countries like Germany, the health care system is available for everyone; it is advanced and includes new technology. At the same time, the demographic situation is not favorable for the development of society, and there is an increasing number of elderly people. According to official statistics from 2019, the average life expectancy is 78.6 years, and for female new-borns, the calculated estimate of life expectancy is even 83.4 years.[1] It is not rare that 90-year-old persons still undergo a great number of operations, which are not only very expensive but which sometimes are unnecessary. Generally, the health care and the social system pay for it; however, it must be said that there are also economic interests involved and economic efficiency becomes more and more important. In other countries, where the health system is not as good or as available, it is rather the other way around. However, the question needs to be raised, what is proportional, and what is not proportional? There is a twofold danger either to do too much or to not do enough. How can a balance be found? The following considerations are meant to offer some basic principles and criteria in order to find orientation.[2]

---

1 "Durchschnittliche weitere Lebenserwartung in Deutschland nach Geschlecht und Altersgruppen laut der Sterbetafel 2017/2019," *Statista*, in de.statista.com/statistik/daten/studie/1783/umfrage/durchschnittliche-weitere-lebenserwartung-nach-altersgruppen/ [15.1.2022].

2 A good overview about the literature to this topic is provided by Marina Casini et al., "La riflessione sul 'fine vita.' Aspetti giuridici ed etico-clinici dell'eutanasia," in *Medicina e Morale* 59 (2010): 987-1005.

PRELIMINARY ETHICAL REFLECTION

The enormous progress of medicine has opened horizons of hope and well-being, but it has raised also concerns regarding the end of life. On the one hand, there is a growing fear toward involuntary euthanasia, the fear of being mistreated by doctors and medicine. On the other hand, there is a growing fear that physicians might submit the dying to treatments that inhumanly prolong an inevitable death. This will increase even more, since many elderly and sick people have to face the last moments of their life in the cold and technical environment of a hospital, often abandoned and alone. They are frequently treated just as an anonymous "case" guarded by a monitor and linked to a series of machines. Indeed, sometimes these people just want to die peacefully, but it is denied them.

All of this arouses fear, and this fear regarding medical treatments leads some people to wish to be freed from such treatments. Sometimes, even euthanasia is proposed as an antidote against a "therapeutic obstinacy." It is not easy to define therapeutic obstinacy and sometimes it is overdramatized. It can be applied "not only when technical measures are employed on someone who is practically dead, [...] but when intervention with medical or surgical treatments (except for ordinary treatments) is done in a way that is 'disproportionate' to the foreseeable effects."[3] An appropriate decision at the end of life is challenging because it is different in every situation. However, this concept is mostly referred to as the initiation or continuation of medical treatments of a dying person that has no other aim than to prolong the patient's life. The main problem becomes the right application of appropriate means. This is a delicate topic, which has many moral implications.

In the year 2002, there was a lively debate about "medical futility"[4]

---

3 Sgreccia, PB, 689.
4 Edmund Pellegrino describes the development of the concept "futility" as follows: "For most of the history of medicine futility was taken to be an objective medical judgment which only physicians were qualified to make. This changed thirty or so years ago [status 1999] with the emergence of autonomy, which granted rights of decision and participation to patients and their valid surrogates. [...] As a result, futility is no longer defined solely in medical terms but also in terms of the patient's goals, values, and beliefs, i.e., those things by which we determine whether the decision is indeed 'worthwhile' from the patient's point of view." Edmund Pellegrino, "Decision at the end of life: the use and abuse of the concept futility," in

in the United States.⁵ This concept was used to override the treatment demands of patients, often dominated by a utilitarian perspective. Similar to therapeutic obstinacy, there was no agreement on how to define this concept. Within this debate, the main problem was a conflict between the patient's self-determination/autonomy and the physician's autonomy. Usually, there is even a third "authority" involved: the economic pressure and the guidelines imposed by the government that favors economic interests. Edward Pellegrino († 2013), an American bioethicist and academic, who was for a period the director of the *Kennedy Institute of Ethics at Georgetown University*, suggested a "human approach" towards futility, based on the general distinction between objective and subjective elements and three criteria:

— Effectiveness: The question needs be to be asked, does the treatment make a difference to morbidity? Pellegrino considers effectiveness an objective element, dependant "upon the outcome studies and within the physician's domain of expertise. Effectiveness centers on medical good and on measurable clinical data about prognosis and therapeutics."⁶ Physicians and specialists can evaluate if a specific intervention will resolve the problem. They should find an answer to the symptoms in a positive way.

— Benefit: this is a subjective element and refers to what is valuable to the patient according to his own perception. It centers on the good and goal of the patient, for example, when a patient says this or that treatment is worthwhile for him. It is not quantifiable and therefore subjective; it refers to the perception of the patient regarding the validity of the treatment for himself.

— Burden: this element is objective and subjective at the same time. It refers "to the physical, emotional, fiscal, or social costs imposed on

---

Correa and Sgreccia, *Dignity of the Dying Person*, 219–41, here 225–26. Regarding this topic, see also the article by Felipe E. Vizcarrondo, "Medical Futility in Pediatric Care," in *NCBQ* 19 (2019): 105–20.

5   Cf. Robert A. Burt, "The medical futility debate: Patient choice, physician obligation, and end-of-life care," in *Journal of Palliative Medicine* 5 (2002): 249–54. The concept of medical futility is neither very clear nor universally accepted. Some distinguish between treatments that are a) physiologically futile; b) quantitatively-qualitatively futile; c) socially futile. Cf. Francisco Javier Insa Gómez and Pablo Requena Meana, "Is Medical Futility an Ethical or Clinical Concept?," in *NCBQ* 17 (2017): 261–73, especially 262–63.

6   Edward Pellegrino, "Decision at the end of life," 227.

the patient by the treatment. Since they are objective and subjective the domain of both the doctor and patient is necessary. One needs to consider both the burden imposed on the medical team, and the burden on the patient. It is difficult to justify morally this category."[7]

Yet, regarding therapeutic obstinacy or futility, the guiding criterion must always be to seek the true good of the patient in its entirety. But what is the true good of the patient? Not everything technically possible is ethically admissible and the agony of the dying should not be prolonged. On the other side, it is sad enough to know that many topics related to the concept of therapeutic obstinacy/futility are often connected to interests that go beyond the good of the patient. Certain groups and even politicians in favor of euthanasia make reference to this concept in order to promote a culture of death and to give in to economic pressure.

Therapeutic obstinacy can be a serious problem, especially if it is unreasonable. Still, any solution will depend on the vision of man and on how the true good of the person is defined. This must be the starting point. Therefore, the following criterion can provide orientation: everything possible must be done, but only the possible and in the best way possible. Therapeutic measures and palliative care have to be proportioned and administrated in the right way; it has to correspond to "the twofold dimension of the principle of justice to promote human life (*suum cuique tribuere*) and to avoid harming another (*alterum non laedere*)."[8]

To Do Everything Possible

Before considering if a treatment is proportionate or not, the difference between person and treatment must be called to mind. The withholding or withdrawing of a treatment is intrinsically related to the person's intent, which, if it is to be morally licit, must not be suicidal. In this sense, the doctors are supposed to do "everything possible" to restore health to the patient, and to keep him alive. Especially since the Hippocratic Oath was changed,[9] it is important to stress this aspect.

Doctors are in a difficult position today because they have to find a way between too many interventions and too few. Therefore,

---

7   Ibid., 228.
8   CDF, SB, I.
9   Cf. chapter IV, Post-Modernity.

it is necessary to look for the true good of the patient, even in the state of chronic or terminal pathology. To do "everything possible" implies, first of all, to recognize that the life of the human person has transcendent value.[10] This concept, if it were well understood and applied, could offer a solution to many problems and avoid any type of discrimination based on a reductionist view. It refers to a non-measurable element, which is not conditioned by external circumstances, such as the state of health, race, sex, etc. It refers to the intrinsic value of man. To recognize this aspect one does not necessarily need to believe in God, even though it will be helpful. The transcendent value of man can be grounded in natural law or in the nature of the person, which John Paul II has called "sacredness of life."[11]

It goes beyond the categories of time and space. In other words, the life of a person who has lived for many years does not necessarily have more value than the life of a person who dies young. This is reflected in the life of the saints, such as St. Thérèse of Lisieux, St. Maria Goretti, and many others, especially when including eternal life in the consideration. From this perspective, one act of sincere forgiveness might be more important than a thousand days living in hatred or with indifference. Let us take the example of a lady who went to the doctor and was diagnosed with brain cancer in its final stage. After accepting the unavoidable and being prepared through the sacraments, she was able to say before she died that she loved her husband more than before. There is a transcendent value of life and this value gains special importance at the last moment of life. Therefore, the goal of life must not be to grow old but to live well in the eyes of God. The Book of Sirach confirms: "A moment's affliction brings forgetfulness of past delights; when a man dies, his life is revealed. Call no man happy before his death, for by how he ends, a man is known" (Sirach 11:27f).

To do everything possible means, above all, to recognize the dignity of man, whatever his physical condition might be. Every

---

10 Sgreccia describes this with the following words: "The person, capable of self-consciousness and self-determination, surpasses the material world in terms of novelty and ontological level and value." Sgreccia, PB, 122–26, here 123.
11 See John Paul II, EV, 39–40. See also Baiju Julian and Hormis Mynatty, *Catholic Contribution to Bioethics: Reflections on "Evangelium Vitae"* (Bangalore: ATC Publication, 2007), 19–45.

human person has a transcendent value and it must be recognized and protected, no matter what type of measures might be applied. Therefore, accompaniment is of great importance; it "involves the exercise of the human and Christian virtues of *empathy* (*en-pathos*), of *compassion* (*cum-passio*), of bearing another's suffering by sharing it, and of the *consolation* (*cum-solatium*), of entering into the solitude of others to make them feel loved, accepted, accompanied, and sustained."[12] To do everything possible should include the fact that dying is a preparation for eternal life.

To Do Only the Possible

If the true good of the patient demands to do "everything possible," it also demands to do "only the possible." In other words, all that is truly beneficial to the person should be done and things are to be avoided that are futile, useless, or harmful. A new sense of responsibility and respectfulness must be proposed in order that doctors may stick to their own competence and do only the possible according to the current means offered by science and medical technology. They have to know that they are not supposed to go beyond their "frontiers." This is a critical aspect, especially within a growing specialization. Today, doctors are experts in some fields of specialization and research, but often they lack a broader perspective. Considering the human person only through the perspective of a certain specialization—which is often defined by medical procedures and techniques—is not enough and will lead to a reductive vision of man. As a consequence, it will not be possible to recognize the true good of the person. It is not enough to keep the organs alive or the function of some biological tissue, but rather the entire person needs to be taken into consideration. The human person is much more than the totality of his cells.

For example, when a medical intervention can only prolong the process of death, the true good for the person could mean to interrupt the medical procedure already started.[13] Regarding this delicate topic, the *Declaration on Euthanasia* from 1980 has provided further clarifications, affirming that the refusal of treatment is not an equivalent of suicide but corresponds to the acceptance of the

---

12   CDF, SB, V, 10.
13   Cf. Pius XII, "Address to an International Congress of Anesthesiologists," 24.11.1957, in *NCBQ* 2 (2002): 309–14.

human condition.[14] This aspect is of great importance in understanding the meaning of "to do only the possible." Death, as part of the human condition, needs to be accepted when inevitable. But whenever man is reduced to the conditions of physical health and methods, this will lead to one of the two extremes: a) therapeutic obstinacy, wherein procedures are undertaken to prolong life as long as possible; or b) attempts to end life indirectly or directly. Therefore, Gonzalo Miranda rightly affirms that the acceptance of death is intrinsically linked to the sense of life, which finds its ultimate inspiration in love.[15]

In society today the acceptance of death becomes ever more difficult, since only a few have actually assisted a dying person, and death is less and less present in public. Relatives especially have difficulties in accepting death. The *Guardian* described a situation in an article in February 2016:

> My father spent 10 days dying. He was 84 and he had lost his wife—my mother, whom he adored, and without whom he felt life was a lot less worth living—three years earlier. He died of old age, and it was entirely natural. The process, though, did not feel that way at all, at least not to me. Dad had been bedridden for months and was in a nursing home. He stopped eating one day, then started slipping in and out of consciousness. Soon he stopped drinking. For 10 days my sister and I sat by his bedside, holding his hand, moistening his lips. Slowly his breathing changed, became more ragged. During the last few days, the tips of his fingers turned blue. His skin smelled different. His breath gradually became a rasp, then a rattle. It sounded awful. We were sure he was in pain. The doctor reassured us he wasn't; this was a human body dying naturally, shutting down, one bit at a time. We had not, of course, talked about any of this with Dad beforehand; we had no plans for this, no idea of what he might have wanted. It would have been a very difficult conversation. The doctor said he could give him something that would make him at least sound better, but it would really be more

---

14   Cf. CDF, DE, IV. The *Catechism of the Catholic Church* adopted these formulations in CCC, 2278.
15   Cf. Gonzalo Miranda, "The meaning of life," 311.

for us than for my father. "My job," the doctor said, "is about prolonging people's lives. Anything I give to your father now would simply be prolonging his death." So we waited. When it finally came, death was quite sudden, and absolutely unmistakable. But those 10 days were hard. Death is foreign to us now; most of us do not know what it looks, sounds and smells like. We certainly don't like talking about it. In the early years of the 20th century, says Simon Chapman, director of policy and external affairs at the National Council for Palliative Care, 85% of people still died in their home, with their family. By the early years of this century, fewer than 20% did. A big majority, 60%, died in hospital; 20% in care homes, like my father; 6% in hospices, like my mother. "Death became medicalized; a whole lot of taboos grew up around it," Chapman says. "We're trying now to break them down."[16]

In this case, the doctor did what we can call "only the possible." He did not prolong the process of death but alleviated the pain of the patient. The family was able to be present and—if they were Catholic—they would have been able to prepare the dying with the sacraments and to accompany him with prayer. The integral good of the person, which is related to what Pope Pius XII called the principle of totality,[17] must be taken into consideration.

Yet, there are always two dimensions involved regarding the application of the medical treatment: a subjective and an objective dimension. Both are usually in close relation to each other. The Pontifical Council *Cor Unum* offered guidelines in 1976,[18] presenting some *Questions of Ethics Concerning the Fatally Ill and the Dying* on June 27, 1981. The document says that some criteria

> are objective: such as the nature of the measures proposed, how expensive they are, whether it is just to use them, and what options of justice are in the matter of using them.

---

16 Jon Henley, "At my father's bedside, I learned what death looks like," *The Guardian*, 3.2.2016, in www.theguardian.com/lifeandstyle/2016/feb/03/death-hospital-nhs-end-of-life-palliative-care-family [15.1.2022].
17 Cf. chapter I, The Magisterium of the Church on Bioethics.
18 Cf. Pontifical Council *Cor Unum*, "Actions de santé pour un promotion humaine," in *Enchiridion Vaticanum*, vol. 5, *Documenti ufficiali della Santa Sede 1974-1976* (Bologna: Edizioni Dehoniane Bologna, 1979), 1232-51.

> Other criteria are subjective: such as not giving certain patients psychological shocks, anxiety, uneasiness, and so on. It will always be a question, when deciding upon measures to be taken, of establishing to what extent the means to be used and the end being sought are proportionate.[19]

These criteria are helpful for coming to the right understanding of what it means "to do only the possible," especially when considering ill and dying people. In this sense, it might happen that relatives, due to their subjective criteria, perceive the process of dying in a totally different way than the dying person does. It might also happen that one patient strongly desires to live, even while being in a precarious state, and is willing to submit to difficult therapies. It could be that he needs this time to prepare himself for the final encounter with God, to become reconciled with his family, etc. The *Declaration on Euthanasia* takes into account the subjective dimension and affirms that in "numerous cases, the complexity of the situation can be such as to cause doubts about the way ethical principles should be applied." Then the CDF adds: "In the final analysis, it pertains to the conscience either of the sick person, or of those qualified to speak in the sick person's name, or of the doctors, to decide, in the light of moral obligations and of the various aspects of the case."[20]

At this point it will not be necessary to go into further detail; however, all this leads to the conclusion that decisions must be taken on a case-by-case basis and special attention needs to be paid to guaranteeing the true integrity of the person. This will be possible only if clear principles are applied. The document issued by the Pontifical Council *Cor Unum* says that the

> fundamental point is that the decision should be made according to rational arguments that have taken well into account the many and various aspects of the situation, including what effect will be had upon the family. The principle to follow is, therefore, that no moral obligation

---

[19] Pontifical Council *Cor Unum*, "Questions of Ethics Regarding the Fatally Ill and the Dying," 27.6.1981, in www.academyforlife.va/content/dam/pav/documents/papi/documentisantasede/ENGLISH/fatally_ill_and_dying_ENG.pdf [15.1.2022], 2.4.2.
[20] CDF, DE, IV.

to have recourse to extraordinary measures exists; and that, incidentally, a doctor must follow the wishes of a sick person who refuses the measures.[21]

To Do Things in the Best Way Possible

It is not enough to do "only the possible." Everything regarding life must be done in the best way possible. The human person is not an object, and therefore, should not only be treated according to therapeutic "quantity" and "quality" criteria.

Especially when the patient is close to death one must tell the truth. Often, as a type of defense mechanism, the dying isolates "himself from his misfortune, discussing his own serious illness or death as though it belonged to another, and which sometimes takes on a maniacal tone (I've never felt better in my life). In any case, it has to do with a misunderstanding of reality."[22] It is a fact that physicians and hospital staff sometimes do not know how to treat the question of death, which might lead to a situation of negation. Some shy away from telling the truth about the real situation of the dying, in order to "protect" the patient and not to disturb him. Mario Bizzotto describes what happens frequently:

> The truth is denied him, and his relationship with others is hidden behind masks. The patient moves towards the end without knowing the truth and for the most part without wanting to know it, and sometimes those around him find it easier to say nothing. Thus communication is broken. Two people who are frank with each other can communicate, they can leave their solitude, but when two masked people talk to each other they tell lies, remaining cut off in their isolation.[23]

However, it would be a big mistake to leave people in this erroneous way of considering their life-reality, especially because it would deprive them of the opportunity to be prepared for death. To make dying people believe they would remain in a "state of shadow" and

---

21 Pontifical Council *Cor Unum*, "Questions of Ethics," 2.4.3.
22 Leonardo Ancona, "Psychological and spiritual assistance: the truth when faced with death," in Correa and Sgreccia, *Dignity of the Dying Person*, 267-86, here 270.
23 Mario Bizzotto, "Concealment of death," in Correa and Sgreccia, *Dignity of the Dying Person*, 31-52, here 41f.

"go with the clouds" will not help them to die in peace. Death and the acceptance of death need to be integrated with life, and for this, spiritual and psychological assistance should be offered. This is the only way to prepare someone for death. Yet, it is important to communicate the truth in a "human way" that means being very personal, taking the time to listen and to accompany the person. This is for sure a work of mercy. The truth must be measured according to the capacity of the patient to accept it. His state of mind needs to be taken into consideration, particularly when delivering bad news to a patient, such as cancer in its final stage.[24] The seriousness of the situation should not be hidden, especially when the patient is already close to death. Death is the most important step in life, and each person has the duty and the right to be well prepared for this moment. "The truth remains a fundamental requirement in order for a moral act to be objectively positive."[25] When the truth is offered in a positive way, it leads to good results and to a better preparation. The Gospel says that the Truth will set you free (cf. John 8:32) and this truth must be addressed even by the dying. Any decision at the end of life requires the informed consent of the patient. In other words, an adequate understanding of the situation is necessary.

In this context, only a few aspects can be taken into consideration that help to "make the best possible" decision. However, one of the most important and most neglected aspects is to assist elderly people and especially the dying. Since the process of death is more and more rationalized and submitted to the criteria of economic sufficiency, it is important to show them that they have a dignity, that they are not abandoned, that suffering has a meaning, and that they need to be prepared for the final encounter with God. Taking the neccesary time in these very moments is an authentic expression of love.

CONSERVING / PROLONGING LIFE

A preliminary ethical reflection will be helpful to facilitate the distinction between ordinary/proportionate and extraordinary/disproportionate means, which can be considered as

---

24 Sgreccia affirms that communicating the truth must be commensurate with the subject's capacity to receive it in a healthy manner, including diagnosis, prognosis, therapeutic alternatives and foreseeable consequences. Cf. Sgreccia, PB, 692–95.
25 Ibid., 693.

synonyms.[26] Originally, the terms "ordinary" and "extraordinary means" were used, and these concepts have a long history both in medicine and ethics; according to William Smith they are over 400 years old.[27] Starting with Francisco de Vitoria, O. P. († 1546), the distinction between ordinary and extraordinary means was introduced. Commenting on St. Thomas and based on man's natural inclination to self-conservation, he raised the question of whether the conservation of self by food is obligatory. Taking into consideration different circumstances, he held the position that there must be a balance between the burden of the means and the benefit provided, according to which the patient needs to decide.[28] In other words, the individual is not bound to prolong his life at all costs. Francisco Suárez, S. J. († 1617) treated the question regarding the necessity that a man has of guarding his life.[29] In his disputation *De iustitia et iure* Juan de Lugo († 1660), a Spanish Jesuit and Cardinal, treated many moral questions, such as suicide, the conservation of one's life, and mutilation. He offered a case-study affirming that mutilation, if it is accompanied by very intense pain, becomes an extraordinary means of conserving life and ceases, therefore, to be obligatory.[30] According to him, man is not bound to employ extraordinary means to conserve his life. In his ethical evaluations regarding ordinary-extraordinary means, he gave much room to the consideration of the circumstances. Several other authors wrote about the same topic, providing further

---

26 The use of both terms will be clarified step by step. For now, cf. Grattan T. Brown, "B. Ordinary and Extraordinary Means," in Edward J. Furton et al. (eds.), *Catholic Health Care Ethics: A Manual for Practitioners* (Philadelphia: National Catholic Bioethics Center, 2009), 15-19, here 18. The *Declaration on Euthanasia* suggested speaking of "proportionate and disproportionate" instead of "ordinary-extraordinary" means. This aspect will be addressed later on in this chapter. Cf. CDF, DE, IV.

27 William B. Smith, "Judeo-Christian Teaching on Euthanasia: Definitions, Distinctions and Decisions," in *Linacre Quarterly* 54 (1987): 27-42, here 27. Henke presents a good overview of the historical development: cf. Donald E. Henke, "A History of Ordinary and Extraordinary Means," in *NCBQ* 5 (2005): 555-75.

28 Cf. Francisco de Vitoria, *Relectiones theologicae, relectio IX, De temperantia* (Lyon, 1587), 1; 9; 12.

29 Cf. Francisco Suárez, *Opera Omnia*, E. Berton (ed.) (Paris, 1858), tom. XII, disp. 9, sect. 3.

30 Cf. Juan de Lugo, *De iustitia et iure* (Rome: 1663), disp. X, 21.

distinctions. Saint Alphonsus Liguori († 1787) affirmed that there is no obligation to use costly and uncommon medicine or to employ extraordinary and very difficult means, such as amputation, in order to conserve life.[31]

Daniel Anthony Cronin, later Archbishop of Hartford from 1992 to 2003, wrote a doctoral dissertation with the topic: *The Moral Law in Regard to the Ordinary and Extraordinary Means of Conserving Life*, published in 1958.[32] The text has been lightly edited for a new edition published in 2011 with the title: *Ordinary and Extraordinary Means of Conserving Life*.[33] In his work, he discussed different aspects, and he presented a comprehensive analysis of the Church's moral tradition pertaining to the ordinary and extraordinary means of conserving human life. He makes some important distinctions, which have not lost their actuality even today. The following explanations will take the results of his research into consideration, including some distinctions and updates.

Ordinary Means — Some Basic Considerations

In view of the ordinary means, it will be helpful to consider briefly their nature. The first and most important principle Cronin offers is that the ordinary means of conserving one's life must offer some hope of a beneficial result.[34] This criterion is important in order to distinguish between ordinary and extraordinary means. If, for example, for the dying person there is no benefit from consuming food and nourishment, because it would only prolong the process of dying, it would be considered an extraordinary means. The question remains: how much hope of benefit must such a means offer? Generally speaking, they must be worthwhile in quality, duration, and regarding the effort of the means used. Cronin summarizes: "In a word, the use of a means must offer a *proportionate* hope of benefit or else it is not an ordinary

---

31 See the historical overview provided by Víctor Ronald La Barrera Villarreal, "Il Principio di proporzionalità terapeutica nell'assistenza alla fase finale della vita," Tesi di Dottorato di Ricerca in Bioetica (Rome: Università di Roma, 2004), 78–84.
32 Daniel A. Cronin, *The Moral Law in Regard to the Ordinary and Extraordinary Means of Conserving Life* (Rome: Pontifical Gregorian University, 1958).
33 Daniel A. Cronin, *Ordinary and Extraordinary Means of Conserving Life* (Philadelphia: National Catholic Bioethics Center, 2011).
34 Ibid., 122.

means."[35] In this context, the objective and subjective elements, mentioned above,[36] should be included since they will facilitate the distinction. These considerations are to be applied even to the taking of food and water, which are generally considered to be natural means of conserving life. Based on the argumentation provided by Juan de Lugo, Cronin affirms that "any means, whether natural or artificial, must give proportionate hope of success and benefit; otherwise it is not an ordinary means and is thus not obligatory."[37] Certain factors indicate a certain relativity regarding the foundational criteria, which are not the same as relativism. They depend on the age of the individual, the person's psychological and physical conditions, and financial status.[38] In this sense, the ordinary means have a "relative nature," because of the elements involved.

Also, the notion of danger or risk is helpful when explaining the nature of ordinary means. They have to be proportionate to the benefits. If a procedure does not offer a proportionate hope of success it cannot be considered an ordinary means. Cronin affirms: "There is a definite relation between the notion of proportionate hope of benefit and the nature of ordinary means. The more a means involves difficulty, the more definite must be the hope of proportionate success and benefit."[39] In other words, the moral obligation is not to fulfill the impossible.

Cronin mentions another element when referring to ordinary means, which he calls the notion of being common. To determine "common" the relative factors have to be taken into consideration; however, it is referred to "the usual care that most men

---

35 Ibid., 123.
36 Cf. chapter VII, To Do Only the Possible.
37 Cronin, *Ordinary and Extraordinary Means*, 124.
38 Depression at the end of life might also affect the treatment. Patients with a major depressive disorder may refuse reasonable and beneficial medical care. Unrelieved depression could make additional medical treatments become burdensome. Jeri Gerding concludes that for "some patients at the end of life who do not respond to antidepressant medication or other treatment, it is reasonable to consider that major depression itself, combined with other health issues, may make treatment itself excessively burdensome and extraordinary." Jeri Gerding, "Extraordinary Means and Depression at the End of Life," in *NCBQ* 14 (2014): 697–710, here 710.
39 Cronin, *Ordinary and Extraordinary*, 128.

normally give their lives."⁴⁰ Luke Gormally counts among them the provision of nourishment, shelter, and a warm and hygienic environment.⁴¹ These aspects are considered "common," as they correspond to human dignity.

Cronin mentions also another "relative factor" describing the nature of ordinary means, which he calls "keeping with one's status." This is an individual and merely relative indicator, which implies a relation with one's financial and social condition, but also his physical and psychological outlook.⁴²

In his analysis based on solid research of the history of moral theology, Cronin mentions further that an ordinary means should not be too difficult. But what does it mean, since difficulties are intrinsically linked to any application of means? It cannot signify that the means must be entirely free of difficulty but from excessive difficulties. The notion is generic and usually called a reasonable difficulty.⁴³

Experts consider ordinary means usually as obligatory since it corresponds to the dignity of the human person to provide basic care. This aspect will be addressed with more detail later on.⁴⁴

Extraordinary Means — Some Basic Considerations

The means of conserving one's life can include also extraordinary means, which are morally non-obligatory. In the history of moral theology, Cronin individuated five elements that are helpful for the right understanding of extraordinary means.

Based on the moral norm to avoid evil and to do good, Cronin deduced from it a certain impossibility. On one side, man is bound to avoid certain things, such as abortion since it is an intrinsically evil act that can never be morally right. On the other side, there are limits within the obligation of conserving one's life. If there is a grave inconvenience, which can refer to different aspects (relative factors), self-conservation is not obligatory. Other authors use instead concepts such as "grave inconvenience" or "moral

---

40 Ibid., 130.
41 Cf. Luke Gormally, "Palliative treatment and ordinary care," in Correa and Sgreccia, *Dignity of the Dying Person*, 252-66, here 264.
42 Cf. Cronin, *Ordinary and Extraordinary*, 130-33.
43 Cf. ibid., 133-39.
44 Cf. chapter VII, Approaching a Definition.

impossibility."[45] Cronin underlines that an affirmative precept is not binding if there is a proportionately grave inconvenience. John DiBaise considers this the case when risky and experimental treatments are about to be applied.[46]

He enumerates a second criterion describing the nature of extraordinary means, which he calls great effort or excessive hardship. If an intervention requires excessive effort it would be considered a moral impossibility. "If the means involves effort which constitutes a grave inconvenience for the individual concerned, even though most men would find the means reasonable, the means is nevertheless an extraordinary means for this individual."[47]

The third element is presented as excruciating or excessive pain; it can render an element of conserving life an extraordinary means. One of the most common examples used in the tradition of moral evaluations is amputation; especially within the period when anesthesia did not yet exist and when the mortality rate was at least twenty-five percent. Since this has changed profoundly, due to the progress of medicine and technology, it is possible that means which were considered extraordinary in the past can now be considered ordinary.[48] Other authors mention in this context the burdens of a treatment that may be more than the patient can cope with, exceed any promised benefit, or is simply inappropriate.[49]

A fourth element is extraordinary expenses and the very best medicine. Moral theologians always took into account the expenses, since unreasonable expenses can constitute a moral impossibility and thus render means extraordinary. This "relative norm" is sometimes difficult to evaluate since the progress of science has brought and continues to bring substantial improvements. Also, the costs of medical and surgical treatments increase continuously.[50]

---

45 Cf. Cronin, *Ordinary and Extraordinary*, 141.
46 Cf. DiBaise, "Euthanasia and Quality of Life," 423.
47 Cronin, *Ordinary and Extraordinary*, 147.
48 Cf. ibid., 148-52.
49 Cf. DiBaise, "Euthanasia and Quality of Life," 423.
50 Gregory Webster analyzed the increase of expenses. He mentioned for example the biotherapeutic treatments. "In the United Kingdom, a National Institute for Health and Care Excellence mock technology appraisal analysis projected that a $649,000 price for a CAR-T therapy would be justified for young patients with acute lymphoblastic leukemia. Stem cell transplants

Any ethical reflection on this criterion will have to include the health system, possible private insurance, public funds, etc. Medical expenses have to be considered in the light of the individual's financial condition.[51]

The fifth element is described as intensive fear or repugnance. The emotion of fear of a particular procedure can be so intense that it constitutes a moral impossibility, and in this case, a means could be considered extraordinary; nevertheless, an irrational type of fear should be eliminated. The concept of repugnance is disputed; historically it was related especially to amputation and to the fact that someone did not want to live with a mutilated body.[52] However, a treatment can be considered also psychologically repugnant to the patient.

Approaching a Definition and Its Consequences

Even after presenting some criteria, it might still be difficult to distinguish between ordinary and extraordinary means, due to the relative factors and the fast development of medicine and technology. Not only have moral theologians developed a distinction between ordinary and extraordinary means, but also secular medicine. Edmund Pellegrino defined ordinary means as a "treatment that is effective, serves some beneficial goal of the patient, and/or carries burdens which can be outweighed by the effectiveness and benefit."[53] Even though this definition is helpful, Daniel Cronin offered a more precise definition, including all major elements, which were mentioned above: "*Ordinary means* of conserving life are those means commonly used in given circumstances, which this individual in his present physical, psychological, and economic condition can reasonably employ with definite hope of proportionate benefit."[54]

Daniel Cronin provides also a definition of the extraordinary means: "*Extraordinary means* of conserving life are those means

---

and follow-up treatment can cost as much as $800,000." Gregory Webster, "Financial Toxicity. Treatment Expense and Extraordinary Means," in *NCBQ* 18 (2018): 227–36, here 229.
51   Cronin, *Ordinary and Extraordinary*, 152–56.
52   Cf. ibid., 158.
53   Pellegrino, "Decision at the end of life," 228.
54   Cronin, *Ordinary and Extraordinary*, 160.

not commonly used in given circumstances, or those means in common use which this individual in his present physical, psychological, and economic condition cannot reasonably employ or, if he can, will not give him definite hope of proportionate benefit."[55] Extraordinary or disproportionate means would equate to a futile treatment, ineffective and burdensome. In other words, ordinary means become beneficial treatments, and extraordinary treatments provide little or no beneficial outcome for the patient. These considerations show that the meaning of ordinary and extraordinary is "not tied to the state of technological progress. Technology is a means which, itself, is judged by its effectiveness, benefits, and burdens."[56] This signifies that these principles and distinctions can be put to practice only if a sound anthropology is the starting point for the reflection.

The *Declaration on Euthanasia* does not present a proper definition, but mentions that the distinction "ordinary / extraordinary" had led to some misunderstandings and it suggests instead the use of the distinction "proportionate / disproportionate."[57] However, the way in which the ordinary-extraordinary means distinction is presented does correspond to the explanations provided in the declaration.[58] Jos Welie argues that the suggested distinction proposed by the CDF has proven to be less clear than the former since the latter includes the relative factors and includes the progress made in the treatment of sickness.[59] For that reason, it will be helpful

---

55   Ibid.
56   Pellegrino, "Decision at the end of life," 228.
57   Kevin O'Rourke affirms this aspect. The danger of using the distinction ordinary-extraordinary means consisted in applying them only in a technical sense. When health-care professionals discovered these terms, they applied them according to their abstract technical understanding. This is the reason why the CDF suggested using the terms proportionate and disproportionate. However, the original meaning was quite different. Cf. Kevin D. O'Rourke, "The Catholic Tradition on Forgoing Life Support," in *NCBQ* 5 (2005): 537-53, here 544.
58   However, the declaration offers some principles which need to be taken into consideration, such as the "degree of complexity or risk, its cost and the possibility of using it, and comparing these elements with the result that can be expected, taking into account the state of the sick person and his or her physical and moral resources." CDF, DE, IV.
59   Jos Welie argues that the alternative terms proportionate/disproportionate "are certainly not clear either, and may be even less clear than the

to consider them in the following considerations as synonyms.

These considerations shed some more light on the question whether there is an obligation of using extraordinary or disproportionate means to conserve life. Experts usually agree that ordinary means are *per se* obligatory means of conserving life; meanwhile, extraordinary means are *per se* not obligatory. Even though the theory might sound easy, the application can be a real challenge, as we are going to show in the next chapter.

Elio Sgreccia presents another helpful distinction. As far as moral duty is concerned he suggests distinguishing between obligatory, optional, and illicit means.[60] Whenever an ordinary means is deemed to be proportionate to the benefits it should be considered obligatory; whenever the same means proves to be extraordinary for the patient, it would be optional, depending on the circumstances. Meanwhile, a disproportionate means for preserving the life that is incapable of procuring any benefit or is simply harmful would be illicit. In other words, the distinction between ordinary and extraordinary means is not solely based on technical procedures but must take into consideration the whole human person. From this perspective to refuse extraordinary means corresponds to the acceptance of the human condition. However, concerning a correct application, the principle of double effect must be taken into consideration in some cases.[61]

The distinction between ordinary-extraordinary (proportionate -disproportionate) is based on relative norms, not on absolute norms, which might cause some confusion in its application. The obligation of conserving life rests with the individual and should be determined in accordance with the conditions of the individual. Yet once "the means are then determined as ordinary means for this individual, they are obligatory."[62]

Nutrition and Hydration

In light of the above-mentioned considerations, it may be helpful to shed some light on the use of nutrition and hydration

---

ordinary/extraordinary distinction." Jos V. M. Welie, "When Medical Treatment Is No Longer in Order," in *NCBQ* 5 (2005): 517–36, here 526.
60 Cf. Sgreccia, PB, 686.
61 Cf. chapter V, Principle of Double Effect.
62 Cronin, *Ordinary and Extraordinary*, 162.

and whether it is obligatory to apply them or not. There were several cases brought up in the mass media, in which nutrition and hydration were considered extraordinary means and therefore not obligatory *per se*, especially when provided artificially. And indeed, this might be the case when the procedure is harmful to the patient, impossible to be implemented or when it would only prolong the process of dying.

The case of Marjorie Nighbert, a businesswoman who had suffered a stroke, is totally different. Marjorie was from Florida, and she was disabled, but not terminally ill. She had once told her brother, however, that she didn't want a tube in the case of terminal illness, and he interpreted her remark to mean that she wouldn't want a tube if she required one to stay alive. He had her tube removed. She was still capable of asking for food and water, however, and did. The issue went to court. A judge appointed a lawyer to conduct a twenty-four-hour investigation, during which feeding resumed, into whether Nighbert was competent to make her own "medical" decisions. The lawyer reported that while she may have been competent when the dehydration started, she was not competent after several weeks of it. That was enough for the judge to rule that she had not been competent to request food and water. The dehydration and starvation resumed, and Nighbert died.[63]

In this case, the issue is not about maintaining or prolonging life, but about ending life. The woman died because of involuntary indirect euthanasia, which is murder. However, the question remains, whether nutrition and hydration are ordinary means, especially when provided artificially and if their refusal or removal is ever ethically acceptable.[64]

Pope Pius XII had already offered some general ethical principles, based on natural reason and Christian morality. In 2007 the CDF referred to Pius XII, who had already affirmed that "the patient

---

63 Ramesh Ponnuru, *The Party of Death: The Democrats, the Media, the Courts, and the Disregard for Human Life* (Washington, D. C.: Regnery Publishing, 2006), 138.
64 Guevin presents a helpful explanation of the word "artificial." Etymologically it comes from the Latin words *ars* and *facere* and means literally "to make art." The word applies therefore "to the entire gamut of medicines, treatments, and operations used in the practice of the healing arts. Something as 'ordinary' as antibiotics is no less artificial than the more 'extraordinary' ventilator or gastrointestinal tube." Benedict M. Guevin, "Ordinary, Extraordinary, and Artificial Means of Care," in *NCBQ* 5 (2005): 471–79, here 477.

and those caring for him have the right and the duty to provide the care necessary to preserve health and life. On the other hand, this duty, in general, includes only the use of those means which, considering all the circumstances, are ordinary, which do not impose an extraordinary burden on the patient or on others."[65] However, this was not referred to as the interruption of the ordinary means such as hydration and nutrition with the intention of killing. He stated already in 1957:

> At the same time, the artificial administration of water and food generally does not impose a heavy burden either on the patient or on his or her relatives. It does not involve excessive expense; it is within the capacity of an average health-care system, does not of itself require hospitalization, and is proportionate to accomplishing its purpose, which is to keep the patient from dying of starvation and dehydration. It is not, nor is it meant to be, a treatment that cures the patient, but is rather ordinary care aimed at the preservation of life.[66]

Years later some debates arose since some scholars quoted these affirmations without respecting the context, trying to justify the possibility of refusing or removing artificial nutrition and hydration. However, the Pope's statement did not open the doors to euthanasia. In 1981 the Pontifical Council *Cor Unum* affirmed that it "remains the strict obligation to apply under all circumstances those therapeutic measures which are called 'minimal': that is, those which are normally and customarily used for the maintenance of life (alimentation, blood transfusions, injections, etc.). To interrupt these minimal measures would, in practice, be equivalent to wishing to put an end to the patient's life."[67]

Alimentation is considered "minimal care," which has to be granted. The *Declaration on Euthanasia* stated that it is permitted to refuse extraordinary care, due to the proportion in the use of remedies.[68] In 2004 Pope John Paul II asserted that the adminis-

65 CDF, Commentary, 11.7.2005, in www.vatican.va/roman_curia/congregations/cfaith/documents/rc_con_cfaith_doc_20070801_nota-commento_en.html [15.1.2022].
66 CDF, Commentary.
67 Pontifical Council *Cor Unum*, "Questions of Ethics," 2.4.4.
68 CDF, DE, IV.

tration of water and food, even by artificial means, does not have to be considered a medical act and is therefore mandatory.[69] This affirmation had created some controversy since it is difficult to evaluate the status of a person in a PVS.[70] However, the CDF affirms that hydration and nutrition are not treatments or cures but ordinary care and therefore they are considered ordinary means. The CDF is aware that the "vegetative state," advanced Alzheimer's, serious mental illness, etc. impose a real burden on families; nevertheless, the Church affirms that it is a right and a duty to assure this ordinary care. Commenting on the *Declaration on Euthanasia* from 1980, the CDF confirmed in 2007 once again the necessity of guaranteeing the ordinary care aimed at the perseveration of life: "Still less can one interrupt the ordinary means of care for patients who are not facing an imminent death, as is generally the case of those in a 'vegetative state'; for these people, it would be precisely the interruption of the ordinary means of care which would be the cause of their death."[71]

In other words, patients and doctors may refuse all types of treatments except nutrition and hydration, even if they need to be administered by artificial means.[72] Elio Sgreccia counts among ordinary means also aspiration of bronchial secretions and the cleansing of bedsores.[73] The letter *Samaritanus Bonus* from 2020 clarifies:

> It is not lawful to suspend treatments that are required to maintain essential physiological functions, as long as the body can benefit from them (such as hydration, nutrition, thermoregulation, proportionate respiratory support, and the other types of assistance needed to maintain bodily

---

[69] John Paul II, Address on "Life-Sustaining Treatments and the Vegetative State," 4.
[70] Cf. Patrick Guinan, "Is Assisted Nutrition and Hydration Always Mandated?," in *NCBQ* 10 (2010): 481–88.
[71] CDF, Commentary.
[72] "The administration of food and liquids, even artificially, is part of the normal treatment always due to the patient when this is not burdensome for him: their undue suspension could be real and properly so-called euthanasia." Cf. Pontifical Council for the Healthcare Workers, *The Charter for Health Care Workers* (Vatican City: Libreria Editrice Vaticana, 1995), 120. See also: Ann M. Heath, "Advance Directives to Withhold Oral Food and Water in Dementia," in *NCBQ* 16 (2016): 421–34.
[73] Cf. Sgreccia, PB, 686.

homeostasis and manage systemic and organic pain). The suspension of futile treatments *must not involve the withdrawal of therapeutic care.*[74]

Permanent "Vegetative" State

Only one year before his death, John Paul II addressed the participants of an International Congress on "Life-sustaining Treatments and Vegetative State: Scientific Progress and Ethical Dilemmas." When he addressed this group on March 20, 2004, he was already greatly affected by his own illness.[75] He noticed that the so-called "vegetative state" has scientific, ethical, social and pastoral implications, since the person in this state "shows no evident sign of self-awareness or of awareness of the environment, and seems unable to interact with others or to react to specific stimuli."[76] He states the high number of diagnostic errors regarding the vegetative state since not a few persons have been able to emerge from it. The PVS refers to "those patients whose 'vegetative state' continues for over a year."[77]

This criterion is only a "conventional prognostic judgment"; there were patients who recovered afterward, as well as those who did not, which is the large majority. John Paul II mentioned that some people cast doubts on the "human quality" of these people being in a vegetative state since they show no sign of self-awareness or of their environment. However, the Pope considers the concept "vegetative state" problematic in itself, since it might reduce the human person to certain criteria offered by medicine and demean the patient's individual dignity and value. He affirmed: "A man, even if seriously ill or disabled in the exercise of his highest functions, is and always will be a man, and he will never become a 'vegetable' or an 'animal'. Even our brothers and sisters who find themselves in the clinical condition of a 'vegetative state' retain

---

74   CDF, SB, V.2. *Samaritanus Bonus* mentions a "proportionate respiratory support" without further clarifications. However, it needs to be understood within the context of the basic distinction between ordinary and extraordinary means. Cf. also ibid., V.6.
75   Cf. John Paul II, Address on "Life-Sustaining Treatments and the Vegetative State."
76   Ibid., 2.
77   Ibid.

their human dignity in all its fullness."[78]

A person being in the "vegetable state" is a human person and retains his dignity. Often, they perceive things, they feel, and they hear what is said. The Canadian Scott Routley was in a PVS for more than a decade. According to the previous description of the concept "vegetative state," this would suppose that the human person does not perceive anything, because whatever is considered "vegetative" would necessarily exclude the rational capacity, like thinking and feeling, but this is not the case. Scientists used a special scanner and asked Scott to imagine certain situations. The scanner detected blood flow to different parts of the brain and the scientists were able to prove that a patient being in a PVS is able to respond on a spiritual level.[79] This calls into question the option proposed by some to interrupt the nutrition and hydration of these patients. For this reason, John Paul II also requested that basic health care, such as nutrition, hydration, cleanliness, warmth, etc. have to be granted to these patients.[80] He concluded: "it is necessary to promote the *taking of positive actions* as a stand against pressures to withdraw hydration and nutrition as a way to put an end to the lives of these patients."[81]

In 2005 the CDF was asked by some bishops in the United States how to deal with artificial nutrition and hydration for people in a PVS. The answers were approved by the Pope—in this case by Benedict XVI—and therefore form part of the Magisterium. It will be helpful to take a closer look:

> First question: Is the administration of food and water (whether by natural or artificial means) to a patient in a "vegetative state" morally obligatory except when they cannot be assimilated by the patient's body or cannot be administered to the patient without causing significant physical discomfort?
> Response: Yes. The administration of food and water even by artificial means is, in principle, an ordinary and

---

78 Ibid., 3.
79 Fergus Walsh, "Vegetative patient Scott Routley says 'I'm not in pain,'" *BBC*, 13.11.2012, in www.bbc.com/news/health-20268044 [15.1.2022].
80 Cf. John Paul II, Address on "Life-Sustaining Treatments and the Vegetative State," 4.
81 Cf. ibid., 5.

proportionate means of preserving life. It is therefore obligatory to the extent to which, and for as long as, it is shown to accomplish its proper finality, which is the hydration and nourishment of the patient. In this way suffering and death by starvation and dehydration are prevented.[82]

This style of question-answer corresponds to the classical way of presenting doubts; whenever a bishops' conference or individual bishops have questions, they are supposed to receive answers. This is intrinsically related to the office of the Magisterium of the Church, which has to provide orientation to direct the faithful towards the way of salvation. The criteria offered by the CDF are precise and correspond to the tradition of the Church. The following answer given by the CDF is to be understood according to this same logic:

> Second question: When nutrition and hydration are being supplied by artificial means to a patient in a "permanent vegetative state," may they be discontinued when competent physicians judge with moral certainty that the patient will never recover consciousness?
>
> Response: No. A patient in a "permanent vegetative state" is a person with fundamental human dignity and must, therefore, receive ordinary and proportionate care which includes, in principle, the administration of water and food even by artificial means.[83]

Hydration and nutrition are always considered ordinary and therefore obligatory means. The same principles have to be applied, as described above. However, at this point some suggest distinguishing between means and mechanism; means would refer to water and food, which are not considered to be medical care and are therefore obligatory ordinary means.[84] Meanwhile the artificial delivery—for example the feeding tube—is considered a

---

82 CDF, "Responses to certain questions of the United States Conference of Catholic Bishops concerning artificial nutrition and hydration," 1.8.2007, in www.vatican.va/roman_curia/congregations/cfaith/documents/rc_con_cfaith_doc_20070801_risposte-usa_en.html [15.1.2022].
83 Ibid.
84 Barbara Golder, et al., "Assisted Nutrition and Hydration as Supportive Care during Illness. Bedside Application of Catholic Moral Teaching," in *NCBQ* 16 (2016): 435-48, especially 437-40.

mechanism, which may not be obligatory. On the one hand, this distinction might be helpful, if everything is ordered to the good of the whole person, as it corresponds to the Christian concept of man, and if the principle of double effect is applied. On the other hand, it might be dangerous since it could open the doors to indirect euthanasia, whenever the human person is considered according to a functional point of view.[85]

Suffering—Palliative Care

Pain and suffering play an important role, especially when considering the end of life. How much must people endure, especially if they do not see any sense in suffering? The modern world has difficulties with suffering since science cannot give answers. Without any doubt, suffering is linked to the transcendental value of life, which is mostly lacking in today's society. However, this changes when considering pain and suffering from a Christian perspective. Pope John Paul II wrote an Apostolic Letter on the Christian meaning of human suffering *Salvifici Doloris*. He affirmed that suffering

> seems to be particularly *essential to the nature of man*. It is as deep as man himself, precisely because it manifests in its own way that depth which is proper to man, and in its own way surpasses it. Suffering seems to belong to man's transcendence: it is one of those points in which man is in a certain sense "destined" to go beyond himself, and he is called to this in a mysterious way.[86]

This is not the place to present this topic exhaustively.

---

[85] This was reaffirmed by the CDF in 2020: "One must never forget in such painful situations that the patient in these states has the right to nutrition and hydration, even administered by artificial methods that accord with the principle of ordinary means. In some cases, such measures can become disproportionate, because their administration is ineffective, or involves procedures that create an excessive burden with negative results that exceed any benefits to the patient." CDF, SB, V, 8.

[86] John Paul II, Apostolic Letter *Salvifici Doloris*, 11.2.1984, in www.vatican.va/content/john-paul-ii/en/apost_letters/1984/documents/hf_jp-ii_apl_11021984_salvifici-doloris.html [15.1.2022], 2. Mary Drahos recognizes even a healing power in suffering, explaining how the right understanding of suffering could help to overcome euthanasia and assisted suicide. Cf. Mary Drahos, *The Healing Power of Hope: Down-to-Earth Alternatives to Euthanasia and Assisted Suicide* (Ann Arbor: Charis Books, 1997).

Nevertheless, a few basics have to be mentioned. Suffering affects the whole person with all his dimensions, that is to say, the spiritual, psychological, and physical dimension.[87] Any consideration regarding suffering has to take them into account. There are different types of suffering such as guilty suffering, caused through personal guilt, "innocent suffering," and the suffering caused by the limitations of nature. Since suffering affects all the different dimensions of the human person, a sense of the uselessness of suffering would do great harm to the person. Christianity provides a profound meaning to suffering since the world was saved through the salvific suffering of Jesus Christ.

According to this perspective, Jesus Christ fulfilled the prophecy of Isaiah who predicted the "suffering servant" (cf. Isa 53:78), and the cross is the symbol of salvation. In this perspective, suffering gains a redeeming and saving power if it is accepted with love for God. Already St. Paul observed that every faithful who participates in the suffering of Christ participates in his redemption. He wrote: "Now I rejoice in my sufferings for your sake, and in my flesh I am filling up what is lacking in the afflictions of Christ on behalf of his body, which is the church" (Col 1:24).

Suffering can also acquire a purifying dimension, especially at the moment before death. It might serve the dying as a preparation for that final encounter with God. There is much talk of the duty of physicians to help patients avoid suffering but rarely does one mention that a physician should help the patient to find the meaning of suffering, especially when it is impossible to eliminate it. Benedict XVI wrote in his encyclical letter *Spe Salvi*: "It is not by sidestepping or fleeing from suffering that we are healed, but rather by our capacity for accepting it, maturing through it and finding meaning through union with Christ, who suffered with infinite love."[88] Such an approach would transmit hope to people and inspire confidence, even in the most difficult moment of life. As the German Pope mentioned, "Often the deepest cause of suffering is the very absence of God."[89] The person who believes in God has an advantage, because "we even boast of our afflictions, knowing that affliction produces endurance, and endurance, proven

---

87 Cf. CDF, SB, II.
88 Benedict XVI, SS, 37.
89 Benedict XVI, DCE, 31c.

character, and proven character, hope, and hope does not disappoint because the love of God has been poured out into our hearts through the Holy Spirit that has been given to us" (Rom 5:3-5). The salvific suffering of Jesus Christ and the hope of eternal life makes a big difference. Meanwhile, the opposite of salvation is not only temporal suffering but "the definitive suffering: the loss of eternal life, being rejected by God, damnation."[90]

Even though suffering has a special meaning for Christians, people do not need to suffer unnecessarily. Some people are not able to bear much suffering and for them, it would be important to assist them with palliative care. Also for that reason, the CDF confirmed:

> Palliative care is an authentic expression of the human and Christian activity of providing care, the tangible symbol of the compassionate "remaining" at the side of the suffering person. Its goal is "to alleviate suffering in the final stages of illness and at the same time to ensure the patient appropriate human accompaniment" improving the quality of life and overall well-being as much as possible and in a dignified manner. [...] Palliative care should include spiritual assistance for patients and their families.[91]

In bioethical debates, pain, suffering, and palliative care are mostly considered from a technical point of view. This is not the place to explain with detail palliative treatments; nevertheless, some basic affirmations will be provided. According to Luke Gormally they "enable the dying person to live as fully as possible while dying—in so far as they control physical symptoms which would interfere with other worthwhile activities (such as prayer, conversing with family and friends, seeking reconciliation with others, and so on)."[92]

Sedation and palliative care are advanced and of great help especially in the last phase of life. However, sedation would be inappropriate if leading to mental distress. Painkillers that cause unconsciousness need special attention, as Pius XII already affirmed.[93] Generally speaking, a person has to satisfy moral

---

[90] John Paul II, Apostolic Letter *Salvifici Doloris*, 14.
[91] CDF, SB, V, 4.
[92] Gormally, "Palliative treatment," 252-66, 256.
[93] Cf. Pius XII, "Address to an International Congress of Anesthesiologists," 309-14.

duties and family obligations and should be able to prepare himself with full consciousness for the final encounter with God.[94] For that reason, the Magisterium of the Church affirmed: "It is not right to deprive the dying person of consciousness without a serious reason."[95] This recommendation has to be understood as a general guideline, which needs to include objective and subjective dimensions. If there were, for example, unsolved interpersonal conflicts or long-hidden memories with guilty content, it would be wrong to apply complete sedation. In the case of tremendous suffering and physical pain, being prepared and at peace with God, one's neighbor, and oneself, this might nevertheless be possible.

The question often arises as to whether it is licit or not to make use of analgesic treatments that may shorten life or may suppress the patient's state of consciousness. Pope Pius XII provided some answers years ago. In a speech of November 24, 1957, and in an allocution the following year, the Pope spoke of the lawfulness of such a procedure, in as much as the purpose of the action is not the killing or the suppression of consciousness in the sick person, but only to alleviate his suffering.[96] This aspect needs to be well understood. The goal of these treatments is not to end the life of the patient (subject) or to offer a merciful killing,[97] but the goal of these treatments has to be oriented towards the object of the action, which is to be achieved. In these cases, the principle of "double effect" needs to be applied.[98] The secondary effect, in this case, the abbreviation of life or the suppression of consciousness, are side effects, but not the intended goal.

According to the explanations provided by Pius XII suppression of consciousness "is permitted if there are no other means and

---

94 This was affirmed by the CDF in 2020: "From a pastoral point of view, prior spiritual preparation of the patients should be provided in order that they may consciously approach death as an encounter with God." CDF, SB, V, 7.
95 Ibid., 145.
96 English translation published in Pius XII, "Address to an International Congress of Anesthesiologists," 309-14.
97 The CDF affirmed: "The sedation must exclude, as it direct purpose, the intention to kill, even though it may accelerate the inevitable onset of death." CDF, SB, V, 7.
98 See chapter V, Principle of Double Effect.

it does not impede the fulfillment of religious and moral duties. Moral evaluation of suppression of consciousness thus depends on the concrete circumstances."[99]

Concluding this chapter, one last aspect shall be mentioned. According to Elio Sgreccia palliative care aims "at reducing the symptoms of the illness and relieving pain."[100] He adds: "Methods of palliative care are commonly understood to mean treatments for the benefit of patients suffering from illnesses that are no longer curable, aimed at controlling the symptoms more than the underlying pathology, through the application of procedures that allow the patient to enjoy a better quality of life."[101] Whenever ambiguous concepts such as "quality of life" are involved the topic proves to be difficult since clear guidelines and definitions are missing.

Kevin Belgrave and Pablo Requena have brought to evidence that there are different practices of sedation for symptom management at the end of life, such as "terminal sedation," "palliative sedation," "continuous deep sedation," "controlled sedation," "total sedation, proportionate palliative sedation," etc.[102] Concepts such as "terminal sedation" are ambiguous, since they might imply or lead to euthanasia or assisted suicide. Today the technical-clinical approach prevails; meanwhile, an ethical-theological reflection is more and more missing. However, neither medicine nor progress per se can provide ethical guidelines. For that reason, both authors conclude that there is a need for guidelines, especially since there is a "significant push for expedient and economic means of controlling both suffering and costs at the end of life."[103] It seems that only the Magisterium of the Church, basing its affirmations on faith and reason, is capable of offering these guidelines focusing on a holistic perspective of man. Especially in "times of suffering, the human person should be able to experience a solidarity and a love that takes on the suffering, offering a sense of life that extends beyond death."[104]

---

99   Kevin Belgrave and Pablo Requena, "A Primer on Palliative Sedation," in *NCBQ* 12 (2012): 263-81, 279.
100 Sgreccia, PB, 687.
101 Ibid.
102 Kevin Belgrave and Pablo Requena, "A Primer on Palliative Sedation," 267.
103 Ibid., 281.
104 CDF, SB, V, 4.

Concerning the Living Will

The chapter on ordinary and extraordinary means concludes with some comments on the living will. No detailed proposals will be made, but those criteria will be mentioned that are necessary for an ethical evaluation and orientation. This topic is of great relevance since choices have to be made, especially when the decision-making capacity is diminished or even lost. Some recommend preparing an advanced directive for such an eventuality, especially when looking to present a morally justified way for medical care at the end of life.

There are mainly two major challenges regarding end-of-life decisions and the so-called living will, which need to be mentioned: a) therapeutic obstinacy; b) right-to-die mentality. Patients and physicians find themselves somewhere between both extremes. They do too much or not enough. Even though these aspects have been explained already before, they thus gain a new actuality with regard to the eventuality of diminished decision-making capacity. For that reason, a living will is required or requested.

In the beginning, the living will was closely related to the right-to-die movement, as Javier Bustos has shown.[105] The development of the living will is linked to "efforts to promote euthanasia in the United States."[106] For that reason, the Catholic Church, which is opposed to euthanasia, was initially also opposed to the living will.

However, a correct understanding will depend on some basic ethical values based on a truly well-formed conscience, which must not be confused with a false understanding of self-determination. As a result, it is important to clarify some concepts right at the beginning:

A *living will* is the regulation of medical wishes when someone is incapacitated; sometimes *Health Care Directive* is used as a synonym. A living will is different from a testament or last will, which is a document indicating how the assets are to be divided after death. Medical treatment cannot be specified in the last will. Thus, a living will often includes a *power of attorney*; it is the legal power to act for another person. The acting person can have a broad or limited legal authority and comes into effect when the decision-making

---

105 Cf. Javier I. Bustos, "The Uncertainty of Living Will," in *NCBQ* 13 (2013): 243–51.
106 Ibid., 246. A more detailed description is provided in ibid., 245–46.

capacity is diminished or lost. A living will can end for a number of reasons such as when the patient revokes it, a court invalidates it or the patient dies. The so-called *guardianship order* that includes powers to deal with financial affairs, personal welfare, and the adult's property is often related to it. It presupposes the legal advice necessary to avoid problems and complications.

A living will provides the security or feeling that one has arranged one's affairs well and will not become a burden for others or himself. It is also due to the fact that one does not want one's own relatives to make a difficult decision, providing a therapeutic obstinacy or rashly ending the life, spending a great amount of money, and basing the decision-making on totally different criteria. Nevertheless, the living will does not solve all problems, and sometimes it creates new ones. What will happen, if the patient changes his mind, but the power of attorney is already given? What about if the person in charge does not respect the medical wishes or cannot respect them due to an objection of conscience?

This becomes even more confounded when taking into account the so-called "presumed will" of the patient, which is difficult to describe and to define. It is supposed to be based on some concrete indications, considering the patient's prior written and/or oral statements, including even ethical and religious convictions. This will make it very difficult to determine, especially if it involves legal consideration. Autonomy and self-determination within the tension between the two extremes, mentioned above, create usually other problems. This difficulty is compounded by the fact that living wills are generally promoted by presenting singular cases of illness and burden. However, a singular case is never a reliable criterion even though it might have an impact and move the sentiments. For that reason, the Church has always chosen the contrary approach, offering general criteria, which need to be applied to singular cases. This is the way which will be chosen for further considerations.

Advance Healthcare Directive as a Guide

Javier Bustos presents a very balanced view of the living will. The following explanations will rely also on his interpretation. A living will concerns different types of medical treatment in the event that someone is not capable of deciding for himself.

It "presupposes that if we are incapacitated when that situation arrives and are unable to communicate any decision, someone else will interpret and carry out the wishes we have described in the living will."[107] It assumes that the person has lost or is about to lose the human faculties of intellect and will necessary for decision-making. In the case of a living will such a person would not entrust the choices regarding the end-of-life to another person but establishes how to proceed in a written document. Nevertheless, in most cases, it will be impossible to take a precise decision in advance because it is almost impossible to foresee the concrete circumstances at the end of life. A disease may develop differently than expected and vary from person to person.

For that reason, Bustos affirms that a living will "should be understood as a *guide* subjected to interpretation by human conscience." He adds: "Decisions regarding life-sustaining treatment and other medical procedures must be made by someone who understands not only the wishes of the patient (expressed in the living will) but also the concrete circumstances of the situation—medical, social, and personal—and God's will."[108] Therefore, it can be said that a living will does not take the place of a decision at the end of life, but can serve as a guide subjected to interpretation according to the changing situation. Even the most detailed living will cannot resolve all problems; sometimes it even lacks flexibility since it suggests that everything is solved, which is simply not possible. The United States Conference of Catholic Bishops affirms, therefore: "No matter how well-crafted, such a document can never predict all the possible problems that may occur at a later time or anticipate all future treatment options. A living will can be misinterpreted by medical providers who might not understand the patient's wishes."[109]

A correct application of the living will presupposes that it is recognized as a guide and is applied by a well-formed agent. Otherwise, it could become a pretext for assisted suicide and euthanasia. The *Catechism of the Catholic Church* offers general criteria helpful for

---

107 Ibid., 247.
108 Ibid.
109 USCCB, "Advance Medical Directives: Planning for Your Future," 2014, in www.usccb.org/about/pro-life-activities/respect-life-program/2014/advance-medical-directives.cfm [15.1.2022].

this context: "Everyone is responsible for his life before God who has given it to him. It is God who remains the sovereign Master of life. We are obliged to accept life gratefully and preserve it for his honor and the salvation of our souls. We are stewards, not owners, of the life God has entrusted to us. It is not ours to dispose of."[110] Autonomy and self-determination have to correspond to a non-negotiable recognition of the dignity of the human person. This is a real challenge since most living wills are lacking precision, are morally problematic because of a lack of flexibility with regard to the changing situation, and often presuppose a blind trust in the physician's suggestions. Tadeusz Pacholczyk points out that there is a better choice than a living will:

> We can choose a *surrogate*, a living person, who will make health care decisions in real time on our behalf if we are rendered unable to do so. The proposed surrogate (also called a "health care proxy") is someone who cares deeply about us, who loves us, and is reasonably able to make decisions in accord with our known wishes and with our best medical and spiritual interests in mind. Filling out a form to designate our health care proxy is something that each of us should do as a sensible way to prepare for difficult end-of-life situations that may arise. Preparing such a document can also prompt us to begin discussing these important topics more effectively with our families and loved ones.[111]

Walter Ramm also considers it important to appoint first of all a surrogate, delegating the power of attorney in cases where one's own decision-making capacity might be diminished.[112] However, it would be more reasonable to call the living will an advanced healthcare directive, which serves as a guide, leaving instructions for treatment that need to be interpreted according to the circumstances, including a specific type of power of attorney delegated to a surrogate.

---

[110] CCC, 2280.
[111] Tadeusz Pacholczyk, "Should I Have a Living Will," in www.catholiceducation.org/en/science/ethical-issues/should-i-have-a-living-will.html [15.1.2022].
[112] Walter Ramm, *Die Patientenverfügung*, No. 13, 6th ed. (Absteinach: Schriftenreihe der Aktion Leben e.V., 2011), 1–35, here 30.

Guiding Criteria for an Advance Healthcare Directive

The explanations have shown that any directive regarding advanced healthcare needs solid criteria. Javier Bustos suggests in this context using the classical three elements, necessary for the evaluation of a moral act: a) object of the action; b) intention; c) circumstances.[113]

> a. The object of the desired outcome must be morally good. Any form of so-called merciful killing, euthanasia, etc., have to be excluded. Generally speaking, the ordinary means have to be guaranteed, the extraordinary not necessarily.[114] The impossibility of foreseeing how a disease will develop beforehand shows once again the limitations of an advanced healthcare directive and the need to appoint a surrogate.
> b. The intention should not be compromised by a functional or utilitarian understanding of life and death. This becomes relevant especially with regard to suffering.[115] The final intention should be directed to participation in eternal life, which John Paul II described with the following words: "Eternal life is therefore the life of God himself and at the same time the life of the children of God. [...] The dignity of this life is linked not only to its beginning, to the fact that it comes from God, but also to its final end, to its destiny of fellowship with God in knowledge and love of him."[116]
> c. The circumstances are difficult to foresee since they may change depending on the physical, mental, and spiritual conditions of the person. Age, dealing with suffering, family issues and other factors may have a major impact. However, the circumstances cannot make an evil act good. At this point the problems regarding the living will become evident: "The person writing a living will may choose the administration of morally acceptable procedures, but the actual circumstances at the time of

---

113 Cf. Bustos, "Uncertainty of Living Will," 248–50.
114 Cf. chapter VII, Ordinary Means.
115 Cf. chapter VII, Suffering/Palliative Care.
116 John Paul II, EV, 38.

the interpretation of the living will (when its author is no longer capable of making a decision) could indicate that those procedures are, in fact, immoral."[117]

In conclusion, it must be said that only if all three elements are good will the results from the entire cause be good.[118] There are different models of how to create a living will. Besides the elements analyzed above, the best way to be prepared is to live according to God's will, which helps one confront all eventualities with interior calm and peace.

---

117   Bustos, "Uncertainty of Living Will," 250.
118   Cf. chapter V, Principle of Double Effect.

VIII
Death — Brain Death

CONSERVING OR PROLONGING LIFE IS INSEPArably connected to the definition of death as well as organ donation; this becomes evident especially when referring to organ donation *ex cadavere*. From an ethical point of view, it is clear that organs can be extracted only from dead persons, as otherwise it would be murder.[1] For that reason, the definition of death is crucial and the question must be raised: when is the human person dead? What kind of indications do we have?

Anyone involved in medical care knows that dead organs are not of any use, they must be alive and in good shape, that's the only way one can use them for transplantation. Already at this point one could be tempted to ask how is it possible to extract living organs from dead bodies? Is it possible at all? The answer depends on which definition of death one adheres to. All this needs to be investigated in this chapter in order to provide, if possible, a solid answer regarding the question, whether it is licit or not to donate organs and to transplant them.

This topic becomes even more important, considering it from the perspective of those urgently in need of organs. It is a fact that without the donation of organs, some people would not be able to survive, and the waiting lists are often quite long. In September 2020 there were 109,000 people on the national waiting list in the U.S. alone.[2] Sometimes it takes more than 5 years to get, for example, a new kidney.

---

1 This is a growing reality, often related to organ traffic. In some parts of the world people are killed for the extraction of their organs; this is for example reported from China. Cf. Maria Vittoria Cattanìa and Toni Brandi (eds.), *Cina Traffici di morte: Il commercio degli organi dei condannati a morte* (Milano: Guerini e Associati, 2008). Organ donation after euthanasia becomes also an increasing issue. Cf. Frans J. van Ittersum and Lambert Hendriks, "Organ Donation after Euthanasia," in *NCBQ* 12 (2012): 431–37.
2 U.S. Government Information on Organ Donation and Transplantation, Organ Donation Statistics, in www.organdonor.gov/statistics-stories/statistics.html [15.1.2022].

However, there are also attempts to "create" new organs from embryonic stem cells. Manufacturing and destroying human embryos is widely practiced and important organizations such as the European Union are offering a great amount of money for the research, over €80 billion between 2013 and 2020.[3] Unlike organ donors, in these cases, the mitochondrial DNA is bequeathed from generation to generation. However, ethical debates arise whether to consider them also "donors."[4] The success rate is still problematic since embryonic stem cells are known for producing tumors in the transplanted adult organism.[5]

The question remains: what can be done if, for instance, a boy needs a new kidney or heart? Suppose that there is a dying person of 80 years and this young boy of 12 years urgently needs a new kidney or heart? Wouldn't it be an act of charity, even of self-surrender, if the dying man would offer his kidney or heart to the young man? These are complex questions and not easy to answer; however, they are related to the question of when is a person dead. For this reason, it is necessary to approach in a first step the topic "death," in order to provide answers regarding organ transplantation in a second step.

Since bioethics is an interdisciplinary discipline it will be important to clarify first the broader perspective in order to approach the concrete situation. Medicine and biology usually operate the other way around, providing specialized and detailed information. However, to come to an ethical decision, it is necessary to offer an overview of the different dimensions, considering the human person as a whole. Otherwise, the risk would be high of getting lost in technical data and within a specific situation, not being capable of presenting any ethical evaluation.

On the one hand, medical technicians and physicians and those associations promoting the transplantation of organs arrange

---

3   The European parliament decided to spend over €80 billion for research until 2020, starting in 2013. Cf. Patricia Cassidy, "EU Commission rejects petition to stop funding embryonic stem cell research," *BioNews*, 2.6.2014, in www.bionews.org.uk/page_424657.asp [15.1.2022].
4   Cf. Jo Markette, "Three's a Crowd: An Argument Against Mitochondrial Replacement," in *Ethics & Medics* 41 (2016): 2-4.
5   Cf. Jacques Suaudeau, "Cellule Staminali," in Elio Sgreccia and Antonio Tarantino (eds.), *Enciclopedia di bioetica e scienze giuridica*, vol. III (Naples: Edizioni Scientifiche Italiane, 2010), 103-28, especially 105-17.

debates about this topic focusing especially on the needs of the patients. On the other hand, the discussion about death, which is the necessary pre-condition for dealing with the topic of transplantation of organs, is banned from most parts of society, public life, and public discourse. Consequently, the question "what comes after death" isn't asked anymore, not even the question "what is death" and "when is someone dead"? Death is mainly discussed as a scientific fact and not from a broader perspective. Mario Bizzotto says: "The more the scientific interest is emphasized, the more attention is diverted from the real problem, which is the human problem. [...] Not speaking of death could be seen as immaturity and lack of realism."[6]

SOME BASIC CONSIDERATIONS REGARDING DEATH

The reasons for this lack of realism can differ. However, the dominating postmodern culture seems to avoid debates about the end of life and therefore, debates about the meaning of life and of human existence. This is also due to a cultural problem: in the name of secularism the (religious) roots are widely abandoned or cut off. For that reason, the human person and also the human body after death is increasingly treated as an object and not as a subject, losing its dignity.[7] This finds also an expression in the cremation of the dead, a topic that will be considered later on.

Yet, the agony of death, suffering, funerals, and other related rites are often obscured; they have lost their meaning in society and often they even disappear from public life. The dramatic moment of death loses its significance. This is also reflected in the tendency to avoid having the presence of the corpse in the churches for the funeral mass, being confronted with the awful signs of death. People tend to ignore the thought of death; they do not want to face it, even though they shall have to. A mentality, dominated by the paradigm of technology and science, insinuates that power over death has been placed in the hands of men. On the one hand, death is often postponed even in the process of dying; on the other hand, death is caused by drugs and medication. All this leads to a changed mentality, considering death more and

---

6   Bizzotto, "Concealment of Death," 31.
7   Cf. Ashley Fernandes, "The Loss of Dignity at the End of Life," in *NCBQ* 10 (2010): 529–46.

more from a perspective that relies on medicine and technology. This has become even more the case, because most people die in hospitals under the surveillance of machines and specialized personal and not at home amidst their family.

Putting it differently, in many parts of society death is hidden and its meaning and consequence are lost. This might be one of the reasons why it is so unpopular for priests to preach about death and the Last Things such as heaven and hell, since society does not want to hear about it anymore. Recognizing death would mean recognizing that life is limited and that one needs to think about eternity. It shows that the most important questions of life cannot be answered by progress or science.

In other words, there is a predominating medicalized concept of death, which is a result of the progress of technology. To a certain degree, it is possible to overcome suffering and even the anguish of death through the progress of science. The pharmaceutical industry provides drugs and all types of painkillers that profoundly change the moment of death. It will be helpful to illustrate this through one example, which was made public in the *New York Times* in 2009:

> In some of the rooms in the hospice unit at Franklin Hospital, in Valley Stream on Long Island, the patients were sleeping because their organs were shutting down, the natural process of death by disease. But at least one patient had been rendered unconscious by strong drugs. The patient, Leo Oltzik, an 88-year-old man with dementia, congestive heart failure and kidney problems, was brought from home by his wife and son, who were distressed to see him agitated, jumping out of bed and ripping off his clothes. Now he was sleeping soundly with his mouth wide open. "Obviously, he's much different than he was when he came in," Dr. Edward Halbridge, the hospice medical director, told Mr. Oltzik's wife. "He's calm, he's quiet." Mr. Oltzik's life would end not with a bang, but with the drip, drip, drip of an IV drug that put him into a slumber from which he would never awaken. That drug, lorazepam, is a strong sedative. Mr. Oltzik was also receiving morphine, to kill pain. This combination can slow breathing and heart rate, and may make it impossible

for the patient to eat or drink. In so doing, it can hasten death. [...] Doctors who perform it [terminal sedation] say it is based on carefully thought-out ethical principles in which the goal is never to end someone's life, but only to make the patient more comfortable.[8]

This example shows how life is stripped of its finitude, expressed in suffering and anguish. Natural death is submitted to artificial science, which subjects the last moment of life to the standards of technique, risking the reduction of man to an object. Death is depersonalized and more and more arranged according to desires and preferences; in the case of unconsciousness relatives usually assume this role. A depersonalized concept of death submits death to the progress of technology, to the criteria of utility, and often to arbitrary criteria. This has changed also the understanding of medical ethics.[9] The secularized society is not capable of offering a meaning of death that goes beyond an immanent perspective. For that reason, death is considered according to the immanent perspective of science and technology. In this logic, death becomes something impersonal, it is part of a process submitted to technology, but it has lost its human dimension.

As a consequence, there is a shift in the understanding of the physician. Once, the doctor was a witness of death; now there is a tendency that he becomes the lord over death. This has become true already in the Netherlands.[10] This creates a new mentality, which leads to medical paternalism. Michael Nair-Collins describes it as "limiting the liberty or autonomy of another by acting contrary to or without regard for her wishes, based on the justification that doing so is in the best interest of that person."[11] This leads to a growing separation between the physician and the patient. Manfred Spieker noticed that the "patient turns from a suffering subject who receives compassion and solidarity from society into an

---

8   Anemona Hartocollis, "Hard Choice for a Comfortable Death: Sedation," *New York Times*, 26.12.2009, in www.nytimes.com/2009/12/27/health/27sedation.html [15.1.2022].
9   Cf. Giovanni Maio, *Mittelpunkt Mensch: Ethik in der Medizin. Ein Lehrbuch* (Stuttgart: Schattauer, 2012), 85-116.
10   Cf. chapter IV, A Look at the Current Situation.
11   Michael Nair-Collins, "Brain Death, Paternalism, and the Language of 'Death,'" in *Kennedy Institute of Ethics Journal* 23 (2013): 53-104, here 75.

object that burdens society."[12] However, if the physicians decide, how do they know what is best for the people? How can they, for example, define "unbearable suffering" in a concrete situation? Can psychological suffering be considered sufficient, as in Belgium and the Netherlands, to end life?

There is another aspect, which needs to be taken into consideration in this context. Especially in the last century, certain ideologies submitted death to the progress of technology. Due to this development, it became possible for the first time in history to destroy millions of lives. The concentration camps and the gulags reflect this mentality, but also several wars, abortion, and the practice of euthanasia. Since the industrial revolution this has become a serious issue and there are increasing possibilities, which might threaten entire nations.[13]

Through the internet and television, people are continuously distracted; they fall into dependency on a kind of narcotic, which keeps them away from worrying and thinking about things like death and the meaning of life. An egocentric mentality spreads rapidly; people are concerned only about themselves according to an immanent perspective. Also for that reason, a cure for the dying based on proximity, with human and spiritual support, is more and more missing. From this perspective most people are abandoned; they only receive medical care and are exposed to the television. Some decades ago, this was totally different. Especially the religious sisters took care of the dying, they prepared them well for death and they were close to the dying, sitting with them through the night. The current mentality is not capable of providing this anymore; for that reason, Anthony Ughetti requested a new *ars moriendi* that "respects the dignity of human life through natural death."[14]

Without any doubt, it is painful to face death, but this is the only way to accept the human condition. An attitude that neglects death

---

12 Manfred Spieker, "The Legal Language of the Culture of Death in Europe," in *NCBQ* 14 (2014): 647–57, here 653.

13 Sidel presents an overview about the historical development of the use of biological and chemical weapons and their impact. Cf. Vitor W. Sidel, "Armi chimiche e biologiche," in Giovanni Russo (ed.), *Bioetica ambientale* (Torino: Editrice Elle Di Ci, 1998), 235–50.

14 Anthony C. Ughetti, "A Contemporary *Ars Moriendi* for End-of-Life Care," in *Ethics & Medics* 44 (2019): 1–2.

will fail to conform with the reality of human existence; then many things become possible, such as euthanasia, suicide or even the crime of abortion. Bizzotto writes: "The decision to put an end to life is a refusal to confront death and therefore it confirms and reinforces its concealment. There is a tendency to substitute human death with a technological and commercialized death, to substitute the natural with the artificial."[15] The artificial interpretation of life will lead to an artificial interpretation of death. In other words, whenever life is submitted to erroneous parameters, so also is death. This happens for example when death is considered only as an artificial process, rejecting the condition of a human being.

PSYCHOLOGICAL EFFECTS AND DEATH

Also, psychological effects related to death need to be taken into consideration. Today, people prefer to speak about death in an indirect way or in reference to others; talking about their own death is usually suppressed. This is also due to increasing psychological pressure, which has a great influence on people. So-called social media and the predominant mentality in society, do not know how to deal with death anymore. At most, they offer tips on how to communicate the loss of someone,[16] but usually, they do not transmit any spiritual meaning that goes beyond some etiquette. During the time of the national socialists, when totalitarianism and propaganda were in favor of euthanasia, there were still strong ethical concerns and public opposition.[17] Yet, during the last decade, these ethical concerns have disappeared more and more, which has had an impact also on the psychological effects.

Psychology, a term that derives etymologically from the Greek *psyché* (in Latin: *anima*) and *logos*, is difficult to define since it undergoes continuous development. Yet, in general terms, it can be described as the scientific study of human behavior and experience,[18] with an emphasis on the conscious or unconscious mental experiences and relationships. Whenever the spiritual dimension

---

15 Bizzotto, "Concealment of Death," 51.
16 Cf. Mark Ray, "Addressing Loss on Social Media," 7.8.2019, in www.nextavenue.org/addressing-loss-on-social-media [15.1.2022].
17 Friedlander, *The Origins of Nazi Genocide*, 188.
18 Cf. Silvestro Paluzzi, *Manuale di psicologia* (Rome: Urbaniana University Press, 1999), 30.

of man is weakened or reduced, this will cause effects on the psychological makeup of persons. This can be shown for example in the practice of confession, which has diminished among Catholics within the last years. However, people continue to experience the burden and consequences of sin, but they do not know how to deal with it anymore. At the same time the number of people, looking for psychological help and support is increasing rapidly.[19] This is not the place to explain these things in more detail, but statistics indicate that mental illness has a great impact on people. The psyche depends on the spiritual dimension, which includes different types of relationships, with God, the neighbor, and oneself. Whenever they are neglected, it will affect the psychological dimension of the person; this becomes even more true in the moment of death. Luciano Sandrin affirms therefore that living "and dying intersects not only in personal experience but also a proper characteristic of a relationship. [...] Acceptance of death means recognizing and accepting the limits which 'constitute' our life: an attitude which, even in psychological terms, takes the name of *humility*."[20]

The process of dying, as well as life, consists of relationships. It implies a therapeutic and even more a spiritual liaison, which should not be neglected. Whenever it is reduced to a technical-medical dimension, man will be treated as an object and not as a person. Death is unnatural to human nature because it is a radical rupture with all dimensions of human existence. For that reason, it is usually accompanied by anxiety and suffering. It separates what are meant to be united: soul and body. The anxiety is at the same time "natural," because it is supposed to help the person prepare for the last moment of life.

In these moments also psychologists—for example, the American Psychological Association—offer help. "They can assess mood, mental functioning, and pain; treat depression, anxiety, and other

---

19 According to the Mental Health Statistics in the United States, "almost half of the adults (46.4 percent) will experience a mental illness during their lifetime." It says: "5 percent of adults (18 or older) experience a mental illness in any one year, equivalent to 43.8 million people." Rubina Kapil, "5 Surprising Mental Health Statistics," 6.2.2019, in www.mentalhealthfirstaid.org/2019/02/5-surprising-mental-health-statistics/ [15.1.2022].
20 Luciano Sandrin, "Psychological effects of refusal of death," in Correa and Sgreccia, *Dignity of the Dying Person*, 53-62, here 62.

mental health problems; provide end-of-life counseling to the dying and their families; and advocate for good medical care."[21] All these aspects are of importance. However, a realistic psychology must confront death respecting all dimensions of the human being and not just apply an overtaxing through treatments. It must help people to be at peace with God, neighbor, and self and it must include a reasonable response to suffering and anxiety. Mario Bizzotto noticed: "The model of Christian death is that of the crucifix, which has nothing to do with the worn-out phraseology of devotional language. A person with faith conquers the fear of death but is not exonerated from suffering. Hope in its turn does not ignore a situation of trial, but presupposes it; it is not an analgesic which suspends pain, but a force for confronting it."[22] Psychology needs to include these different dimensions, to provide help and support especially in the last moments of life.

DEATH FROM A PHILOSOPHICAL PERSPECTIVE

Given the multidiscipline approach of bioethics, it will be helpful to include some philosophical and theological considerations.[23] Even though within a philosophy based on realism, death and life after death were always given special importance, it might be sufficient to rely on Robert Spaemann († 2018) to offer a brief presentation from this perspective, since his point of departure is a holistic vision of man.

He affirmed that human life is directed towards the future, it is "part of the future that in it the actually present moment of time has already come to belong to the past."[24] In other words, the present moment is intrinsically linked to the future and becomes part of it. At the same time, the present moment is passing by and becomes part of the past. Spaemann affirms that we "cannot think that what happened once will one day not have been."[25]

---

21 American Psychological Association, "Death & Dying," in www.apa.org/topics/death/index.aspx [15.1.2022].
22 Bizzotto, "Concealment of death," 45.
23 Josef Pieper noticed that there are various dimensions of death and the process of dying goes beyond the physical death. Cf. Josef Pieper, *Death and Immortality*, 14-22.
24 Robert Spaemann, "Death-suicide-euthanasia," in Correa and Sgreccia, *Dignity of the Dying Person*, 123-31, here 123.
25 Ibid.

That's the reason for the memory (*memoria*): the past becomes part of eternity, and eternity assumes an eternal mind, in which the past remains in its actuality and this is, according to Spaemann, a proof for the existence of God. Within this context, he also mentions that love transcends the presence towards the future and the past. The German philosopher uses these considerations in order to explain the reality of life and death.

According to this perspective, life is some type of activity, death is instead pure passivity. Death is something passive. Man can accelerate it, can provoke it, but naturally, it happens as something passive to man. The human person is aware of death; he can consciously anticipate death: "Accepting death is *the* ultimate *actus humanus*, because it can no longer be understood in terms of merely vital needs. The human being is that being which, unlike all other living beings, does not merely try to escape death until the last moment, only in order to perish nevertheless, but that being which truly is 'capable' of its death."[26]

In this context, it will be helpful to call briefly to mind the meaning of the concept of the so-called *actus humanus*. Thomas Aquinas distinguishes between an *actus hominis* and an *actus humanus*. In the *Summa Theologiae*, he provided a definition helpful for any ethical consideration: "sin is nothing else than a bad human act. Now an act that is a human act is due to its being voluntary, [...] whether it be voluntary, as being elicited by the will, e.g. to will or to choose, or as being commanded by the will, e.g. the exterior actions of speech or operation."[27] The *Catechism of the Catholic Church* has adopted this concept when it states in #1749: "Freedom makes man a moral subject. When he acts deliberately, man is, so to speak, the father of his acts. Human acts, that is, acts that are freely chosen in consequence of a judgment of conscience, can be morally evaluated. They are either good or evil."[28]

Robert Spaemann refers to this concept when he speaks about the acceptance of death, which he considers an *actus humanus*. Meanwhile, the *actus hominis* is a "normal performance of the human person, such as breathing, which does not require the will nor

---

26 Ibid., 124.
27 Thomas Aquinas, STh, I-II, q. 71, a. 6.
28 CCC, 1749.

conscious thought." Even though death is pure passivity, it should be perceived as an *actus humanus*, because in this way the human person admits the present and participates in the future. This becomes especially true, when the person accepts death voluntarily, which will affect the future (eternal life). From this perspective, some important conclusions can be made.

Ending one's own life with artificial means destroys the meaning of death because the attempt is made to escape from pure passivity (death) by changing death into an act. Robert Spaemann concludes:

> It splits the human being into an acting, i.e. the killing, part and a passive part which gets eliminated and drags the one acting along with it into this extinction. The suffering itself is not transformed. [...] In suicide human beings do not gain their self; rather, it is the extreme form of the non-identity of human beings. [...] The non-pathological or "philosophical" suicide is therefore the most fundamental violation of human dignity.[29]

The denial of death degrades death to a non-human act. This would contradict the very nature of death, which aims towards the future.

DEATH FROM A THEOLOGICAL PERSPECTIVE

As has often been remarked, bioethics is an interdisciplinary subject, which should not be reduced to the presentation of some medical or biological facts. Any reduction of man to an object will do injustice to him and his dignity. Human dignity is a concept that is related not only to philosophy but especially to theology and to Christian theology. It is based on Sacred Scripture and it was developed and fully understood in Tradition and interpreted through the Magisterium of the Church.[30] Today, the word "dignity" has many confusing meanings; even euthanasia is justified by referring to "dignity."

Some experts in bioethics distinguish between "basic dignity," which can never be taken from us, and "personal dignity," which

---

29 Spaemann, "Death-suicide-euthanasia," 124.
30 Cf. Enrique Colom, *Scelti in Cristo per essere santi, IV. Morale sociale* (Rome: Edusc, 2008), 116-19.

is the self-perception and the way others treat the patient.³¹ This distinction would allow that "personal dignity" could be degraded or removed by pain, sickness, or suffering. However, this Cartesian distinction is not helpful at all, since it relativizes the intrinsic dignity of the human person. Even though a person might feel undignified because of his suffering or pain, the dignity remains intact, because it arises from the very nature of man. Christianity includes a duality between soul/body and natural/supernatural, but it excludes dualisms. For that reason, John Paul II said: "The dignity of the dying is rooted in the fact that they are created by God and personally called to immortal life. This hope-filled vision transfigures the destruction of our mortal body."³² According to this perspective, the soul is the substantial form of the body within an intrinsic unity of the whole.

Therefore, it is important to include a brief theological consideration of death. Regarding the further explanations it must be assumed that theology is, as the encyclical letter *Lumen Fidei* states, a reflection on faith and therefore on revelation; a perspective is offered that goes beyond the realm of the visible material world.³³

According to a Christian understanding, the human person is created in "the image and likeness" of God (Gen 1:26) and the divine image is present in each man. The most profound reason for the dignity of man is the fact that the human person is endowed with "a spiritual and immortal soul."³⁴ The constitution *Gaudium et Spes* affirms: "Since all men possess a rational soul and are created in God's likeness, since they have the same nature and origin, [...] the basic equality of all must receive increasingly greater recognition."³⁵ The immortal soul is not generated by one's parents, but immediately created by God and therefore does not perish, even when separated from the body.³⁶ The concept of

---

31 Cf. Fernandes, "Loss of Dignity," 535–38.
32 John Paul II, "Discourse of Holy Father John Paul II," in Correa and Sgreccia, *Dignity of the Dying Person*, 7–10, here 9.
33 Cf. Francis, LF, 36.
34 GS, 14.
35 GS, 29.
36 Pope Pius XII affirmed: "for the Catholic faith obliges us to hold that souls are immediately created by God." Pius XII, Encyclical Letter *Humani Generis*, 12.8.1950, in www.vatican.va/content/pius-xii/en/encyclicals/documents/hf_p-xii_enc_12081950_humani-generis.html [15.1.2022], 36.

soul is crucial to understand death from a Christian perspective. The Magisterium of the Church has clarified this concept, which acquires a special meaning when related to death.[37]

Death is the consequence of sin (cf. Rom 5:19).[38] However, man was created to be immortal. Death contradicts human nature and was introduced into this world because of the bad use of the *actus humanus*, which caused the state of original sin in which we are born. Death is the separation of the soul from the body,[39] it separates what was meant to be intrinsically united and it is already an indication of the resurrection of the dead. Since soul and body form an intrinsic unity, the problem remained how to justify the immortality of the soul when the body is submitted to corruption.

Elio Sgreccia summarizes in this regard the teaching of St. Thomas, who found a profound and still valid explanation:

> Aquinas arrived at the statement that the human soul has the privilege of surviving the dissolution of the body: besides being the substantial form, the soul is the subsisting form because it has an autonomous being, as is evident from the fact that it performs operations independently of the body. These operations can be identified in the consciousness that the soul has of all bodies, in its knowledge of what is universal, and in self-consciousness.[40]

At the moment of death, the immortal soul is separated from the body; when this life-giving principle is separated, the natural body is no longer sustained in life and falls into corruption and decay. The very nature of the soul—it is a spiritual reality—already indicates its immortality and therefore, it does not cease to exist. Also for that reason, the value and dignity of the soul cannot be measured by certain functions or intellectual activities.

---

37 See GS, 14-16: 22. A good summary is offered in CCC, 1703-1705.
38 The *Catechism of the Catholic Church* summarizes: *"Death is a consequence of sin. The Church's Magisterium, as authentic interpreter of the affirmations of Scripture and Tradition, teaches that death entered the world on account of man's sin. Even though man's nature is mortal God had destined him not to die. Death was therefore contrary to the plans of God the Creator and entered the world as a consequence of sin."* CCC, 1008.
39 See CCC, 1005.
40 Sgreccia, PB, 138.

At the moment of death, the soul goes back to its origin; it goes directly and immediately into the presence of God, where it is judged.[41] God respects the freedom of man and the decisions that the person has taken in his lifetime. For that reason, the last moment of life is so important, since the life-decision becomes definitive at the moment of death. The *Catechism* offers the following explanation:

> The Church encourages us to prepare ourselves for the hour of our death. [...] If you aren't fit to face death today, it's very unlikely you will be tomorrow... Praised are you, my Lord, for our sister bodily Death, from whom no living man can escape. Woe be to those who will die in mortal sin! Blessed are they who will be found in your most holy will, for the second death will not harm them.[42]

Within this context and from a perspective of faith the word "compassion" receives a new meaning. It does not primarily mean avoiding suffering and pain, but accompanying and preparing the dying person, that he may enter into eternal life. This can include means to ease pain and means of sedation, but it consists primarily of a preparation for the final encounter with God. The Christian meaning of death is totally different from other conceptions because Jesus Christ has given a new meaning to death (cf. Phil 1:21); he opened the gates to eternal life through his death. Christians who die with Christ will live with him (cf. 2 Tim 2:11). Thérèse of Lisieux, as many other saints, accepted death even though she was suffering a great deal. She wrote before her own death in the afternoon of 30th September 1897: "I am not dying; I am entering into life."[43]

The Catholic Church considers the separation of soul and body as the definition of death; it expresses its complex reality. However, how can this definition be applied for medicine and science? The soul as a spiritual entity cannot be submitted to the positivistic mentality of science, which—according to the limits of its methodology—can verify only material things.[44] According to

---

41 Benedict XII, Constitution *Benedictus Deus*, DH, 1000-1002.
42 CCC, 1014, citing the *Imitation of Christ* and St. Francis of Assisi.
43 Thérèse of Lisieux, *Story of a Soul: Autobiography*. trans. John Clarke, 3rd ed. (Washington, D.C.: ICS Publications, 2017), 271.
44 A precise overview about death, Christianity, and the Magisterium of the Catholic Church according to the teachings of Pope John Paul II is

Christian tradition, the soul is not the same as the intellect, since the soul is the principle of life and this principle is not localized in an organ or limited to any one power.

When the process of bodily corruption starts, there are clear indications of death. Yet, this would be too late for any type of transplantation of organs. The question remains of how to "translate" the theological definition of death into a medical language. In 1957, Pope Pius XII addressed this problem during an International Congress of Anaesthesiologists: "It remains for the doctor, and especially the anesthesiologist, to give a clear and precise definition of 'death' and the 'moment of death' of a patient who passes away in a state of unconsciousness. Here one can accept the usual concept of complete and final separation of the soul from the body; but in practice one must take into account the lack of precision of the terms 'body' and 'separation.'"[45] This requested precision, as the Pope called it, is not easy to provide, especially since any concept of death has to be compatible with Christian anthropology.

DETERMINING THE MOMENT OF DEATH

The response provided by Pope Pius XII indicated that the determination of death—from a medical perspective—does not fall under the expertise of the Church, but has to be provided by physicians trained in this field. It is up to them to interpret the signs of death since it is part of their life work. In other words, the way in which the Catholic Church describes death has not always a counterpart in the language of medical science. However, the Pope affirmed that in "case of insoluble doubt [...] it will be necessary to presume that life remains, because there is involved here a fundamental right received from the Creator, and it is necessary to prove with certainty that it has been lost."[46]

From a theological point of view, there can never be a "half-dead" person and this is part of the difficulty, determining the moment of death, which is usually a process. This becomes even more challenging, since—from a medical point of view—the distinction can be made between the death of various organs and the death

---

presented by Francesco Brancato, *L'ultima chiamata: Giovanni Paolo II e la morte* (Firenze: Giunti Editore, 2006).
45 Pius XII, "Address to Anesthesiologists," 312.
46 Pius XII, "Prolongation of Life," 300.

of the individual person. For that reason, Pope Pius XII affirmed that "human life continues for as long as its vital functions, distinguished from the simple life of organs, manifest themselves spontaneously or even with the help of artificial processes." He added: "A great number of these cases are the object of insoluble doubt, and must be dealt with according to the presumption of law and of fact of which We have spoken."[47] The Pope offers considerations of a general nature and affirms the difficulty of any attempt to define the moment of death.

In past centuries the death of the organs and the death of the whole person had been considered mostly as coinciding, proven by the so-called secure signs of death, such as dead spots, rigor mortis, and decay.[48] Through the progress of science and technology, "the difference between the life of the person and the life of the body has become apparent. The difference is most dramatically exposed in the body of the brain-dead patient."[49] This is also due to the fact that new definitions of death usually rely on what was called before insecure signs of death, such as unconsciousness, cardiac and respiratory arrest, immobility, paleness, and low body temperature.[50] And indeed, due to the progress of medicine and technology, it is possible that signs once considered "insecure" turn out to be secure signs. This presupposes that science can prove this with certainty. To understand this progress, it will be helpful to consider briefly the historical development.

Physicians base their definitions of death on the results of medicine; like medical technology, they continuously develop. In the 17th century, the discovery of the blood circulatory system made physicians conclude that the putrefaction of a body is the only certain sign of death.[51] At that time there was a widespread fear of being buried alive and this criterion was supposed to respond to this fear. As the development of medicine further advanced, it turned out that this criterion was not practical anymore. The

---

47 Ibid., 301.
48 Cf. Regina Breul and Wolfgang Waldstein, *Hirntod-Organspende. Brisant und ehrlich*, 2nd ed. (Illertissen: Media Maria, 2014), 19.
49 Edward J. Furton, "Brain Death, the Soul, and Organic Life," in *NCBQ* 2 (2002): 455–70, here 467.
50 Cf. Breul and Waldstein, *Hirntod-Organspende*, 19.
51 Cf. Corrado Manni, "A report on cerebral death," in Correa and Sgreccia, *Dignity of the Dying Person*, 102–18, here 103.

cardiocirculatory criterion was introduced; the diagnosis of death became verifiable even without instruments displaying heart activity.

This criterion is still in force; however, in this context, the main emphasis will be given to the brain-death definition. In her critical analysis, Doyen Nguyen has brought out the problem of how this criterion is applied. After removing life support a person is declared dead within the brief time-window of 25 minutes after asystole. The so-called "controlled cardiac/circulatory death" uses a timeframe that permits organ harvesting. Nguyen concludes that "donors are still alive (though dying) at the time of organ removal."[52]

The cardiocirculatory criterion remained the only one valid for the diagnosis of death until 1959. That year the French neuroscientist and medical researcher Michel Valentin Marcel Jouver († 2017) published a significant report in the medical journal *Electroencephalography and Clinical Neurophysiology*, focusing on four cases of "death of the central nervous system"; they were "characterized by persistent apnoeic coma, the absence of brain stem and osteotendinous reflexes."[53] The author inserted bipolar electrodes into the thalamus and did not register any electric activity. He compared the situation to patients using an isolated heart-lung system and "concluded that if spontaneous respiration is not revived in 24 hours, all intensive treatment should be suspended as this indicates 'the death of the central nervous system,' and this system 'is a necessary condition for resuscitation.'"[54]

The presentation of these criteria marked the beginning of a new definition of death. Only some months later there were similar experiences in other countries. French neurologists called this state a "coma dépassé," a term that caused confusion, since coma cannot be a sufficient criterion for death. Coma is usually a transitory condition, while death marks an irreversible status. In the beginning, encephalic death was called an "irreversible coma." Only in 1988 did the French National Medical Academy ban the

---

52 Doyen Nguyen, NDD, 499. Nguyen adds that the controlled cardiac/circulatory death criterion applied is "a veiled form of euthanasia; it is the immediate precursor of the overt practice of organ donation after euthanasia, now established in Belgium and the Netherlands." Ibid., 500. Nguyen points out that there is an intrinsic link between organ donation after euthanasia and these criteria of death.
53 Manni, "A report on cerebral death," 104.
54 Ibid.

term "coma dépassé," which had become counterproductive for the transplantation of organs since no one wants to extract organs from a person in a coma.[55]

Before approaching the definition of brain death, which has become the determining criterion in our days, it is important to call to mind once again that death is usually a process unless someone is shot or killed or dies immediately. This is a major difficulty for physicians, who need to have a concrete and very precise definition of death. This difficulty becomes even more obvious when considering that some activities persist even after death in other parts of the body. Nails and hair continue to grow; there can even be reflexes some 24 hours after death. The problem of being able to determine the moment of death consists precisely in the fact that it includes four levels, such as a conceptional basis, general physiological standards, operational criteria, and specific tests to prove that the established standards have been satisfied.[56]

The determination of the moment of death has become difficult[57] since there is a new category of "dead" donors, "which include both heart-beating and non-heart-beating donors, that is, patients whose deaths are determined by the 'brain death' criterion, or by the 'controlled cardiac/circulatory death' criterion."[58] Is it justified to confirm that the death of certain organs corresponds to the death of the whole person? This question becomes even more delicate regarding the transplantation of organs.

BRAIN DEATH — DEATH OF THE WHOLE PERSON?

The following explanations will rely above all on the 2017 doctoral thesis of Doyen Nguyen, who provides a critical analysis from the perspective of Christian ethics on *The New Definitions of Death for Organ Donation*.[59] Her work presents the most important issues

---

55 Cf. ibid., 105.
56 Cf. Alexander Morgan Capron and Leon R. Kass, "A Statutory Definition of the Standards for Determining Human Death: An Appraisal and a Proposal," in *University of Pennsylvania Law Review* 121 (1972): 87–118, here 102-3.
57 Regarding the historical development of criteria for brain death, cf. Alphonse D. Walder, "The Artificial Prolongation of Life and the Determination of the Exact Moment of Death," in Carlos Chagas (ed.), *Pontificia Academia Scientiarum*, vol. 60 (Vatican City: Libreria Editrice Vaticana, 1985), 75-84.
58 Nguyen, NDD, 3-4.
59 Ibid.

related to brain death and organ transplantation. Further, in the succeeding considerations, the concepts "brain death," "cerebral death," or "encephalic death" are used as synonyms.

Manfred Lütz points out an important detail regarding the origin of the brain death criteria, which were established in 1968 by the Ad Hoc Committee of the Harvard Medical School, defining brain death as an "irreversible coma."[60] This definition was due to a utilitarian approach; the "commission looked for a criterion sufficient to disconnect the machines in terminal patients. [...] The second utilitarian aim of the Harvard Declaration was the transplantation of organs. Taking organs from corpses is a customary medical practice."[61] In other words, chronologically speaking the new definition came into existence right after the first successful organ transplantations had been realized. The Report of the Ad Hoc Committee of the Harvard Medical School says:

> Our primary purpose is to define irreversible coma as a new criterion for death. There are two reasons why there is need for a definition: (1) Improvements in resuscitative and supportive measures have led to increased efforts to save those who are desperately injured. Sometimes these efforts have only partial success so that the result is an individual whose heart continues to beat but whose brain is irreversibly damaged. The burden is great on patients who suffer permanent loss of intellect, on their families, on the hospitals, and on those in need of hospital beds already occupied by these comatose patients. (2) Obsolete criteria for the definition of death can lead to controversy in obtaining organs for transplantation.[62]

The way in which the Committee of the Medical School of Harvard justified the new definition of death might prompt surprise.

---

60 Ad Hoc Committee of the Harvard Medical School, "A Definition of Irreversible Coma," in *Journal of the American Medical Association* 205 (1968): 337-40, here 337.
61 Manfred Lütz, "Statement against the 'A report on cerebral death' by prof. Corrado Manni," in Correa and Sgreccia, *Dignity of the Dying Person*, 119-22, here 121-22. The Pontifical Academy of Sciences rejected this argument regarding the genesis of brain death. However, Nguyen has shown in her study that Lütz was right. Cf. Nguyen, NDD, 45-51.
62 Ad Hoc Committee of the Harvard Medical School, "A Definition of Irreversible Coma," 337.

It is said that the improvement of supportive measures leads to the situation that the heart of patients still beats, but the brain is irreversibly damaged and therefore, they are a great burden. The argumentation is quite frankly based on utilitarianism. As the report says, one of the two reasons to change the definition of death is the obtaining of organs for transplantation.

The following criteria for brain death were established: 1. Unreceptivity and Unresponsitivity; 2. No Movements of Breathing; 3. No Reflexes; 4. Flat Electroencephalogram.[63] The Ad Hoc Committee stated that there is a shift from the heart as the central organ (in the past) to the brain and its functions to determine death. It is—at least for our time—surprising that while presenting a new definition of death the committee quoted quite extensively Pope Pius XII and some of his ethical reflections. It seems that the Ad Hoc Committee felt the need to justify their position.[64] However, brain death was defined as an "irreversible coma."[65] Later on, this definition was modified and is commonly related to "the irreversible loss of the capacity to integrate and coordinate the body's physical and mental functions."[66]

Worldwide, there are more than 37 brain death definitions, some of which vary a lot. This new definition of death has caused and continues to cause debates and evokes contra positions. The main problem consists in the practice of relating the life of the person to the function of an organ, in this case, the encephalon. For that reason, some conclude that "the death of the encephalon equals the death of the person."[67]

In the US there are, according to the President's Commission study group, two ways of determining death that meet these requirements: "An individual who has sustained either 1) irreversible cessation of circulatory and respiratory function, or 2) irreversible cessation of all functions of the entire brain, including the brain stem, is dead. A determination of death must be made in accordance with accepted medical standards."[68]

---

63   Cf. ibid, 337-38.
64   Ibid., 340.
65   Ibid.
66   Corrado Manni, "A report on cerebral death," 106.
67   Ibid.
68   President's Commission for the Study of Ethical Problems in Medicine

For that reason, there is the so-called "dead donor rule," according to which it must be assured that procuring organs should never kill patients and the procurement of organs may begin only after the donor has died.[69] However, the question remains: does the definition of brain death respect this rule?[70] At this point, it will not be necessary to discuss these issues in great detail since this was already done by Doyen Nguyen, who provides a precise overview. Yet, it will be worth mentioning the position of the Magisterium of the Church regarding this new definition of death and to mention some of the most problematic issues regarding the definition of brain death.

The Magisterium of the Church and Brain Death

A few years after the President's Commission study had provided a definition of death in 1981, the Pontifical Academy of Sciences offered its own definition. "A person is dead when he has suffered irreversible loss of all capacity for integrating and coordinating physical and mental functions of the body. Death has occurred when: a) spontaneous cardiac and respiratory functions have irreversibly ceased, or b) there has been an irreversible cessation of all brain functions."[71] The Academy affirmed that "it appears that cerebral death is the true criterion of death since the definite cessation of cardio-respiratory functions leads very rapidly to cerebral death."[72]

---

and Biomedical and Behavioral Research, *Defining Death: Medical, Legal and Ethical Issues in the Determination of Death* (Washington, D. C.: U. S. Government Printing Office, 1981), 73.

69 Cf. James M. DuBois, "Organ Transplantation: An Ethical Road Map," in *NCBQ* 2 (2002): 413-53, here 418. Based on these principles Nguyen concludes that the Uniform Determination of Death Act needs to be revised since it is an "inherent incoherence." Doyen Nguyen, "Does the Uniform Determination of Death Act Need to Be Revised?," in *The Linacre Quarterly* 87 (2020): 317-33, here 329.

70 Just like the body of a living person, the brain-dead body is warm, with still functioning vital organs. None of these features are present in the heart-dead body. Cf. Robert Truog and Walter Robinson, "Role of Brain Death and Dead-Donor Rule in the Ethics of Organ Transplantation," in *Critical Care Medicine* 31 (2003): 2392.

71 Carlos Chagas (ed.), *The Artificial Prolongation of Life and the Determination of the Exact Moment of Death*, Pontifical Academy of Science (Vatican City: Libreria Editrice Vaticana, 1985), 113.

72 Ibid.

DuBois comments on this statement that it did shape practice, but did not end the debate. One of the main questions, however, remains: is it sufficient to delegate the definition of death to physicians, and are they capable of presenting a medical definition of death that respects the human person and death with all their dimensions? How can a definition of death, based only on a technical perspective, cope with death as a process?

Although Pope John Paul II approved neurological criteria for the determination of death, it is worth considering some details. On 29th August 2000, he addressed the 18th *International Congress of the Transplantation Society* inviting them to promote a culture of life and human dignity, underlining that vital organs can be removed only after the death of a person. After that, he addressed the problem of how to be completely certain that a person is dead. He confirms first the classical definition of death: "It results from the separation of the life-principle (or soul) from the corporal reality of the person. The death of the person, understood in this primary sense, is an event which *no scientific technique or empirical method can identify directly.*"[73] He calls the biological signs that follow death "criteria" for ascertaining death used by medicine today, yet he admonishes that they "should not be understood as the technical-scientific determination of the *exact moment* of a person's death, but as a scientifically secure means of identifying *the biological signs that a person has indeed died.*"[74] He calls in mind that the criteria were changed from "the traditional cardio-respiratory signs to the so-called '*neurological*' criterion." Following the logic established by Pope Pius XII, he quotes the commonly accepted definition of brain death as the "complete and irreversible cessation of all brain activity (in the cerebrum, cerebellum and brain stem)."[75]

The position of Pope John Paul II is prudent. Following the logic of Pope Pius XII, he stated that the Church does not make technical decisions but has the duty to compare the definitions

---

73 John Paul II, Address to the 18th International Congress of the Transplantation Society, 29.8.2000, in w2.vatican.va/content/john-paul-ii/en/speeches/2000/jul-sep/documents/hf_jp-ii_spe_20000829_transplants.html [15.1.2022], 4.
74 Ibid.
75 Ibid., 5.

of death provided by science to the Gospel, evaluating if they correspond to the dignity of man. He added:

> Here it can be said that the criterion adopted in more recent times for ascertaining the fact of death, namely the complete and irreversible cessation of all brain activity, if rigorously applied, does not seem to conflict with the essential elements of a sound anthropology. Therefore, a health-worker professionally responsible for ascertaining death can use these criteria in each individual case as the basis for arriving at that degree of assurance in ethical judgment which moral teaching describes as "moral certainty." This moral certainty is considered the necessary and sufficient basis for an ethically correct course of action. Only where such certainty exists, and where informed consent has already been given by the donor or the donor's legitimate representatives, is it morally right to initiate the technical procedures required for the removal of organs for transplant.[76]

The Pope takes into account the facts presented by science, evaluating them according to the ethical criteria deriving from natural law and Revelation. However, death is recognized as the "complete and irreversible cessation of *all* brain activity." John Paul II added that if it is rigorously applied, it "does not seem to conflict with the essential elements of a sound anthropology."[77] The problem regarding this definition consists exactly in the word "all" and "irreversible," because, as we are going to see, later on, the brain-death definition in use does not include all brain activities and there were cases when it became even reversible.

Yet, several Conferences of Catholic Bishops, for example, the United States Conference of Catholic Bishops, have issued *Ethical and Religious Directives for Catholic Health Care Services*, in which they affirm: "The determination of death should be made by the physician or competent medical authority in accordance with responsible and commonly accepted scientific criteria."[78] The bishops from the US do not present a specific definition of death

---

76 Ibid.
77 Ibid.
78 USCCB, "Ethical and Religious Directives for Catholic Health Care Services," in Furton et al., *Catholic Health Care Ethics*, 389–400, here 397-98.

but delegate it to the physicians or competent medical authorities.

Pope John Paul II addressed this issue on various occasions, Doyen Nguyen presents a good overview.[79] Yet, in 2005, the Pope addressed this topic for the last time in a message to the participants of a conference organized by the Pontifical Academy for Science. He summarizes the position of the Church choosing a balanced position: "On the one hand, the Church has encouraged the free donation of organs and on the other hand she has underlined the ethical conditions for such donation, emphasizing the obligation to defend the life and dignity of both donor and recipient."[80] The Pope states that death presupposes Christian anthropology since the human person is a substantial unity of soul and body and the soul as its substantial form is the life principle.

In 2008 Pope Benedict XVI presented a similar view, affirming that organs can be extracted only *ex cadavere*. He states that the scientific community has to provide certainty and that in such a delicate area "there cannot be the slightest suspicion of arbitrariness and where certainty has not been attained the principle of precaution must prevail."[81] For that reason, he encouraged the scientist to undertake an investigation to discover reliable criteria within an interdisciplinary reflection. Benedict XVI continued to present a very balanced position towards the definition of death, without however pronouncing himself regarding the definition of brain death. His successor has not taken any position concerning this topic.

A Critical Analysis of the Brain-Death Definition

The German-born philosopher Hans Jonas († 1993) declared his opposition to the concept of brain death only a few weeks after its publication, confirming that the boundary line between life and

---

[79] Doyen Nguyen, "Pope John Paul II and the neurological standard for the determination of death: A critical analysis of his address to the Transplantation Society," in *The Linacre Quarterly* 84 (2017): 155-86.

[80] John Paul II, Letter to the Pontifical Academy of Sciences, 1.2.2005, in www.vatican.va/content/john-paul-ii/en/speeches/2005/february/documents/hf_jp-ii_spe_20050201_p-acad-sciences.html [15.1.2022].

[81] Benedict XVI, Address to the Participants at an International Congress Organized by the Pontifical Academy for Life, 7.11.2008, in w2.vatican.va/content/benedict-xvi/en/speeches/2008/november/documents/hf_ben-xvi_spe_20081107_acdlife.html [15.1.2022]. The Vatican English translation mistakenly says "arbitration" instead of "arbitrariness"; the other languages use the correct term.

death wouldn't be clear.[82] The debates continue until this very day. There are many critical analyses of the brain-death definition; some authors are opposed.[83] Yet, the definition of death is crucial, because human organ donation post mortem is at stake. Doyen Nguyen presents a precise analysis of the definition, offering much detailed information.[84] In this context, only some of the most important objections are going to be mentioned.

The new definition of brain death is problematic since it defines the human being by the mind. Manfred Lütz stated: "This is absolutely against Christian anthropology and ends up directly with Peter Singer. In this case, severely mentally handicapped and advanced Alzheimer patients would no longer be human beings."[85] Even more problematic is the affirmation: "Even though the soul of the brain-dead person has departed, various organs of the body continue to function if oxygenation of the blood is maintained by mechanical ventilation."[86] Such a conception would imply a total misunderstanding of the soul as *forma corporis*; its presence would be reduced to the functioning of an organ, which would question the immortality of the soul.

James DuBois affirms that organ transplantation within the realm of cadaveric organ donation led to changing the definition of death since it needed a "special kind of determination of death. Specifically, it requires a determination of death that is made very soon after, or prior to, the loss of circulation to major organ systems (other than the brain, which may lose circulation long before the other organs). In other words, it requires that the death of the human being be determined before his or her transplantable organs die."[87] This topic was already mentioned above,[88] yet, it would bring to evidence a false anthropology, based on an extreme Cartesian dualism.

---

82 Cf. Hans Jonas, *Technik, Medizin und Ethik: Zur Praxis des Prinzips Verantwortung* (Frankfurt am Main: Suhrkamp Verlag, 1985).
83 Paul Byrne and George Rinkowski, "'Brain Death' is False," in *Linacre Quarterly* 66 (1999): 42-48. The topic is extensively covered in Roberto de Mattei (ed.), *Finis Vitae: Is Brain Death Still Life?* (Soveria Mannelli: Consiglio nazionale delle ricerche, 2006).
84 Cf. Nguyen, NDD, 31-357.
85 Lütz, "Statement against the 'A report on cerebral death,'" 120.
86 Furton, "Brain Death, the Soul," 467.
87 DuBois, "Organ Transplantation," 417.
88 Cf. chapter VIII, Brain Death—Death of the Whole Person?

When referring to the cessation of all brain activities, usually the interbrain (diencephalon) is not included, nor the hypothalamus (ὑπό [hypo] "under" and θάλαμος [thalamós] "room, chamber"), which is the supreme regulatory center for all vegetative and endocrinal processes, such as body temperature regulation, sexual behavior, fluid, and food acceptation, etc. Regina Breul argues that for that reason the circulatory regulation, temperature regulation, autonomic, and hormonal regulation still work in the so-called "brain dead." A brain-dead person has inner breathing, that is, the gas exchange between blood and tissues is still working. A really dead person cannot be ventilated anymore. The brain dead may have spontaneous heart activity and blood pressure. They are warm, have metabolic processes. They can develop diarrhea and constipation, they are able to produce antibodies, can overcome infections, show vegetative reactions such as redness and sweating, and have muscle contractions.[89] Nguyen has discovered evidence that the definition of brain death does indeed imply a selective discarding of functions when referring to the "whole brain death."[90] As distinct from coma, death is by definition irreversible. The dead donor rule corresponds to the very nature of death since organs can be removed only from donors who are dead. As Nguyen had shown, the notion of irreversibility itself is not an empirical concept, it can be inferred only in retrospect.[91] Confronting the definition of brain death with the position of Peter Singer makes Nguyen conclude that this would actually weaken our defense of the beginning of life. The exaltation of the brain led some to the concept of "brain life"; the idea "that, (i) since human life ends on the basis of definable neurological end-point criteria, then conversely there must exist some definable neurological starting-point criteria which identifies the beginning of life; and (ii) together, the concepts of 'brain life' and 'brain death' would provide 'a consistent biological definition of humanness.'"[92] This type of reasoning would put into doubt the Church's position regarding the ontological status of the embryo and it would shed new light on abortion as a possible

---

89 Cf. Breul and Waldstein, *Hirntod-Organspende*, 17.
90 Cf. Nguyen, NDD, 101-11.
91 Cf. ibid., 113.
92 Ibid., 198.

option.[93] Any attempt to define "brain life" would follow arbitrary criteria. Nguyen concludes, therefore: "Such arbitrariness also parallels the arbitrariness of the Harvard Committee in equating 'irreversible coma' with death."[94] However, there were a few cases of people who recovered after they were declared brain dead.[95] Some women declared brain dead were even able to give birth to their children. This is the case of Robyn Benson, who was pregnant in the 22nd week when she suffered a cerebral hemorrhage. The doctors said she was artificially kept alive, to give birth to her child.[96] After birth the doctors turned off the machines and she died. For more than two months the woman had lived in this way giving birth to her child.

Even though it is not necessary to get into more detail regarding a more specific medical analysis of brain death,[97] it can be concluded that the "new biological definition of death lacks coherence, a fact which is readily apprehended at the level of the empirical medical evidence and which, through rigorous and critical analysis, can also be ascertained at the biophilosophical and metaphysical levels."[98]

According to a significant number of scientists, *post mortem* donors are not truly dead and therefore, the dead donor rule is

---

[93] The instruction *Dignitas Personae* defined in the very first sentence: "The dignity of a person must be recognized in every human being from conception to natural death." CDF, DP, 1.

[94] Nguyen, NDD, 199.

[95] The case of baby Kaleb Crook, who recovered almost entirely, became quite popular in 2018. Cf. Vanessa Chalmers, "Baby boy who was declared brain dead miraculously survives after his life support was switched off by doctors," *Daily Mail*, 10.12.2018, in www.dailymail.co.uk/health/article-6478937/Baby-boy-declared-brain-dead-miraculously-survived-life-support-switched-off.html [15.1.2022].

[96] Cf. Ian Austen, "Brain-Dead, a Canadian Woman Remains a Silent Partner Awaiting Birth," *New York Times*, 6.2.2014, in www.nytimes.com/2014/02/07/world/americas/brain-dead-a-canadian-woman-lives-on-as-a-silent-partner-awaiting birth.html [15.1.2022]. In a more recent case, a "brain dead" woman gave birth to a girl after being kept on life support for three months. Cf. Phoebe Eckersley, "Brain-dead woman gives birth to a baby girl after she is kept on life support for three month following a brain hemorrhage," *Daily Mail*, 27.8.2019, in www.dailymail.co.uk/news/article-7399705/Brain-dead-woman-gives-birth-baby-three-months-life-support.html [15.1.2022].

[97] Cf. Nguyen, NDD, 359-425.

[98] Ibid., 427.

not the guiding principle anymore. This is reflected in the fact that it is routine to give pain medication to organ donors. "This has been considered as a way to ensure that the donor does not suffer during vital organ procurement."[99] Doctors taking organs from brain-dead donors have to make sure they are paralyzed,[100] something that does not happen to someone who's truly dead. In October 2021, some scientists announced a new achievement. Reuters presented it in an article as follows: "U. S. surgeons successfully test pig kidney transplant in human patient."[101] The dilemma is, they were talking about a brain-death-diagnosed person to whom a pig's kidney had been transplanted "without triggering immediate rejection by the recipient's immune system."[102] The success consisted in the fact that the results "looked pretty normal." According to the surgeons, everything worked well for three days. However, this fact contradicts everything that could be said in favor of the definition of brain-death, because it would be impossible to make a donated organ—even, as in this case, when coming from a pig—work in a dead person.

> The German Federal Agency for Political Education points out that the assumption that cardiac arrest and physical disintegration occur immediately and necessarily after cerebral death has been [...] refuted by some 175 documented cases (to 1998) in which between brain death and cardiac arrest at least one week and up to 14 years occurred. The cases of "chronic brain death" refute the hypothesis of the close causal and temporal relationship between brain death and

---

99 David Rodríguez-Arias at al., "Donation After Circulatory Death: Burying the Dead Donor Rule," in *The American Journal of Bioethics* 11 (2011): 36-43, here 41.

100 Nguyen refers to a document of the American Academy of Neurology, affirming that the "manifestations of reflexes and movements in brain-dead individuals have not been disclosed to the public at large. Such manifestations have been the principal source of 'emotional discomfort and cognitive dissonance' to health professionals (especially nurses) caring for brain-dead donors in preparation for organ harvesting, however." Nguyen, NDD, 479.

101 Nancy Lapid, "U. S. surgeons successfully test pig kidney transplant in human patient," *Reuters*, 20.10.2021, in www.reuters.com/business/healthcare-pharmaceuticals/us-surgeons-successfully-test-pig-kidney-transplant-human-patient-2021-10-19 [15.1.2022].

102 Ibid.

death of the entire organism. In addition, serious diagnostic errors in brain death diagnosis are mentioned.[103]

Josef Seifert concludes, consequently, that this new conception of death leads to a new conception of human life since human life is identified just with brain functions or with those aspects of biological life that depend on brain functions or with conscious life that depends on "those cerebral functions that are not just necessary for integrated biological life but also for consciousness."[104] At the same time, as shown above, not all brain functions cease to function, but primarily the upper brain. From a different perspective, authors conclude that the "patient is not dead at the moment of organ retrieval because brain death is not rigorously demonstrated and can only be assumed in [donation after circulatory death]."[105] However, the problem regarding the dead donor rule remains even after cardiac arrest, because it has to be assured that it is irreversible and whenever this is shown, it might be too late for the extraction of organs.[106]

This chapter will be concluded with a final consideration regarding brain death from a theological point of view. Based on sound anthropology the soul has to be considered the life principle of the body and consequently, death is the separation of the soul from the body. The nature of the rational soul does not permit a precise determination of the moment of death when it occurs naturally since death is a process and there is no observable evidence. For that reason and from a medical perspective it is not possible to affirm nor to prove the contrary that the soul of a brain-dead person is already departed, as, for example, Edward Furton claims.[107] Since the nature of the rational soul is spiritual, it would be a dangerous reduction to conclude that the soul resides in the brain, even

---

103 Cf. Sabine Müller, "Wie tot sind Hirntote? Alte Frage—neue Antworten," vom 9.5.2011, in www.bpb.de/apuz/33311/wie-tot-sind-hirntote-alte-frage-neue-antworten?p=all [15.1.2022].

104 Josef Seifert, "A philosophical refutation of the identification of 'brain death' with human death or its criterion," in *Studia Bioethica* 2 (2009): 19-25, here 19.

105 Rodríguez-Arias et al., "Donation After Circulatory Death," 39.

106 Cf. ibid., 38.

107 Furton claimed that "the soul of the brain-dead person has departed": Furton, "Brain Death, the Soul," 467.

though there is a certain link. Furton compares the brain-dead person to the use of embryonic stem cells and concludes that the embryo had been destroyed and no longer exists, even though the cells continue to live with a number of biological functions.[108]

Even though these aspects are related to a highly speculative theology the conclusions seem not to be correct. A "destroyed embryo" as well as a "destroyed man"—the adjective is not precise at all—are most probably not dead at all. However, the comparison limps. If such a comparison is undertaken, it would probably be more fitting to compare a "brain dead" person, who is artificially kept alive, to cryopreserved embryos. They are also kept alive artificially and the spiritual soul is—which contradicts the nature of human existence—bound by machines and under the dominance of technology to a certain status, which is something between death and life. The person is prevented from dying—even though being in the process of dying—due to the progress of medicine and technology. From this perspective one could consider applying the same moral judgment to the brain-dead as to cryopreserved embryos; they are the result of a therapeutic obstinacy.

Doyen Nguyen points out three main contradictions of the doctrine of the "whole-brain death": "1. the biological reality manifested by brain-dead patients, 2. the holistic understanding of life and organism according to contemporary biophilosophy, and 3. the Church's teaching on human nature."[109] Since the death of the person is a process, consisting of the total disintegration of an integrated and unitary whole that is the person himself, the neurological criteria are not sufficient for declaration of death; especially, when an intact cardio-respiratory system is functioning. The complete cessation of all brain activity cannot be adequately assessed since irreversibility is a prognosis, not a medically observable fact. It must be concluded that the diagnosis of brain death as well as controlled cardiac/circulatory death wouldn't have any meaning if it were not for the sake of organ transplantation. This would effectively end most of the human organ transplantation, but it would make possible the restoration of social respect for the sanctity of human life.[110]

---

108 Cf. ibid., 469.
109 Nguyen, NDD, 508.
110 Cf. ibid., 437-38.

IX
Organ Donation

THE DEFINITION OF BRAIN DEATH IS OF GREAT importance when it is used as a legal definition and constitutes the presupposition of legislation concerning organ donation. Organs are a rare and essential resource. According to the *U.S. Government Information on Organ Donation and Transplantation*, "17 people die each day waiting for an organ transplant" (2020) and "90% of U.S. adults support organ donation but only 60% are actually signed up as donors."[1] Organ donation has the potential that people benefit in remarkable ways. The Catholic Church recognizes this in the *Catechism of the Catholic Church*: "*Organ transplants* are in conformity with the moral law if the physical and psychological dangers and risks to the donor are proportionate to the good sought for the recipient. Organ donation after death is a noble and meritorious act and is to be encouraged as an expression of generous solidarity."[2] John Paul II considered organ donation even as an act of "solidarity and self-giving love."[3] The act of self-giving love becomes more evident if one reads the "stories of hope" described by the Network for Organ Sharing.[4]

Individual cases of people in urgent need of new organs move the hearts of the people, especially when made public. However, ethical evaluation of organ donation has to take into consideration not only the need of the individual person but also medical indications and—above all—the definition of death. For that reason, it will be helpful to take a closer look at the historical development of organ transplantation.

---

1 U. S. Government Information on Organ Donation and Transplantation, Organ Donation Statistics, in www.organdonor.gov/statistics-stories/statistics.html#glance [15.1.2022].
2 CCC, 2296.
3 John Paul II, Address to the Participants of the First International Congress of the Society for Organ Sharing, 20.6.1991, in www.vatican.va/content/john-paul-ii/en/speeches/1991/june/documents/hf_jp-ii_spe_19910620_trapianti.html [15.1.2022], 5.
4 "United Network for Organ Sharing, Stories of Hope," in unos.org/transplant/stories-of-hope/ [15.1.2022].

BIOETHICAL CHALLENGES AT THE END OF LIFE

SOME HISTORICAL NOTES

Due to the rapid progress of surgical techniques and medical science, the transplantation of organs is a relatively recent development. Within the last decades, more and more vital organs have been transplanted successfully.

According to some sources, the first transplantation of a lower limb was effected miraculously by Cosmas and Damian, both physicians and saints in the third century.[5] Yet, 16 centuries later and due to some important developments in the medical field, the idea of replacing organs was brought up. In the first step, experimentations were undertaken on animals, developing effective techniques also for human application. Certain medical developments were the pre-condition for organ transplantation; some of the most important are going to be mentioned briefly:

- 1901: Discovery of the blood groups (ABO-System). The Austrian physician, immunologist, and biologist Karl Landsteiner, Nobel Prize laureate in 1930, discovered in 1901 the different blood types, which have a vital role in the safe use of blood transfusions. Based on his findings it was possible for the first time to successfully perform blood transfusion in 1907.[6]
- 1902: First kidney transplantation in animals. The first kidney transplantation was accomplished by Emerich Ullmann, an Austrian surgeon and researcher, a former assistant to Louis Pasteur. The first transplanted kidney of a dog remained functional for 5 days.[7]
- 1944: Discovery of tissue compatibility and immune response. During the Second World War, the discovery was made that the rejection of transplanted organs involved an immune response. Peter Medawar, a British biologist, was named for his findings the "Father of transplantation."[8]
- 1954: First successful kidney transplant as a living donation. It was realized at the Peter Bent Brigham Hospital in Boston

---

5 Cf. Marco Castagneto, "Trapianti," in Sgreccia and Tarantino, *Enciclopedia di bioetica e scienza giuridica*, vol. XII (Naples: Edizioni Scientifiche Italiane, 2017), 275–91, here 277.
6 Cf. Christopher D. Hillyer, et al., *Blood Banking and Transfusion Medicine: Basic Principles & Practice*, 2nd ed. (Philadelphia: Churchill Livingstone, 2007), 15.
7 Cf. Clyde F. Barker and James F. Markmann, "Historical Overview of Transplantation," in *Cold Spring Harbor Perspectives in Medicine* (2013), 3:a014977, 3.
8 Cf. ibid.

by Joseph Murray.[9] Ronald donated one of his own kidneys to his brother Herrick, his identical twin, who was dying of kidney disease. Between 1954-1973 about 10,000 kidney transplants were performed.

- 1959: First successfully transplanted kidney from genetically different individuals. The person lived for another 26 years.[10]
- 1967: First successful heart and liver transplants took place in Cape Town, South Africa.[11] The patient died after 18 days of pneumonia; his immune system was overridden. A second patient (1968) had already lived with the transplanted heart for 19 months. This surgery was considered a major historical event, which was made public all over the world. Transplantation reached a new degree of popularity.
- 1983: First successful lung transplantation in Toronto, Canada.[12]

Technological and scientific advances offer new possibilities with far-reaching medical innovations. The invention of the heart-lung machine, immunosuppressant medicine, as well as other developments, paved the way for the transplantation of organs. The medical-technical preconditions made organ transplantation possible and the year 1968 marks a major turning point, since this year, as we have seen, the recognition of the irreversible coma as a new definition of death was accepted.

TERMINOLOGY

Before approaching an ethical evaluation of organ transplantation it will be helpful to make some useful distinctions regarding the terminology by which is most commonly known: organ donation.

First of all, a fundamental distinction must be made between a living organ donor and a cadaver organ donor. A famous case of a living donor is Frank-Walter Steinmeier, the former opposition leader and later president of Germany. In 2010, he donated to his 48 year-old wife Elke a kidney; otherwise, she would have died.

---

9   Calvin R. Stiller, "Organ and Tissue Transplants. I. Medical Overview," in Warren Thomas Reich (ed.), *Encyclopedia of Bioethics*, vol. 4 (New York: Macmillan Publisher, 1995), 1871-82, here 1871.
10 Ibid., 1872.
11 Ibid.
12 Ibid.

The waiting period in Germany for patients in need is quite long, on average six years. Steinmeier decided to undergo the operation and interrupted his political work for some weeks. The operation worked out well.[13] Yet, this type of donation is not free of risks. Usually, it is said that one of 3,000 living donors dies during the surgery. Living organ donation is growing worldwide; it refers to the donation of organs (or tissues) from a living donor, most commonly one kidney, a portion of a lung, and lobe of the liver.

The organ donation from deceased persons offers more options to donate and extract organs: "Eight vital organs that can be donated: heart, kidneys (2), pancreas, lungs (2), liver, and intestines. Hands and faces have also recently been added to the list. Tissue: cornea, skin, heart valves, bone, blood vessels, and connective tissue, bone marrow and stem cells, umbilical cord blood, peripheral blood stem cells (PBSC)."[14] According to the US Department of Health & Human Services, every 10 minutes a new person is added to the waiting list, but only 2 of 1,000 people die in a way that allows for organ donation. Yet 33,611 transplants were performed in 2016 while 17 people die each day waiting for a transplant.

Any organ donation post mortem is dependent on the definition of death and the so-called informed consent. However, death is usually declared on the basis of cardiopulmonary or neurological (brain death) criteria. It must be assured that the donor is dead (*ex mortuo*).[15]

Transplants and grafts are "an organ or tissue obtained from a donor," which is inserted into the host organism."[16] Elio Sgreccia makes a distinction between life-saving transplants "in which the patient is doomed to die if he does not receive a transplant" and non-life-saving transplants, which "are supposed to improve the patient's life quality."[17] Dead or preserved tissues are more properly called implants.[18]

---

13 Cf. Kate Connolly, "Germany's opposition leader breaks from politics to donate kidney to wife," *The Guardian*, 23.8.2010, in www.theguardian.com/world/2010/aug/23/steinmeier-sabbatical-kidney-donation [15.1.2022].
14 U. S. Department of Health & Human Services, General Donation Questions, in www.organdonor.gov/about/facts-terms/donation-faqs.html [15.1.2022].
15 Cf. chapter VIII.
16 Sgreccia, PB, 629.
17 Ibid., 659.
18 Ibid., 629.

When a tissue is transferred within the same organism, it is called an autologous transplant. This method is usually undertaken for the sake of reparation (after burns) or for aesthetic reasons (beauty). The term homologous transplant refers to a tissue transferred from one donor to another; it can include nerves, bone tissues, pancreas, etc. When the transplant involves tissues from other species it is called heterologous transplant or xenotransplant. Already in the 60s the first attempts were undertaken in this field. In the 1980s an infant girl got a transplanted heart of a chimpanzee; she survived for a short time.[19]

Regarding the process for the extraction of organs, it will be helpful to mention some other concepts. In the case of a cadaver organ donor and after declaring the patient dead, the organ retrieval begins. The cadaver is transferred to an operating room, where organs and tissues are extracted. Often they are sent directly to the transplant center; the organs are examined according to certain criteria and checked if they are intact and in good condition. "The heart or lungs are removed first; for heart-lung transplants, the heart and lungs are removed together. The liver and small bowel are usually removed next, followed by the pancreas and kidneys."[20] The whole process of extracting organs and tissues follows a precise order, starting with pre-death procedures to facilitate organ transplantation and viability. There are recipient and donor criteria for any organ to be transplanted. An organ evaluation follows, considering a "present or past medical history of cancer, drug abuse, or other biological risks [...], viral serologies for human immunodeficiency virus (HIV), hepatitis B virus (HBV), and hepatitis C virus (HCV) are all negative."[21]

This is followed by the so-called tissue retrieval. After removing the organs, tissues are extracted. "The eyes or corneas are usually the first tissues removed. Often the entire eye is removed, placed in a sterile container with a solution, and sent to the nearest eye bank."[22] This is followed by an organ and/or tissue preservation.

---

19 Ibid., 660.
20 Stiller, "Organ and Tissue Transplants," 1874.
21 Constantino Fondevila et al., "Liver Transplant Using Donors after Unexpected Cardiac Death: Novel Preservation Protocol and Acceptance Criteria," in *American Journal of Transplantation* 7 (2007): 1849-55, 1850.
22 Ibid., 1875.

Elio Sgreccia enumerates three general principles that help to define the problems regarding organ transplantation: "defending the lives of the donor and recipient, protecting personal identity, and obtaining informed consent."[23] It will be helpful to take a closer look at these principles.

Defending the Life of the Donor and of the Recipient

It must be said that a transplant does not solve all problems, especially if it would prolong the life of a seriously ill person, or if the effective benefit for the patient receiving the organ is minimal or not proportional.[24] For that reason, there must be a high probability of success and proportionality between a real improvement of the life and the donor's sacrifice. In the case of a living donor, any substantial harm must be excluded. The principle of totality, as well as the principle of double effect, needs to be applied.

Living organ donation is a kind of mutilation, which is ordinarily forbidden. The *Catechism* states that "it is not morally admissible to bring about the disabling mutilation or death of a human being, even in order to delay the death of other persons."[25] However, a living donation of organs is morally permissible if it does not sacrifice or seriously damage any essential bodily function and if there is a proportion between the harm done to the donor and the anticipated benefit.[26] Generally, it is said that living donation meets these criteria; however, a risk remains.

The possibility of transplanting organs has created a huge black market. Since the waiting lists are long and people die if they don't get a needed organ in time, organs are often procured in an illegal way. Even though these practices are illegal in most countries except Iran, more organs are sold every year.[27] There is also something that can be called transplantation tourism.

Kidneys are traded for around $200,000, depending on whether they are obtained legally or not. In some poor countries, and used

---

23 Sgreccia, PB, 639.
24 Cf. chapter VII, Conserving/Prolonging Life.
25 CCC, 2296.
26 Cf. DuBois, "Organ Transplantation, " 435-36.
27 Even U.S. citizens have received organs in China, at a cost ten times more economical and—because of the reasons described above—with more organs available. Cf. Meiling Wang, et al., *WTO, Globalization and China's Health Care System* (New York: Palgrave Macmillan, 2007), 218.

by criminal organizations, body parts are sold, sometimes even taken from "living donors." This happens especially in China and North Korea. Prisoners sentenced to death are often used to gain organs. The actual transplant operation itself becomes the execution.[28] According to a report published by Canadian human rights activists in June 2016:

> China's hospitals are removing organs from 60,000 to 100,000 prisoners every year. Many of these prisoners were Uyghurs, Tibetans, Christians and Falun Gong believers who were convicted as "political criminals" by the Communist Party. It is a gruesome story. Insiders have come out saying that organs were extracted from prisoners while they were still alive. This is the atrocity that is being withheld from the official statistics showing donors numbering three in every one million people.[29]

On other occasions, living donors simply sell their kidneys to make some extra money. The price is about $7,000 on the black market.[30] In India, for example, there is a flourishing black market and many poor people are exploited. All these are criminal acts and a widespread reality. Nor is the use of organs from anencephalic new-borns permissible since it is difficult to determine brain death in a neonate.[31]

Regarding the dead donor, it has to be assured that through donation the donor is not killed but dies for natural reasons. At the same time, the dignity of the cadaver and personal dignity have to be respected, which is not easy to uphold. Also for that reason cremation is becoming more and more popular. In this way, the exploited body disappears.

Protecting Personal Identity

The personal identity has to be respected in all types of organ donation. This becomes especially evident when a possible transplantation is connected to the patient's thinking capacity (brain)

---

28   Cf. Cattania and Brandi, *Cina Traffici di morte*, 41–48.
29   "China's Live Organ Harvests Are Happening Worldwide," 11.4.2017, in *The Liberty Web*, eng.the-liberty.com/2017/6673/ [15.1.2022].
30   Cf. Martin Patience, "China's black market for organ donations," *BBC*, 11.8.2015, in www.bbc.com/news/world-asia-china-33844080 [15.1.2022].
31   Sgreccia, PB, 661.

and procreative identity. Head transplantations have been carried out already on animals, such as dogs. They are still in an experimental stage for humans.[32] However, they would severely threaten and compromise personal identity. The Pontifical Council for Pastoral Assistance to Health Care Workers has issued some guidelines in a *New Charter for Health Care Workers*, which indicate: "Not all organs can be donated. From the ethical perspective, the brain and the gonads are ruled out as potential transplants, inasmuch as they are connected respectively with the personal and procreative identity of the person."[33] The personal identity has to be protected and guaranteed.

Informed Consent

Informed consent is a third criterion, which needs to be mentioned, pointing out its importance and limitations. Within the Catholic tradition, the ethical legitimacy of organ donation—whether referring to living or cadaveric donation—depends on informed consent. This is clearly indicated in the *Catechism of the Catholic Church*: "Organ transplants are not morally acceptable if the donor or those who legitimately speak for him have not given their informed consent."[34] Informed consent is widely acknowledged as a basic principle in respect for human dignity, not only within religious but also within secular discourse. DuBois points out: "Failing to inform patients or to solicit their consent to surgically invade their bodies is generally a failure to respect them as person."[35]

While the concept of informed consent as such is relatively accepted, some questions remain controversial. What constitutes a free and responsible decision? How is adequate information presented and how is a sufficient understanding guaranteed? What about minors or adults who are not capable of understanding and decision-making? These questions become even more challenging considering the risks involved, independent of the fact that the organs or tissues are obtained *ex vivo* or *ex cadavere*. Elio Sgreccia

---

32   This aspect is well described in ibid., 641.
33   The Pontifical Council for Pastoral Assistance to Health Care Workers, *New Charter for Health Care Workers*, trans. by The National Catholic Bioethics Center (Philadelphia: National Catholic Bioethics Center, 2017), 88.
34   CCC, 2296.
35   DuBois, "Organ Transplantation," 439.

points out that there "could be no act of donation, no expression of solidarity if there were no well-founded awareness of all the consequences of the gesture."[36] There is even a trend to perceive the cadaver as a "common good" and to drop the dead donor rule. However, different attempts were undertaken to lower or to change the standards for obtaining informed consent, as shown in Germany in 2020. The German Bundestag discussed practically three donation models: informed consent, presumed consent, and presumed consent with relatives' right to object. However, at the end, the politicians decided to stick with the informed consent.[37]

DuBois presents the two most common arguments to lower the informed consent: financial incentives and presumed consent.[38] Based on the demand for organs and long waiting lists there are several attempts to offer a new interpretation of informed consent. Even though, according to the National Organ Transplant Act, it is forbidden to sell organs, financial pressure increases. Medicine is expensive, especially at the end of life, and can become a burden for the whole family. Through certain payments, including travel and housing costs, lost wages, payment to the family, paying for funeral expenses, insurance, reimbursement for living donors, etc., organ donation is made more attractive. Living donors in poor countries or in poor conditions might have limited resources and consider the "donation" as a way to make some money. This is becoming more and more problematic since it might lead to exploiting people in need; at the same time organ donation could lose its altruistic dimension. Yet, it is most problematic that the informed consent would become compromised because submitted to other interests.

The so-called presumed consent is no less problematic since it is difficult to define. In order to increase donation rates some countries, such as Belgium, France, Greece, Spain, Italy, Poland, etc., adopted the criterion of presuming the consent through so-called opt-out laws, which have apparently led to an increase

---

36 Sgreccia, PB, 643.
37 Mark Hallam and Astrid Prange, "German parliament: Explicit consent still necessary from organ donors," 16.1.2020, in www.dw.com/en/german-parliament-explicit-consent-still-necessary-from-organ-donors/a-52022245 [15.1.2022].
38 DuBois, "Organ Transplantation," 441.

of donation rates.³⁹ Even though the presumed consent is gaining popularity, it is highly problematic, since it is not based on medical or objective criteria, but on "a commitment to communal dialogue."⁴⁰ In other words, it is based on arbitrary principles.

Yet, the charter for health care workers indicates some general guidelines, which will be helpful for providing basic criteria. The informed consent of the patient is obtained implicitly "when the medical acts are routine and involve no particular risks" or explicitly "in documentable form when the treatments involve risks."⁴¹ In other words, explicit or implicit authorization is needed, depending on the medical procedure and the "status" of the person. In any case, this will work only if a human relationship is respected, in which the patient is not treated as an object, nor as "an anonymous individual," but as a responsible person. A correctly informed consent implies a fully informed and free choice regarding risks, possible treatments, and consequences.

A consent can be presumed if the patient is incapable of understanding; however, the treatments must be appropriate to the risks and urgency. If the patient has not recovered this capacity and if there is no urgent need to intervene, "the health care worker must communicate the information about the patient's state of health to the legal representative and request consent for the medical treatments from the person who is legally authorized to provide it."⁴²

POSITION OF THE CATHOLIC CHURCH

It has been said that the topic of organ donation *ex cadavere* is intrinsically linked to the definition of death. Controversies regarding the definition of brain death and therefore regarding organ donation from the deceased continue. Manfred Balkenohl, an expert in the field of bioethics, has argued that the new definition of death leads to a fundamental decision: 1) Do relatives,

---

39 Cf. Alejandra Zúñiga-Fajuri, "Increasing organ donation by presumed consent and allocation priority," 3.12.2014, in www.who.int/bulletin/volumes/93/3/14-139535/en/ [15.1.2022].
40 DuBois, "Organ Transplantation," 444.
41 Pontifical Council for Pastoral Assistance to Health Care Workers, *New Charter*, 71.
42 Ibid., 72.

doctors, patients, caregivers, really want to support the burden of an irreversible coma? 2) Do they want to guarantee organ transplantation?[43] However, the question remains, what does the Catholic Church say in this regard? Nevertheless, even within the Catholic Church discussions continue, whether to recognize or not the brain death definition.[44]

Organ donation is also considered as an expression of charity. The *Catechism of the Catholic Church* says: "Autopsies can be morally permitted for legal inquests or scientific research. The free gift of organs after death is legitimate and can be meritorious."[45] The same document calls it an "expression of generous solidarity" and adds: "It is not morally acceptable if the donor or his proxy has not given explicit consent. Moreover, it is not morally admissible to bring about the disabling mutilation or death of a human being, even in order to delay the death of other persons."[46] Since an ethical evaluation regarding living donors was already provided, the following explanations will focus on organ donation from dead donors.

The Church repeatedly states that organs can be extracted only after death and affirms the inviolability and dignity of human life. But what about organ donation *ex cadavere*? On 7th November 2008, Pope Benedict XVI addressed the participants of an International Congress organized by the Pontifical Academy for Life. In his discourse, he did not mention the neurological criterion of brain death. After affirming the importance of informed consent he stated:

> It is helpful to remember, however, that the individual vital organs cannot be extracted except *ex cadavere*, which, moreover, possesses its own dignity that must be respected. In these years science has accomplished further progress in certifying the death of the patient. It is good, therefore, that the results attained receive the consent of the entire scientific community in order to further research for solutions that give certainty to all. In an area such

---

43 Cf. Manfred Balkenohl, "Der Hirntod—Zur Problematik einer neuen Todesdefinition," in idem and Roland Rösler (eds.), *Handbuch für Lebensschutz und Lebensrecht* (Paderborn: Bonifatius Verlag, 2010), 469–86, here 470.
44 Doyen Nguyen provides a precise overview: NDD, 483–93.
45 CCC, 2301.
46 CCC, 2296.

as this, in fact, there cannot be the slightest suspicion of arbitrariness and where certainty has not been attained the principle of precaution must prevail. This is why it is useful to promote research and interdisciplinary reflection to place before public opinion the most transparent truth on the anthropological, social, ethical and juridical implications of the practice of transplantation.[47]

Benedict XVI insists on true death. The question remains, when is a person truly dead and what is the "point of no return"? Doyen Nguyen affirms that the moment of death cannot be confirmed with a "knife-like sharp precision" according to the criteria offered by "controlled cardiac / circulatory death." To make sure that death has truly occurred a waiting period of "20-30 minutes following [normothermic] circulatory arrest" would be necessary.[48] This would for sure aggravate the organ shortage and would effectively end—as Nguyen describes—"90 percent of all human organ transplantation, and possibly 100 percent of unpaired vital organ transplantation."[49] She concludes: "it is a moral choice between the path of the secular utilitarian argument and the path of an authentic culture of life in conformity with Christian morals."[50]

Human life is a precious gift from God, which man must preserve until natural death. But natural life is not an absolute good that should be preserved at all costs.[51] Already Pope Pius XII had confirmed: "Human life continues for as long as its vital functions—distinguished from the simple life of organs—manifest themselves spontaneously or even with the help of artificial processes."[52] Commenting on these affirmations Doyen Nguyen asserts that the "soul manifests itself through multiple, complex,

---

47 Benedict XVI, Address to the Participants at an International Congress organized by the Pontifical Academy for Life, 7.11.2008, in w2.vatican.va/content/benedict-xvi/en/speeches/2008/november/documents/hf_ben-xvi_spe_20081107_acdlife.html [15.1.2022]. The Vatican English translation of this passage has two errors that have been corrected by reference to other language versions.
48 Nguyen, NDD, 485.
49 So quoted in ibid., 486.
50 Ibid.
51 Nguyen mentions several aspects related to this complex issue. The goal is often to prevent death, which becomes manifest in many of the so-called retransplants. Cf. ibid.
52 Pius XII, "The Prolongation of Life," 301.

mutually interacting vital processes (vegetative functions) which are distinct from sensori-motor functions (e.g. brainstem reflexes) and functions of the cognitive order (including consciousness)." She concludes affirming that the "Pope's statement should, therefore, prompt us to exercise prudence and to be more aware that, even at the end of life, *in dubio pro vita.*"[53]

LEGAL SITUATION

The transplant laws aim to increase the safety and availability of organs to their citizens. Organ donation follows death determined by the common criteria, such as brain death and circulatory death. Some proposed using patients in the PVS as organ donors as well as anencephalic infants; also people seeking euthanasia are considered as possible organ donors. Attempts are made to delegate the decision to the autonomy of the patient or to a presumed consent.[54] Governments often advertise and promote organ donation.

Many countries issue specific laws in order to provide a legal framework for organ donation. In 1984 the so-called "National Organ Transplant Act" was approved in the United States, which outlawed the sale of human organs. Organ donation is one of the most regulated areas in the US, offering a national registry for organ matching.[55] In the United States, similar to other countries, the patient's predicted mortality and severity of illness are taken into consideration regarding the waiting list.

In India, the *Transplantation of Human Organs Act* was approved in 1994. The government tried to regulate the situation and to prevent people from commercial dealings with human organs. The act included the brain-death definition and cardiac death criterion as a condition for organ donation, allowing the transplantation of human organs from living and deceased and providing some regulations for monitoring transplantation activities.[56]

---

53 Nguyen, NDD, 489. "When in doubt, favor life."
54 A good overview is presented by Marie T. Nolan and John M. Travaline, "Organ Donation and Transplantation," in Furton, *Catholic Health Care Ethics*, 26.1-26.19, here 26.4-26.8.
55 Cf. United States. National Organ Transplant Act: Public Law 98-507. US Statute Large. 1984 Oct 19;98:2339-48. PMID: 11660818.
56 Cf. Ministry of Law, Justice and Company Affairs, New Delhi, the 11th July 1994, The Transplantation of Human Organs Act, 1994 No. 42 OF 1994.

In Germany, there is a transplantation law, which regulates transplantation and prohibits any type of organ trade under punishment.[57]

From May 2020 presumed consent regarding organ donation was adopted in England. All adults, unless they have signed out with a recorded decision not to donate, will be considered an organ donor. "The British Medical Association has previously called for an opt-out system for England, saying it was backed by almost two-thirds of the public. It said that while 66% of people say they would donate their organs after death, only 39% had signed the organ donor register, the system in England."[58]

Most countries accept the "brain-death definition" as a legal definition and presupposition of organ extraction. In Europe, various countries approved a series of norms, definitions, and rules in order to guarantee a greater uniformity in the legislation. Elio Sgreccia points out that the governments "are invited to provide the opportunity for citizens to declare in advance their willingness to make a post-mortem organ donation on state-issued identification documents and licenses." He states that there is a general drift that "favors the possibility of making use in the member states of 'presumed consent' to obtain organs *post mortem*, unless the subject has explicitly 'opted out' during his lifetime."[59]

---

[57] Cf. Bundesministerium der Justiz und für den Verbraucherschutz, Gesetz über die Spende, Entnahme und Übertragung von Organen und Geweben, in www.gesetze-im-internet.de/tpg/__1a.html [15.1.2022].
[58] Peter Walker, "Organ donation presumed consent could be adopted in England," *The Guardian*, 30.6.2017, in www.theguardian.com/society/2017/jun/30/presumed-consent-organ-donation-could-be-adopted-england [15.1.2022].
[59] Sgreccia, PB, 635.

X

Cremation — Burial — Alkaline Hydrolysis

HISTORICAL DEVELOPMENT

Cremation is of ancient origin and was in use in many cultures. The early Persian Empire practiced cremation, although it was replaced by the ritual of burial in a later period.[1] Phoenicians practiced both burial and cremation and the Greeks practiced above all inhumation. In Rome, both practices were common; cremation was often associated with military honors and widespread from the 2nd century BC.[2] One of the most famous cases of cremation was that of Julius Caesar. Only a few days after he was murdered he was cremated on the Forum Romanum. His biographer Gaius Suetonius Tranquillus († 122 AD) describes this event in the following way:

> When the funeral was announced, a pyre was built in the Campus Martius near the tomb of Julia and on the rostra, a golden shrine modeled after the Temple of Venus Genetrix was placed; inside was an ivory couch covered in gold and purple and at the head was a trophy with the cloak in which he was killed. It was decreed for those bearing gifts, because a day was not considered sufficient time, to bring them to the Campus by whatever street in the city each person wished, regardless of rank or order. [...] Some wanted to cremate him in the cella of the Temple of Jupiter but others in the Curia of Pompey, when suddenly, two men armed with swords and carrying two javelins of burning wax set fire to it and immediately the crowd of bystanders piled dry twigs, even the seats from the tribune and whatever else was available as an offering. Next the musicians and actors tore off the robes taken from the items of his triumph and worn for the

---

1 Cf. Igor M. Diakonoff, *Early Antiquity*, trans. Alexander Kirjanov (Chicago: University of Chicago Press, 1991), 380–82.
2 Cf. Jocelyn M. C. Toynbee, *Death and Burial in the Roman World* (Baltimore: Johns Hopkins University Press, 1996), 33–42.

occasion, shred them and threw them on the fire and veterans of the legions their own armor which they had worn for the funeral; and many matrons threw the jewelry that they were wearing, even the amulets and robes of their children.[3]

Suetonius describes how, before cremation started, the body was put upon a funeral pyre and then burned. The remaining parts, such as bones and teeth, were collected and interned in a funeral urn. This golden urn—today in the museum of the Capitolini—was put at the top of the obelisk, which is nowadays in the center of Saint Peter's Square. The obelisk has a profound symbolic meaning pointing towards immortality. The ashes of Julius Caesar remained at the top of the obelisk which means that he had entered into the immortal memory of the Romans. The Romans were quite superstitious, and they believed that until the ashes/body was interred the spirit (or shade) had not crossed over from this world. Until the middle of the 2nd century AD, cremation was more common in Rome than burial. The ashes of the dead were stored in the so-called *columbarium*, and there were hundreds of them in ancient Rome. Due to the growing population of Rome cremation was more economic, and corresponded to the needs of the city.[4] Nevertheless, the process of cremation was usually related to a religious ceremony; it was not simply submitted to a technical process. Something similar is still done in Hinduism, in which cremation is accompanied by the family and by certain ceremonies.

The Influence of Christianity

The spreading of Christianity had great influence also on burial rites because the Christian vision of man had changed almost everything. According to this perspective, the body is not a burden or a prison, but, as the First Letter to the Corinthians affirms, a "temple of God," in which "the Spirit of God dwells" (cf. 1 Cor 3:16). The sixth chapter affirms this with even more rigor: "But whoever is joined to the Lord becomes one spirit with him. Avoid

---

3   English translation in Mario Erasmo, *Reading Death in Ancient Rome* (Columbus, OH: Ohio State University Press, 2008), 36.
4   Cf. Dorian Borbonus, *Columbarium Tombs and Collective Identity in Augustan Rome* (New York: Cambridge University Press, 2014), 17-37.

immorality. Every other sin a person commits is outside the body, but the immoral person sins against his own body. Do you not know that your body is a temple of the Holy Spirit within you, whom you have from God, and that you are not your own? For you have been purchased at a price. Therefore, glorify God in your body" (1 Cor 6:17-20). Furthermore, the story of Lazarus shows us the Lord resurrecting his body and restoring his earthly life: an anticipated image of the resurrection of the body at the end of time. This is the most crucial and important element for any Christian understanding of death. It is once again the first letter to the Corinthians that provides more insights:

> But if Christ is preached as raised from the dead, how can some among you say there is no resurrection of the dead? If there is no resurrection of the dead, then neither has Christ been raised. And if Christ has not been raised, then empty (too) is our preaching; empty, too, your faith. Then we are also false witnesses to God, because we testified against God that he raised Christ, whom he did not raise if in fact the dead are not raised. For if the dead are not raised, neither has Christ been raised, and if Christ has not been raised, your faith is vain; you are still in your sins. Then those who have fallen asleep in Christ have perished. If for this life only we have hoped in Christ, we are the most pitiable people of all. But now Christ has been raised from the dead, the first fruits of those who have fallen asleep. For since death came through a human being, the resurrection of the dead came also through a human being. For just as in Adam all die, so too in Christ shall all be brought to life. (1 Cor 15:12-23)

According to the Christian understanding, the body has a special significance, as it will rise again from death. In the case of Jesus Christ, it was the same body that suffered, was tortured and crucified, and rose from the dead as a glorious body (cf. Lk 24:30; Jn 20:20). The *Catechism* says: "In his risen body he [Christ] passes from the state of death to another life beyond time and space. At Jesus' Resurrection his body is filled with the power of the Holy Spirit: he shares the divine life in his glorious state, so that St. Paul can say that Christ is 'the man of heaven.'"[5] The body of

---

5   CCC, 646.

the Christian shares in the dignity of "the likeness and image of God"; the whole man is incorporated in Christ and is a temple of the Holy Spirit. The same body will be reunited with the soul at the final resurrection of the dead. The Christian understanding of the human person as a unity of soul and body changed also the way in which one treated the body, even after death, because this body will resurrect and is not just some biologic material. All this had a deep impact on the way in which one treated the human body after death. Christians follow the example of Jesus Christ also in regard to their own death and burial. For that very reason, Christians considered cremation a pagan rite and were—under normal circumstances, except for plagues—opposed to this practice, which was widespread in the whole world.

As Christianity spread, all the more were burial practices changed even in the general society. This was not only due to the biblical understanding but also to the important topic of relics. Already the Second Book of Kings describes how a dead man was restored to life after his corpse touched the bones of the prophet Elisha (2 Kings 13:20-21). In the Gospel of Mark, a woman is healed from hemorrhage after touching the hem of Christ's garment (Mk 5:25-34). The early Christians went to the tombs of the saints to pray and to venerate the relics.[6] They believed in the resurrection of the dead and therefore of the body. St. Thomas Aquinas described the Christian belief in a more systematic way. He held the opinion that the soul retains a relationship with the body, even after separating from the body.

At the resurrection the soul will be reunited with the same body, becoming again the form of the matter, giving identity to it.[7] The relics remain consequently in a certain way connected to the soul of the saint and have special importance. For that reason, it was common practice to venerate the relics and to ask the saints for their intercession, especially at the places of their burial, where they were considered to be present. The basilicas of St. Peter and St. Paul, for example, bring this to evidence. At these places, prayers were offered and the Eucharist was celebrated;

---

6 A good overview is provided by Thomas J. Craughwell, *Saints Preserved: An Encyclopedia of Relics* (New York: Image Books, 2011).

7 Cf. Thomas Aquinas, *Summa contra gentiles*, Tito Sante Centi (ed.), vol. 1 (Bologna: Edizioni Studio Domenicano, 2001), Book II, ch. 79, 10.

the miracles which occurred confirmed this practice until today.[8]

Due to Christianity, by AD 400 the situation regarding burial had changed. Cremation was completely replaced by burial; the only exceptions were rare instances of epidemics or war. In some cultures, cremation had been quite widespread, such as the Germanic culture, but this fact changed due to their Christianisation. Throughout the Middle Ages cremation was mostly forbidden, even by law. Only heretics were burnt, but in these cases, it was considered to be a punishment, such as with John Wycliff and Jan Hus. The latter was burnt at the stake for heresy in Constance during the Council which occurred there. Religious considerations were of great importance and society was influenced by Christianity. A religious indifference as such did not exist and theology had an important role to play. For that reason, inhumation was the common way of burial.

Modern Age

The Modern Age, even though this concept is not very precise, is influenced by the dominion of progress and technology. Religious parameters based on Christianity lost more and more of their importance. This shift is reflected also in burial rites.

The first organized attempt to reinstate cremation began in the 1870s. At the Second International Congress of Medical Science held in Florence, some experts demanded the introduction of this practice in the name of civilization and public health. During the Franco-Prussian war (1870-71) the Prussian army used portable crematoriums.[9] In 1876 the first cremation was performed in Italy by Giovanni Polli († 1880) and Celeste Clericetti († 1887). It was a paradox, since the corpse of Alberto Keller, a German Lutheran businessman and Freemason, was first preserved "by injection and wetting with alcohol, phenol, sodium acetate, and arsenious acid."[10] Only two years later was he cremated. In 1874 the *Cremation Society*

---

8 Cf. Arnold Angenendt, *Heilige und Reliquien: Die Geschichte ihres Kultes vom frühen Christentum bis zur Gegenwart* (München: C. H. Beck Verlag, 1997).
9 Cf. Douglas J. Davies and Lewis H. Mates, *Encyclopedia of Cremation* (Burlington: Ashgate Publishing, 2005), 460.
10 Alessandro Porro, et al., "Modernity in medicine and hygiene at the end of the 19th century: the example of cremation," in *Journal of Public Health Research* 1 (2012): 51-58, here 53.

of Great Britain[11] was founded with the goal of promoting cremation and its legalization through various campaigns, which led to the *Cremation Act 1902*. This act, which has been modified since, is still valid legalizing cremation. In particular, the Freemasons made considerable efforts to obtain a legislative basis for cremation, with the intention of contradicting the doctrine of bodily resurrection.[12] The claim was made that cremation was needed in the name of civilization and public health. The cost factor was added only later on since the costs of the first attempts at cremation were extremely high. These ideas spread very fast reaching the United States in 1876 and Germany in 1891.

At this point, it is not necessary to present a complete overview of the development. However, during the Second World War cremation became popular in a very negative sense. The national socialists used this technique in at least several extermination camps, to make the bodies of the murdered persons disappear. It was used within a process of industrialized killing; the crematoriums worked day and night. This ideology, which was considered to favor technology and progress, made use of cremation also for their state funerals, such as for the murdered German general, Erwin Rommel. It was the best way to hide the crime.[13] The same method is still in use by various regimes.

However, cremation became more and more popular, which is also related to the diminishing influence of Christianity. Great Britain, for example, had a percentage of 1.3% in 1933 being cremated; in 1960 it was 35.7% and in 2018 it was 69.40%.[14] In the United States, it was 54.6% in 2019 and by 2024 it is projected to reach 60.7%, increasing every year by one percent.[15]

---

11 Cf. "History of the Cremation Society of Great Britain," in www.cremation.org.uk/Our-History [15.1.2022].
12 Cf. Renée Mirkes, "The Mortuary Science of Alkaline Hydrolysis," in *NCBQ* 8 (2008): 683-95, here 691.
13 Cf. Charles F. Marshall, *Discovering the Rommel Murder: The Life and Death of the Desert Fox* (Mechanicsburg: Stackpole Books, 2002).
14 The Cremation Society, "Progress of Cremation in the British Islands 1885-2018," in www.cremation.org.uk/progress-of-cremation-united-kingdom [15.1.2022].
15 Cremation Association of North America, "Industry Statistical Information," in www.cremationassociation.org/page/IndustryStatistics [15.1.2022].

A PHILOSOPHICAL PERSPECTIVE

Before considering the biological, and technological facts it is helpful to have a brief philosophical and theological consideration regarding cremation. According to the German philosopher Robert Spaemann († 2018), there is an intrinsic relation between the treatment of the dying and the treatment of the bodies of the deceased. When the treatment of the dying person changes, the treatment of the dead bodies will change also. The central question is once again an anthropological question: what is the human person, what is the body? When the dead body is considered as organic waste or just some leftover organic material, it will be treated as such. Meanwhile, when the human body is considered as the temple of the Holy Spirit, even the body of a deceased person will be treated with respect and dignity. Spaemann makes the point when he refers to some clinical practices. "Clinics that remove corpses immediately to some storage room often do the same thing with the dying themselves."[16] Whenever the person is considered as an object, he will be treated as such.

Philosophical considerations are relevant since cremation was initially strongly promoted by Freemasons.[17] It was supposed to be a blow against the Church and the belief in the resurrection of the dead. According to this perspective man himself becomes the ultimate end, even after death when dealing with the deceased body. For that reason, Spaemann considers the crematories as an anti-Christian statement. Only after many years has cremation lost its ideological character, and only then was the Church able to lift the ban on cremation.

It is well known that in early Christian communities, martyrs were burnt to death, drowned, eaten by animals, etc., and no one doubted the resurrection or the belief in the resurrection. But there is a fundamental difference to the modern process of cremation. The German philosopher mentions that cremation is completely submitted to a technical process today. He compares it to the cremation ritual in India, which takes several hours, in

---

16   Spaemann, "Death-suicide-euthanasia," 129.
17   Cf. Thomas Laqueur, "The burning question—how cremation became our last great act of self-determination," *The Guardian*, 30.10.2015, in www.theguardian.com/books/2015/oct/30/burning-question-how-cremation-became-last-great-act-self-determination-thomas-laqueur [15.1.2022].

which the family and friends participate in the parting procedure. In Western society, it is totally different. Cremation corresponds to an active annihilation of the body itself. Usually, the family does not participate. A machine, run by a computer, does most of it. Spaemann writes about this quite strongly:

> The lifting of the ban on cremation can only be explained by assuming that those responsible for the shift had never seen at first hand the real process involved in this kind of disposal. The brutal violence of this process does not reflect human dignity which can still be seen on the faces of the dead. In an increasingly de-Christianized society, Christians will have to learn again that they are a distinct people, a people with unique ways and customs which differ from those around them.[18]

These aspects are of great importance and they must be remembered when considering the process of cremation. Nevertheless, Spaemann, who was a faithful son of the Church, tried to justify the new position of the Church. He holds the position that there might be a way of accepting cremation according to Christian criteria, but this would imply that it is done in a way that corresponds to human dignity and not to a technical process. The way of dealing with the deceased should not be based on the criteria of a pagan society, but it should be based on distinctively Christian *mores*. How this might be possible with cremation is not easy to explain.

A THEOLOGICAL PERSPECTIVE

Some of the Protestant denominations were the first to accept cremation, claiming that God can resurrect also the ashes, as He created human beings from dust. Besides the difficulties mentioned above, for the Catholic Church there was also the challenge of the Freemasons. They "had advocated cremation over burial as a way of rejecting Catholic dogma."[19] Through cremation, they claimed to contradict the Christian faith in the resurrection and this was another reason the Catholic Church was strongly opposed to cremation.

---

18 Spaemann, "Death-suicide-euthanasia," 131.
19 Mirkes, "The Mortuary Science," 684.

In several interventions, the Holy Office had intervened against cremation; the stance found its most explicit expression in the Canon Law promulgated in 1917. Canon 1203.1 affirmed that "The bodies of the faithful must be buried, and cremation is reprobated. If anyone has in any manner ordered his body to be cremated, it shall be unlawful to execute his wish."[20] Since cremation was considered a public denial of the resurrection of the body, it was strictly forbidden. Catholics who chose to be cremated were to be denied a Christian burial.[21] Even public masses and the last sacraments were to be denied to persons who chose cremation for themselves. However, in exceptional circumstances, as in times of war and epidemic, cremation was allowed. The main reason for condemning cremation were: a) cremation was initially related to Freemasonry and thus considered a public rejection of the faith in the resurrection; b) It is opposed to the piety and respect one must have for the dead.

Within the Catholic Church, cremation remained forbidden. Only during the Second Vatican Council, in 1963, did Pope Paul VI lift the ban on cremation. On May 8th, the Pope authorized the publication of the instruction *De cadaverum crematione*, affirming that cremation in itself does not negate the Church's doctrine of the resurrection of the body and the soul's immortality.[22] The instruction affirmed that as long as Catholics do not deny the resurrection of the body and the immortality of the soul, cremation might be a morally acceptable alternative to burial. Yet, burial was given greater value, and burial as the normative means was to be preserved.

However, some theological problems remain: What about the dignity of the human body if it is burnt and submitted to a technical process? What about Christian anthropology and the tradition of the Church regarding the human remains? Will economic costs and health concerns become the new guiding criteria? Is the destruction of the body and the loss of the memory that was related to a classical tomb, just a smooth development? And what about alkaline hydrolysis, is it only a further development of the same?

---

20 c. 1203 §1, CIC/1917.
21 Ibid., c. 1240 §5.
22 Cf. Suprema Sacra Congregatio S. Officii, Instructio *De cadaverum crematione*, in AAS 56 (1964): 822-23.

A TECHNICAL PERSPECTIVE

Before providing answers to these questions at the end of this chapter, a broader perspective is needed, including the technical perspective of the process of cremation. This is necessary at a time when some governments are attempting to increase their capacities for cremation, since—as in ancient Rome—many cities have a great number of inhabitants. According to an article published in 2014, Mexico City is, for example, pushing cremation because many big cemeteries are simply full.[23] Besides these needs and other reasons, such as economic considerations and health concerns, it will be necessary to take a closer look at the technical procedures. In the modern crematories, almost everything is submitted to a technical process, run by computer-guided systems. Incineration and—this is going to be considered in a second step—alkaline hydrolysis breaks down the body by a chemical reaction.[24] Kent Lasnoski describes this technical process as "sending a body up in smoke" or "dumping the body down the drain". He affirms that the "object, in both cases, is the destruction of the human body by a rapid chemical reaction."[25] These aspects will be described briefly.

Cremation

Following the death of a patient, legal requirements (including a death certificate) are to be completed before the body is released for cremation. Then the bodies are stored in a room and a medical examiner needs to give the authorization, since, unlike after a burial, the body cannot be exhumed once it's been cremated. For that reason, criminal governments or organizations use cremation, as in the case of many communist countries or the national socialists mentioned above. The time between death and cremation can vary; however, it is supposed to occur 48 hours after death. In a second step the body is prepared for cremation; sometimes this can imply

---

23 Cf. "With cemeteries almost full, Mexico City pushes cremation, threatening Day of Dead traditions," 11.12.201, in www.foxnews.com/world/2014/10/28/with-cemeteries-almost-full-mexico-city-pushes-cremation-threatening-day-dead.html [15.1.2022].

24 In 2008, Sister Renée Mirkes, OSF, wrote the first Catholic moral analysis of the process for an academic journal. She argued that alkaline hydrolysis is morally neutral. Cf. Renée Mirkes, "The Mortuary Science."

25 Kent J. Lasnoski, "Are Cremation and Alkaline Hydrolysis Morally Distinct?," in *NCBQ* 16 (2016): 233-42, here 236.

the removal of implants and prostheses, as well as radioactive cancer seeds, which were used to treat cancer. The removal practice might vary from country to country; in some countries, it is forbidden to remove external items, such as glasses, jewelry, etc., in others not. When everything is ready, the body is put into a container made out of flammable materials. The incinerator is usually preheated to about 600 degrees Celsius (about 1,100 degrees Fahrenheit). The doors are opened and the container is moved in. In some cases family members are allowed to assist, sometimes they start even the process of cremation by pressing the start button. The door is closed and the body is subjected to the flame.

The body, composed of 75 percent water, dries out and the skin splits. The muscles begin to extend, the bones become calcified when exposed to the heat. An average human body will produce 4 to 6 pounds of ashes. "The process can take anywhere from 30 minutes, as in the case of a stillborn, to over two hours depending on the body size and stored heat in the chamber."[26] To avoid confusion, in the cremation chamber there is place only for one body. The national socialists used chambers to burn two bodies at the same time; they did not identify the ashes, as the dead body was treated according to their ideology as an inferior material object. However, the temperature is heated to 1,400- and 1,600-degrees Fahrenheit. The industrial crematoria, especially the latest generation, are computerized; emissions and smoke are reduced through new burning systems. Often the human skeleton remains and the bones are swept with a long-handed hoe to reduce them to ashes. Through a magnet, any metal is removed and often recycled. The remains of the bones are pulverized and poured into a container, according to the choice of the family.

In the US the "United States Postal Service offers Priority Mail Express and Priority Mail Express International service for shipping human or animal cremated remains domestically and internationally."[27] In the United States, the regulation of cremation falls usually under state or local government.

---

26   Cremation Association of North America, "An Overview of Cremation," in www.cremationassociation.org/page/CremationProcess [15.1.2022].
27   United States Postal Service, "How to Package and Ship Cremated Remains," Publication 139, September 2019, in about.usps.com/publications/pub139.pdf [15.1.2022].

There were several scandals accompanying cremation, such as, for example, in Georgia in 2002. The crematorium's incinerator was broken and the crematorium left dozens of corpses in the woods and stored in outbuildings.[28] As a consequence, all crematoriums are required to be inspected and licensed. There are still other types of abuses, such as people involved in crematory centers who sold body parts for medical research or sent back the wrong ashes.[29]

Nevertheless, for the relatives, the question remains: what to do with the ashes? Ideas are not lacking. Some keep the ashes at home; others, similar to the practice in the Roman Empire, leave them in a modern type of columbarium. There are also some extravagant ideas. Gene Roddenberry, the creator of *Star Trek*, had his ashes shot into space remaining in earth orbit. The scattering of ashes on land or at sea is becoming more and more popular. Some even offer a GPS position to localize the place of scattering afterward and the ceremony is accompanied by using flower petal mixes or other elements. Ocean funerals are advertised as emotional experiences to honor the deceased.[30] Imagination does not know any limits regarding the scattering of ashes. A cremation institute offers, for example, "52 beautiful ideas of what to do with ashes."[31] This ranges from portraits made from ashes to cremation art, tattoos using ashes, skydiving scattering, aerial scattering, fireworks, ashes used by 3D printers, and ashes used in bullets. One of the most recent developments consists of turning ashes into diamonds. An advertisement is made: "If you desire an everlasting connection to someone close to you, Cremation Diamonds are right for you. Each cremation diamond is a celebration of life, tells a unique story and represents a new beginning. With the closeness offered only by a diamond, you

---

28 Matthew Engel, "More than 100 bodies found as US crematorium gives up grisly secret," *The Guardian*, 18.2.2002, in www.theguardian.com/world/2002/feb/18/matthewengel [15.1.2022].
29 Cf. Michelle Kim, "How Cremation Works, Cremation Regulation and Scandal," 31.3.2009, in science.howstuffworks.com/cremation3.htm [15.1.2022].
30 Cf. Newhaven Funerals, "Ocean Funerals," in newhavenfunerals.com.au/other-services/ocean-funerals/ [15.1.2022].
31 Cremation Institute, "Expert Advice on Cremation, 52 Beautiful Ideas of What to Do with Ashes," in cremationinstitute.com/what-to-do-with-ashes/ [15.1.2022].

will have your loved one with you and in your life at all times."³²
The process is described as follows:

> Place several ounces of the ashes in a crucible that can withstand massive heat. Step 2: Bring the temperature to just over 5,000 degrees Fahrenheit, and allow all of the elements except the carbon to oxidize. Step 3: Continue to heat until the carbon has turned to graphite. The entire heating process will take a few weeks. Step 4: Place the graphite in a core with a metal catalyst and a diamond seed crystal. Step 5: Place the core in a diamond press. Step 6: Bring the temperature to about 2,500 degrees Fahrenheit and the pressure to about 800,000 pounds per square inch. Allow several weeks for the graphite to turn into a rough crystal. Step 7: Remove the crystal and use faceting tools to cut it to your specifications.³³

These practices have nothing to do with Christianity anymore. The human body is submitted to a technical process and arbitrary-individual criteria. Less and less room is left for ethical, moral or religious reflections.

Alkaline Hydrolysis

Alkaline hydrolysis is another method becoming more and more popular. The procedure is considered to be more environmentally friendly as it corresponds to a "natural process." The method was used for the first time in 1888 when a patent was issued to Amos Herbert Hobson, who developed a way to reduce animal carcasses. The interest in that method was revived only in the 1990s.³⁴ How does this procedure, which is also called resomation, biocremation, or water resolution, work?

The Mayo Clinic began using this process in the early twenty-first century, disposing of donated cadavers. The clinic describes the process as follows:

---

32 Cremation Solutions, "Tomorrows [sic] Traditions, Cremation Diamond Information," in www.cremationsolutions.com/cremation-jewelry-for-ashes/cremation-diamonds/cremation-diamond-information [15.1.2022].
33 Cremation Solutions, "Tomorrows [sic] Traditions, How Cremation Diamonds Are Made," in www.cremationsolutions.com/cremation-jewelry-for-ashes/cremation-diamonds/how-cremation-diamonds-are-made [15.1.2022].
34 Cf. Lasnoski, "Cremation and Alkaline Hydrolysis," 234.

Alkaline hydrolysis is similar to many physiological processes that occur naturally in the body. The process converts tissue and cells of the human body into a watery solution of micromolecules, leaving the bone structure of mineral compounds, such as calcium and phosphates. Since Resomation is not a combustion process, it is environmentally friendly and does not produce toxic gases or air pollutants. The remains are reduced to a powder consistency, placed in a temporary container, and may be returned to the family or interred in the Mayo vault at the Oakwood Cemetery.[35]

The clinic emphasizes that the new method would be cheaper (than cremation), more natural and greener. It is a method which only recently has become more popular. "Since then, the process has been appearing more and more often in the United States, Britain, and Australia."[36]

Regarding both methods—either cremation or alkaline hydrolysis—similar ethical evaluations can be made. Kent Lasnoski recommends the following four principles for medical practitioners and ethics committees when considering bodily disposition: "(1) the dignity of the human person and the human body, (2) the doctrine of bodily resurrection, (3) subsidiarity and personal autonomy (the expressed or probable wishes of the deceased), and (4) the common good, including economic, environmental, and health concerns."[37] Lasnoski further distinguishes between objective and subjective criteria; his considerations will serve to provide an ethical evaluation.

AN ANALYSIS OF BURIAL, CREMATION, AND ALKALINE HYDROLYSIS

Based on objective criteria it must be stated that cremation and alkaline hydrolysis have as their object "the destruction of the human body by rapid chemical reaction." Lasnoski adds:

---

35   Mayo Clinic, "Resomation," in www.mayoclinic.org/body-donation/biocremation-resomation [15.1.2022].
36   Lasnoski, "Cremation and Alkaline Hydrolysis," 234.
37   Lasnoski, "Burial, Cremation, and Alkaline Hydrolysis," in Furton (ed.), *Catholic Health Care Ethics*, 25.1–25.15, here 25.4.

In AH, the reaction is hydrolysis (reduction): breaking chemical bonds among organic compounds and molecules by introducing a water molecule in the presence of heat and a basic catalyst. Incineration, of course, is also a chemical reaction: the combustion (rapid oxidation) of organic compounds—that is, the breaking of chemical bonds holding organic compounds and molecules together—through the introduction of heat and oxygen. [...] What remains is bone and ash, similar to the bone remains from AH.[38]

However, there is a difference between the methods. Alkaline hydrolysis offers the possibility of keeping the aqueous and solid remains one hundred percent, while this is not possible for cremation. The first criterion to be considered regarding the bodily disposition is the dignity of the human person and the human body. In burial "the object is to place the body safely away from contamination while allowing ecological decay to occur at its natural rate."[39] In other words, it respects the dignity of the body and corresponds to the second criterion: the doctrine of the bodily resurrection. The third criterion is more difficult to judge. Personal autonomy is a subjective element; however, it must be orientated towards the truth of God. The common good, including economic reasons, is also difficult to judge, especially when death occurs in a poor family. Nevertheless, in burial all four criteria are fulfilled; for that reason, the Church has always considered burial the most appropriate way of bodily disposition.

Regarding cremation and alkaline hydrolysis, this is somehow different. The procedures break down the human body by a chemical reaction. "The object of the act in both cases is the destruction of the human body by a chemical reaction."[40] Even though God, who created the universe from nothing, can resurrect the body from any form, it remains a matter of fact that these methods destroy the human body through a chemical process. Generally speaking, no form of bodily disposition would necessarily contradict the dogma of bodily resurrection. The Christian martyrs,

---

38 Ibid., 25.5.
39 Ibid., 25.6. The further distinction between burial with and without embalming, as presented by Lasnoski, is not necessary for this study.
40 Ibid., 25.5.

as already mentioned, were sometimes burnt or slaughtered, as in the case of Saint Edith Stein, who died in the concentration camp in Auschwitz. In the case of a concentration camp, a tremendous injustice was committed due to a criminal ideology and government. The practices of cremation or alkaline hydrolysis are problematic especially according to this perspective. Lasnoski writes:

> The objective distinction between the act of placing a body at rest and allowing it to decompose naturally, versus the act of destroying it, is morally significant. God occasionally gives the gift of incorruptibility to the human body. Regardless of method, destroying the body largely removes the possibility of this gift, or at least conveys the belief that such a gift is implausible.[41]

The destruction of the body could be considered an implicit denial of the resurrection of the body. According to this perspective, the use of these methods obscures the doctrine. They give a bad example to society and to the mourning community. The body is reduced to biological material, rather than to relics expecting the resurrection of the death. The burial of the whole body would still express this.

Personal autonomy, as seen before, is a subjective criterion. The Church, and also the faithful, are morally bound to act on only those wishes of the deceased that benefit the faith of the deceased. If someone wishes to be buried scattering his ashes in the sea and orders it to be done in his will, a Catholic would not be morally bound to this provision. Analogously the same can be said regarding cremation and alkaline hydrolysis. However, this distinction is important and problematic. At the same time, there are also legal obligations. For the Church, the intention of the action is of great importance. If the person should express through the chosen method a denial of the doctrine of the resurrection, the Church would need to deny the burial. This is a very delicate topic which will be considered later on. One must be very attentive. In these cases, the Church must demonstrate that the deceased denied through his wishes the faith of the Church.

Considering the common good, such as the environmental effects, it must be said that alkaline hydrolysis uses less fuel than

---

41 Ibid., 25.8.

cremation; the process is based on water and pressure and low heat and requires only one-eighth of the energy of cremation. Even though burial might raise more environmental concerns than the other two practices, cremation and alkaline hydrolysis are cheaper than a classical burial, which implies also care of the grave for years to come. Today economic reasoning often dominates the debates, which reflect a cultural trend, since the present culture is submitted to the criteria of technology and banning any reflection that goes beyond death. There is almost a total loss of "memory" (*memoria*), the deceased are almost immediately forgotten after death. On the other side, when for example ashes are turned into diamonds, people want to be reminded of the dead person, even though in a pagan style.

Thus, in both cases, the body is submitted to a technological, industrial, and sterile process. It is reduced to an immanent perspective. Even though these methods might be required in times of epidemics and war, they are under normal circumstances somehow an expression of the culture of death, destroying the body after death. Not only alkaline hydrolysis but also cremation and the way they are realized are symptomatic of the present culture which is not capable of confronting the reality of death and bodily corruption.[42]

There is a fundamental difference between a natural decomposition and the act of destroying the body. However, special attention must be given to the intention of the action, which is an important part of any moral evaluation and to which special attention will be paid when considering the position of the Church. With Lasnoski it can be concluded that "burial accords best with the four moral principles when it comes to the object of the act. It ranks highest at the level of respect for human dignity (which is the most important criterion), and it can be done in a way that ranks second in terms of the common good."[43]

THE CHURCH'S POSITION

The Church's position on burial was already explained above, and it must be affirmed that the Catholic Church has consistently privileged burial as the most fitting disposition. It respects the

---

42 Cf. Lasnoski, "Cremation and Alkaline Hydrolysis," 241. The author focuses above all on alkaline hydrolysis regarding his ethical evaluation.
43 Lasnoski, "Burial, Cremation, and Alkaline Hydrolysis," 25.8.

dignity of the human body, it reflects best the doctrine of bodily resurrection, a correctly-guided personal autonomy as an expression of faith, and corresponds to the criteria of the common good, including the mourning community and the important element of memory. However, since cremation and alkaline hydrolysis are becoming increasingly popular, it will be helpful to unfold the Church's position.

The Canon Law from 1917 had strictly forbidden cremation for the reasons presented above; Catholics who opted for cremation were to be denied a Christian burial. This was changed by the instruction *De cadaverum crematione*. The reasons which led the Catholic Church to change her position regarding cremation are various. In the 60s cremation wasn't considered an expression of an ideology that rejected the Catholic doctrine of the resurrection. There were also non-theological concerns that had a great impact: for many, there is an increasing economic problem since cremation is not as expensive as a classical earthen burial, and the availability of funeral ground in major cities is often limited. In some parts with a very dense population, the prices were simply too expensive and some Catholics could not afford a burial place.

This development is reflected in the current Canon Law from 1983. However, it affirms in Canon 1184 §1: "Unless they gave some signs of repentance before death, the following must be deprived of ecclesiastical funerals: [...] 2/ those who chose the cremation of their bodies for reasons contrary to Christian faith."[44] In other words, if cremation or alkaline hydrolysis is used because of ideological reasons, and if this is explicitly affirmed, the funeral must be denied. This norm reflects a shift of perspective: the old Canon Law from 1917 presupposed that cremation is intrinsically related to ideological reasons. The new Canon Law changed this perspective and asserts that only if evidence is provided should a funeral be denied.

Also, Canon 1176 §3 speaks about cremation: "The Church earnestly recommends that the pious custom of burying the bodies of the deceased be observed; nevertheless, the Church does not prohibit cremation unless it was chosen for reasons contrary to Christian doctrine."[45] Today, cases in which people choose

---

44   c. 1184 §1, CIC.
45   c. 1176 §3, CIC.

cremation for reasons contrary to the faith are rare and they are even more difficult to prove.

In 2016, the CDF issued an Instruction called *"Ad resurgendum cum Christo*, regarding the burial of the deceased and the conservation of the ashes in the case of cremation."[46] The instruction clarifies several concepts related to burial and cremation, but it does not include the most recent method: alkaline hydrolysis. The document calls to mind the Instruction from July 5, 1963, which was the first to permit cremation in certain circumstances. The instruction from 2016 calls to mind that cremation is not per se opposed to the Christian religion. Thus, the instruction notes the increase of its practice and mentions a consulting process through which the CDF was able to issue the following norms related to cremation and the use of the ashes.

The first affirmation is not new at all; nevertheless, it is important to consider that the Magisterium of the Church insists again and again on this aspect: "Following the most ancient Christian tradition, the Church insistently recommends that the bodies of the deceased be buried in cemeteries or other sacred places."[47] The document offers different arguments and mentions above all the theological meaning of death. Burial corresponds best to the dignity of the body, to piety—cemeteries as places of prayer for the faithful departed—and as an act of mercy. Also, the relationship between the deceased and the Church is upheld. For that reason, the instruction states that the practice of burying the bodies of the deceased is to be preferred, "because this shows a greater esteem towards the deceased."[48]

Whenever cremation is chosen, the ashes "must be laid to rest in a sacred place, that is, in a cemetery or, in certain cases, in a church or an area, which has been set aside for this purpose, and so dedicated by the competent ecclesial authority."[49] The reservation of the ashes in a sacred place ensures that they are not excluded

---

46 Cf. CDF, *Ad resurgendum cum Christo*, regarding the burial of the deceased and the conservation of the ashes in the case of cremation, 15.8.2016, in www.vatican.va/roman_curia/congregations/cfaith/documents/rc_con_cfaith_doc_20160815_ad-resurgendum-cum-christo_en.html [15.1.2022].
47 Ibid., 3.
48 Ibid., 4.
49 Ibid., 5.

from prayer and avoids superstitious practices. Especially this question touches the common good because the faithful might be scandalized or led astray. When alkaline hydrolysis is chosen the problem remains of how to deal with the aqueous remains? Will they be poured sewage? This would clearly contradict the dignity of the human body and the doctrine of bodily resurrection.

Regarding the ashes, many of the different practices are related to pantheism, naturalism, or nihilism. It seems that there is a revival of ideas related to Freemasonry. For that reason, the CDF admonishes that it is not allowed to divide ashes among various family members due to respect. Therefore, it is also not permitted to scatter the ashes in the air,

> on land, at sea or in some other way, nor may they be preserved in mementos, pieces of jewelry or other objects. These courses of action cannot be legitimized by an appeal to the sanitary, social, or economic motives that may have occasioned the choice of cremation. When the deceased notoriously has requested cremation and the scattering of their ashes for reasons contrary to the Christian faith, a Christian funeral must be denied to that person according to the norms of the law.[50]

The supernatural good, the primary goal of life, is not sufficiently reflected either in the practice of cremation or in that of alkaline hydrolysis. Christ did not destroy the body, which would correspond to the erroneous conception of dualism, but came to save and redeem also the body. There is a saying that in the way in which someone lives, he dies. As one dies, so shall one be buried. For a Christian, this must above all respect the dignity of the human body and reflect faith in the resurrection, to both of which burial gives witness.

---

50   Ibid., 7f.

Conclusion

WHILE I WAS WRITING THIS BOOK, THE CORONAvirus pandemic broke out, granting a special emphasis to the topic "end of life." The dramatic images of many people dying due to an infection, broadcast by the mass media, have given new importance to death and the challenges associated with it. Many new questions arose, as how to deal with people who are dying and in need of a respirator? What is proportional and what is disproportional with regard to the treatment? How can the distinction between conserving and prolonging life be applied in these situations?

In other words, bioethical challenges at the end of life are of great relevance especially today. This book aims to provide an overview and basic orientation, presenting not only the challenges but trying to offer ethical orientation. In this way and based upon non-negotiable principles, the inviolable dignity of the human person can and must be defended. It is the basic right of all human beings, and governments have the obligation to guarantee its compliance as well as any (bio-)ethical committee; it is the foundation of a rightly-ordered society.

From this perspective, the structure of this book becomes evident. The first three chapters of this book provide the necessary ethical principles and anthropological foundations. The first chapter serves as an introduction and shows that everyone needs to have some basic formation regarding bioethical issues. It is not necessary to be an expert or even a physician; however, some basics, as they are presented in this book, should be known. This leads to a positive approach towards bioethics as an interdisciplinary subject. Since a one-dimensional understanding of man wouldn't do justice to the human person, the introduction presents an integral approach of different subjects, taking into consideration the growing gap between technical progress and ethical-moral responsibility. In this regard, some of the most important magisterial interventions and documents of the Church providing guidelines and orientation are particularly helpful.

The second chapter deals with the spread of what Pope John Paul II called a "culture of death." Tools are offered, permitting an analysis of a culture and considering its foundational elements. This is the precondition to study the actual culture that is characterized by a new prototype, according to which man becomes the new archetype—a vision often opposed to the biblical understanding of man as created in the image and likeness of God. The so-called culture of death, characterized by its acceptance and tolerance of sin, is present in today's society. This shows clearly that bioethics is not just about certain techniques and technological progress, but includes necessarily a spiritual dimension.

The third chapter offers some basic anthropological considerations. Sooner or later all bioethical problems are seen to be related to our conceptions of what the human person is. Even though this is the most salient aspect, it is frequently neglected. For that reason, some of the most basic concepts related to the understanding of the human person are called to mind, since the inviolable dignity of man can be recognized only if its meaning is known. The duality, not dualism, of the human being as a substantial unity between the spiritual form and the physical body is constitutional for any anthropological and ethical evaluation.

The following chapters constitute a second part, which is more practical. Based on the former considerations, specific topics related to the end of human life are analyzed, followed by an ethical evaluation. Especially in the case of euthanasia, history can be considered as another source of orientation; assuming that only those who know history will learn from it. For that reason, chapter four presents a brief overview of the historical development of the idea of euthanasia, and how its meaning changed from antiquity to post-modernity, with far-reaching consequences due to philosophical and theological reflections. This is mirrored in the legislation of several countries and its recent development.

Chapter five presents a classification of the different types of euthanasia as well as precise definitions. There is a difference in the ways in which human life is ended. Euthanasia may be done voluntarily, non-voluntarily, and involuntarily, as well as directly and indirectly. The chapter provides guidelines and distinctions necessary for ethical evaluation. The difference between prolonging life and letting one die needs to be respected. For that reason, special emphasis is given to indirect euthanasia and the principle of double effect.

Suicide and assisted suicide are of increasing relevance today. The explanations of chapter six provide an overview of what for some people, in their hopelessness, seems to be the last resort. The explanations include an ethical evaluation based on the criteria developed within the tradition of the Catholic Church. Assisted suicide, especially when it includes business-like models, is a new challenge for society. People claim to be autonomous especially regarding the ending of their lives. The misunderstanding of human freedom leads frequently to intrinsically evil actions.

Chapter seven explains in detail the difference between ordinary and extraordinary means in health care. Followed by some preliminary reflections, the important distinction between conserving and prolonging life is made. Much confusion is due to the fact that this distinction is not respected. However, ordinary means are directed to conserve once's life and they must offer some hope of a beneficial result. The supply of nutrition and hydration is related to this distinction, as well as an ethical evaluation of so-called permanent "vegetative" state, the meaning of suffering and palliative care, as well as the living will. All these topics have to be integrated into a broader perspective.

Chapter eight deals with death and so-called brain death; a delicate topic because organ transplantation depends partially on this definition. Since the human person cannot be reduced to a merely material dimension, it is necessary to consider death from a four-dimensional point of view, including psychological, philosophical, theological, and scientific aspects. For organ transplantation, the determination of the exact moment of death is of great relevance, especially when it comes to extracting organs. However, does brain death correspond to the death of the whole person? When is a person dead and are the facts provided by science reliable? The chapter includes a critical analysis of the brain-death definition comparing the "brain dead" person, who is artificially kept alive, to a cryo-conserved embryo.

All this has great repercussions for organ donation. The following chapter starts with a reference to history and the development of organ donation. A close look at this topic reveals that there are coincidences between the technical possibility of organ transplantation and the new definition of death as brain death. A precise terminology and some basic criteria allow the topic of organ donation to be approached with more ease. The chapter offers also an ethical evaluation of organ donation, including some reflections on the position of the Catholic Church and the legal situation in different countries.

Finally, the last chapter explains and evaluates cremation, burial, and alkaline hydrolysis. The way in which the body of the departed is treated allows drawing conclusions about how people are treated in general. Whenever the substantial unity of soul and body is not recognized, it will be difficult to guarantee that the (dead) body is treated with respect, and according to its intrinsic dignity. Cremation, as well as the recently developed method of alkaline hydrolysis, corresponds only partially to a healthy anthropology since it implies the destruction of the body through a chemical process. The problems related to cremation and the latter method are brought into evidence, as well as the advantages of classical burial.

This book tries to offer an objective approach towards bioethical challenges at the end of life, which needs to be applied according to concrete circumstances. These criteria are the fruit of the perennial and rich heritage of the Catholic Church. However, they presuppose a fundamental option, which C. S. Lewis once described as follows: "There are only two kinds of people in the end: those who say to God, 'Thy will be done,' and those to whom God says, in the end, '*Thy* will be done.'"[1] In an age of relativism, in which everything is considered equal, there is a fundamental difference between someone who believes in God and someone who does not. In the first case, death receives a new meaning; it is not the end of everything, but the beginning of the new and everlasting life. C. S. Lewis found a beautiful way to describe the consequences of this fundamental option (cf. Mk 16:16). To believe in God provides a new meaning not only of death but also of life in all its dimensions,[2] doing justice to the substantial unity of the spiritual form (soul) and the body.

---

[1] C. S. Lewis, *The Great Divorce* (New York: Macmillan Publishers, 1946), 72.
[2] The CDF affirmed: "The greatest misery consists in the loss of hope in the face of death. This hope is proclaimed by the Christian witness, which, to be effective, must be lived in faith and encompass everyone—families,

Conclusion

The approach chosen in this book is based on faith and reason. However, it puts its emphasis not on the "end" but on "life," recognizing God as the source of true and everlasting life (cf. 1 Jn 1:2). This perspective enables a true ethical orientation by avoiding arbitrary and subjective criteria, founded on the intrinsic dignity of each human person, necessary to confront the bioethical challenges at the end of life.

---

nurses, and physicians. It must engage the pastoral resources of the diocese and of Catholic healthcare centers, which are called to live with faith the duty to accompany the sick in all of the stages of illness, and in particular in the critical and terminal stages of life." CDF, SB, Conclusion.

BIBLIOGRAPHY

MAGISTERIAL DOCUMENTS (CHRONOLOGICALLY ORDERED)

Benedict XII, Constitution *Benedictus Deus*, 29.1.1336, in DH 1000–1002.
Pius X, *Il Catechismo Maggiore di Pio X nel centenario della sua promulgazione*, 15.6.1905 (Vigodarzere: Ares, 2005).
Pius XI, Encyclical Letter *Casti Connubii*, 31.12.1930, in https://w2.vatican.va/content/pius-xi/en/encyclicals/documents/hf_p-xi_enc_19301231_casti-connubii.html [15.1.2022].
Pius XII, Encyclical Letter *Mystici Corporis*, 29.6.1943, in https://w2.vatican.va/content/pius-xii/en/encyclicals/documents/hf_p-xii_enc_29061943_mystici-corporis-christi.html [15.1.2022].
———, Encyclical Letter *Humani Generis*, 12.8.1950, in http://www.vatican.va/content/pius-xii/en/encyclicals/documents/hf_p-xii_enc_12081950_humani-generis.html [15.1.2022].
———, Allocutio, in AAS 49 (1957), 129–47
———, "Address to an International Congress of Anesthesiologists," 24.11.1957, in *NCBQ*, 2 (2002), 309–14.
———, Allocutiones «Societate internazionali Hematologiae», in AAS 50 (1958), 732–40.
Suprema Sacra Congregatio S. Officii, Instructio *De cadaverum crematione*, in AAS 56 (1964), 822–23.
Vatican Council II: The Basic Sixteen Documents, Constitutions, Decrees, Declarations, Austin Flannery, ed. (Northport, N.Y.: Costello Publishing Co., 1996).
Paul VI, Encyclical Letter *Humanae Vitae*, 25.7.1968, in http://w2.vatican.va/content/paul-vi/en/encyclicals/documents/hf_p-vi_enc_25071968_humanae-vitae.html [15.1.2022].
Pontifical Council *Cor Unum*, "Actions de santé pour un promotion humaine," in *Enchiridion Vaticanum*, Documenti ufficiali della Santa Sede 1974-1976, vol. 5 (Bologna: Edizioni Dehoniane Bologna, 1979), 1232–1251.
John Paul II, Encyclical Letter *Redemptor Hominis*, 2.3. 1979, in http://w2.vatican.va/content/john-paul-ii/en/encyclicals/documents/hf_jp-ii_enc_04031979_redemptor-hominis.html [15.1.2022].
CDF, *Declaration on Euthanasia*, 5.5.1980, in http://www.vatican.va/roman_curia/congregations/cfaith/documents/rc_con_cfaith_doc_19800505_euthanasia_en.html [15.1.2022].
John Paul II, Apostolic Letter *Salvifici Doloris*, 11.21984, in http://www.vatican.va/content/john-paul-ii/en/apost_letters/1984/documents/

hf_jp-ii_apl_11021984_salvifici-doloris.html [15.1.2022].

CDF, Instruction *Donum Vitae*. On Respect for Human Life in its Origin and on the Dignity of Procreation Replies to Certain Questions of the Day, 22.2.2987, in http://www.vatican.va/roman_curia/congregations/cfaith/documents/rc_con_cfaith_doc_19870222_respect-for-human-life_en.html [15.1.2022].

John Paul II, Encyclical Letter *Redemptoris Missio*, 7.12.1990, in http://www.vatican.va/content/john-paul-ii/en/encyclicals/documents/hf_jp-ii_enc_07121990_redemptoris-missio.html [15.1.2022].

———, Address to the Participants of the First International Congress of the Society for Organ Sharing, 20.6.1991, in http://www.vatican.va/content/john-paul-ii/en/speeches/1991/june/documents/hf_jp-ii_spe_19910620_trapianti.html [15.1.2022].

———, Encyclical Letter *Veritatis Splendor*, 6.8.1993, in http://w2.vatican.va/content/john-paul-ii/en/encyclicals/documents/hf_jp-ii_enc_06081993_veritatis-splendor.html [15.1.2022].

———, Address at the International Airport of Denver, 15.8.1993, in https://w2.vatican.va/content/john-paul-ii/en/speeches/1993/august/documents/hf_jp-ii_spe_19930815_congedo-denver-gmg.html [15.1.2022].

———, Encyclical Letter *Evangelium Vitae*, 25.3.1995, in http://w2.vatican.va/content/john-paul-ii/en/encyclicals/documents/hf_jp-ii_enc_25031995_evangelium-vitae.html [15.1.2022].

Pontifical Council for the Healthcare Workers, *The Charter for Health Care Workers* (Vatican City: Libreria Editrice Vaticana, 1995).

John Paul II, Encyclical Letter *Fides et Ratio*, 14.9. 1998, in http://w2.vatican.va/content/john-paul-ii/de/encyclicals/documents/hf_jp-ii_enc_14091998_fides-et-ratio.html [15.1.2022].

———, "Discourse of Holy Father John Paul II," in Juan de Dios Vial Correa and Elio Sgreccia (eds.), *The Dignity of the Dying Person* (Vatican City: Libreria Editrice Vaticana, 1999), 7-10.

———, Address to the 18th International Congress of the Transplantation Society, 29.8.2000, in http://w2.vatican.va/content/john-paul-ii/en/speeches/2000/jul-sep/documents/hf_jp-ii_spe_20000829_transplants.html [15.1.2022].

———, Address to the Participants in the International Congress on "Life-Sustaining Treatments and the Vegetative State: Scientific and Ethical Dilemmas," 20.3.2004, in http://www.vatican.va/content/john-paul-ii/en/speeches/2004/march/documents/hf_jp-ii_spe_20040320_congress-fiamc.html [15.1.2022].

———, Letter to the Pontifical Academy of Sciences, 1.2.2005, in http://www.vatican.va/content/john-paul-ii/en/speeches/2005/february/documents/hf_jp-ii_spe_20050201_p-acad-sciences.html [15.1.2022].

Bibliography

CDF, Commentary, 11.7.2005, in http://www.vatican.va/roman_curia/congregations/cfaith/documents/rc_con_cfaith_doc_20070801_nota-commento_en.html [15.1.2022].

John Paul II, *Man and Woman He Created Them: A Theology of the Body*, trans. by Michael Waldstein (Boston: Pauline Books & Media, 2006).

Benedict XVI, Address of his Holiness to the Members of the European People's Party on the Occasion of the Study Days on Europe, 30.3.2006, in https://w2.vatican.va/content/benedict-xvi/en/speeches/2006/march/documents/hf_ben-xvi_spe_20060330_eu-parliamentarians.html [15.1.2022].

CDF, Responses to certain questions of the United States Conference of Catholic Bishops concerning artificial nutrition and hydration, 1.8.2007, in http://www.vatican.va/roman_curia/congregations/cfaith/documents/rc_con_cfaith_doc_20070801_risposte-usa_en.html [15.1.2022].

———, Instruction *Dignitas Personae*. On Certain Bioethical Questions, 8.9.2008, in http://www.vatican.va/roman_curia/congregations/cfaith/documents/rc_con_cfaith_doc_20081208_dignitas-personae_en.html [15.1.2022].

Benedict XVI, Address to the Participants at an International Congress Organized by the Pontifical Academy for Life, 7.11.2008, in https://w2.vatican.va/content/benedict-xvi/en/speeches/2008/november/documents/hf_ben-xvi_spe_20081107_acdlife.html [15.1.2022].

———, Encyclical Letter *Caritas in Veritate*, 29.6.2009, in http://w2.vatican.va/content/benedict-xvi/de/encyclicals/documents/hf_ben-xvi_enc_20090629_caritas-in-veritate.html [15.1.2022].

———, Christmas Greetings to the Roman Curia, 21.12.2012, in http://w2.vatican.va/content/benedict-xvi/en/speeches/2012/december/documents/hf_ben-xvi_spe_20121221_auguri-curia.html [15.1.2022].

Francis, Encyclical Letter *Lumen Fidei*, 29.6.2013, in http://www.vatican.va/content/francesco/en/encyclicals/documents/papa-francesco_20130629_enciclica-lumen-fidei.html [15.1.2022].

———, Encyclical Letter *Laudato Si'*, 24.5.2015, in http://www.vatican.va/content/francesco/en/encyclicals/documents/papa-francesco_20150524_enciclica-laudato-si.html [15.1.2022].

———, Meeting with the Polish Bishops, 28.7.2016, in https://w2.vatican.va/content/francesco/en/speeches/2016/july/documents/papa-francesco_20160727_polonia-vescovi.html [15.1.2022].

———, Post-Synodal Apostolic Exhortation *Amoris Laetitia*, 19.3.2016, in http://www.vatican.va/content/dam/francesco/pdf/apost_exhortations/documents/papa-francesco_esortazione-ap_20160319_amoris-laetitia_en.pdf [15.1.2022].

CDF, *Ad resurgendum cum Christo*, regarding the burial of the deceased and the conservation of the ashes in the case of cremation, 15.8.2016, in http://www.vatican.va/roman_curia/congregations/cfaith/documents/rc_con_cfaith_doc_20160815_ad-resurgendum-cum-christo_en.html [15.1.2022].

The Pontifical Council for Pastoral Assistance to Health Care Workers, *New Charter for Health Care Workers*, trans. by The National Catholic Bioethics Center (Philadelphia: National Catholic Bioethics Center, 2017).

CDF, Letter to the Superior General of the Congregation of the "Brothers of Charity," Regarding the Accompaniment of Patients in Psychiatric Hospitals of the Congregation's Belgian Branch, 30.3.2020, in http://www.vatican.va/roman_curia/congregations/cfaith/documents/rc_con_cfaith_doc_20200330_lettera-fratellidellacarita-belgio_en.html [15.1.2022].

———, Letter *Samaritanus Bonus*. On the Care of Persons in the Critical and Terminal Phases of Life (Vatican City: Libreria Editrice Vaticana, 2020).

OTHER LITERATURE (ALPHABETICALLY ORDERED)

Ayuba, Mahmud Adesina, "Euthanasia: A Muslim Perspective," in *Scriptura*, 115 (2016), 1-13.

Ad Hoc Committee of the Harvard Medical School, "A Definition of Irreversible Coma," in *Journal of the American Medical Association*, 205 (1968), 337-40.

Albert II, "The Belgian Act on Euthanasia of May, 28th 2002," trans. by Dale Kidd, Centre for Biomedical Ethics and Law, Leuven, in *Ethical Perspectives*, 9 (2002), 182-88.

Ambrosius Mediolanensis, *Verginità e vedovanza*, Franco Gori (ed.) (Milano - Roma: Biblioteca Ambrosiana, 1989).

Ancona, Leonardo, "Psychological and spiritual assistance: the truth when faced with death," in Juan de Dios Vial Correa and Elio Sgreccia (eds.), *The Dignity of the Dying Person* (Vatican City: Libreria Editrice Vaticana, 1999), 267-86.

Angenendt, Arnold, *Heilige und Reliquien. Die Geschichte ihres Kultes vom frühen Christentum bis zur Gegenwart* (München: C.H.Beck Verlag, 1997).

Aquinas, Thomas, *Summa Theologiae*, English translation in http://www.newadvent.org/summa/3064.htm [15.1.2022].

———, *Summa contra gentiles*, Tito Sante Centi (ed.), vol. 1 (Bologna: Edizioni Studio Domenicano, 2001).

Aristotle, *The Nicomachean Ethics*, trans. by David Ross (Oxford: Oxford University Press, 2009).

Aristotle, "On the Soul," in Jonathan Barnes (ed.), *The Complete Works of*

Bibliography

Aristotle, vol. 1, 6th ed. (Princeton, NJ: Princeton University Press, 1995).

Ascencio, Juan Gabriel, *Il pensiero culturale. Tra filosofia metafisica e razionalità postmoderna* (Rome: Casa Editrice Ateneo Pontificio Regina Apostolorum, 2004).

Atighetchi, Dariusch, *Islam e Bioetica* (Rome: Armando Curcio Editore, 2009).

Augustine, *The City of God Against the Pagans, Books I–III*, trans. by George E. McCracken (Cambridge: Harvard University Press, 1995).

Bacon, Francis, *The Works of Francis Bacon In Ten Volumes* (London: W. Baynes, 1824).

Balkenohl, Manfred, "Der Hirntod - Zur Problematik einer neuen Todesdefinition," in ibid./Roland Rösler (ed.), *Handbuch für Lebensschutz und Lebensrecht* (Paderborn: Bonifatius Verlag, 2010), 469–86.

Barker, Clyde F. and Markmann, James F., "Historical Overview of Transplantation," in *Cold Spring Harbor Perspectives in Medicine* (2013), 3:a014977.

Bayles, Michael D., "Euthanasia and the Quality of life," in James J. Walter, Thomas A. Shannon (eds.), *Quality of Life. The New Medical Dilemma* (Mahwah, NJ: Paulist Press, 1990), 265–81.

Beine, Karl H., Turczyknski, Jeanne, *Tatort Krankenhaus. Wie ein kaputtes System Misshandlungen und Morde an Kranken fördert* (München: Droemer Verlag, 2017).

Belgrave, Kevin and Requena, Pablo, "A Primer on Palliative Sedation," in *NCBQ*, 12 (2012), 263–81.

Bellarmine, Robert, Robert Bellarmine, "The Art of Dying Well," in John Patrick Donnelly and Roland J. Teske, translators, *Robert Bellarmine: Spiritual Writings* (Mahwah NJ: Paulist Press, 1989), 231–386.

Benzenhöfer, Udo, *Der gute Tod? Euthanasie und Sterbehilfe in Geschichte und Gegenwart* (München: C.H.Beck Verlag, 1999).

Berg, Jessica, "The Effect of Social Media on End-Of-Life Decision Making," in Stuart J. Youngner and Robert M. Arnold (eds.), *The Oxford Handbook of Ethics at the End of Life* (Oxford: Oxford University Press, 2016), 279–90.

Birnbacher, Dieter, "Hilft der Personenbegriff bei der Lösung bioethischer Fragestellungen?," in H.-J. Kaatsch and H. Kreß (eds.), *Ethik interdisziplinär*, vol. 3 (London: LIT Verlag, 2003), 31–43.

Bizzotto, Mario, "Concealment of death," in Juan de Dios Vial Correa and Elio Sgreccia (eds.), *The Dignity of the Dying Person* (Vatican City: Libreria Editrice Vaticana, 1999), 31–52.

Błażek, Magdalena et. al., "Sense of Purpose in Life and Escape from Self as the Predictors of Quality of Life in Clinical Samples," in *Journal of Religion and Health*, 54 (2015), 517–23.

Böckenförde, Ernst-Wolfgang, *Staat, Gesellschaft, Freiheit* (Berlin: Suhrkamp

Taschenbuch Verlag, 1976).

Boethius, *De persona et duabus naturis*, PL 64.

Borbonus, Dorian, *Columbarium Tombs and Collective Identity in Augustan Rome* (New York: Cambridge University Press, 2014).

Brancato, Francesco, *L'ultima chiamata. Giovanni Paolo II e la morte* (Firenze: Giunti Editore, 2006).

Breul, Regina and Waldstein, Wolfgang, *Hirntod-Organspende. Brisant und ehrlich*, 2nd ed. (Illertissen: Media Maria, 2014).

Brown, Grattan T., "B. Ordinary and Extraordinary Means," in Edward J. Furton et al. (eds.), *Catholic Health Care Ethics. A Manual for Practitioners* (Philadelphia: National Catholic Bioethics Center, 2009), 15-19.

Buchs, Stefan, *Ärzteethos und Suizidhilfe. Theologisch-ethische Untersuchung zur Praxis der ärztlichen Suizidhilfe in der Schweiz* (Basel: Echter Verlag, 2018).

Burt, Robert A., "The medical futility debate: Patient choice, physician obligation, and end-of-life care," in *Journal of Palliative Medicine*, 5 (2002), 249-54.

Bustos, Javier I., "The Uncertainty of Living Will," in *NCBQ*, 13 (2013), 243-51.

Byrne, Paul and Rinkowski, George, "'Brain Death' is False," in *Linacre Quarterly*, 66 (1999), 42-48.

Caplan, Arthur L. et al. (eds.), *The Case of Terri Schiavo. Ethics at the End of Life* (New York: Prometheus, 2006).

Capron, Alexander Morgan and Kass, Leon R., "A Statutory Definition of the Standards for Determining Human Death: An Appraisal and a Proposal," in *University of Pennsylvania Law Review*, 121 (1972), 87-118.

Casini, Marina et al., "La riflessione sul 'fine vita.' Aspetti giuridici ed etico-clinici dell'eutanasia," in *Medicina e Morale* 59 (2010), 987-1005.

Castagneto, Marco, "Trapianti," in Elio Sgreccia and Antonio Tarantino (eds.), *Enciclopedia di bioetica e scienza giuridica*, vol. XII (Naples: Edizioni Scientifiche Italiane, 2017), 275-91.

Cattanìa, Maria Vittoria and Brandi, Toni (eds.), *Cina Traffici di morte. Il commercio degli organi dei condannati a morte* (Milano: Guerini e Associati, 2008).

Cessario, Romanus, *Introduction to Moral Theology* (Washington, D.C.: Catholic University of America Press, 2001).

Chagas, Carlos (ed.), *The Artificial Prolongation of Life and the Determination of the Exact Moment of Death*, Pontifical Academy of Science (Vatican City: Libreria Editrice Vaticana, 1985).

Cohn, Felicia and Lynn, Joanne, "Vulnerable People: Practical Rejoinders to Claim in Favor of Assisted Suicide," in Kathleen Foley and Herbert Hendin (eds.), *The Case against Assisted Suicide* (Baltimore and London: Johns Hopkins University Press, 2002), 238-60.

Bibliography

Colom, Enrique, *Scelti in Cristo per essere santi, IV. Morale sociale* (Rome: Edusc, 2008).

Cosentino, Angela Maria, "Vita (Sacralità, Inviolabilità, Indisponibilità)," in *Enciclopedia di bioetica e scienza giuridica*, vol. XII (Naples: Edizioni Scientifiche Italiane, 2017), 853–84.

Craughwell, Thomas J., *Saints Preserved. An Encyclopedia of Relics* (New York: Image Books, 2011).

Cronin, Daniel A., *Ordinary and Extraordinary Means of Conserving Life* (Philadelphia: National Catholic Bioethics Center, 2011).

———, *The Moral Law in Regard to the Ordinary and Extraordinary Means of Conserving Life* (Rome: Pontifical Gregorian University, 1958).

Culwell, Kelly R. et al., "Critical gaps in universal access to reproductive health: Contraception and prevention of unsafe abortion," in *International Journal of Gynecology & Obstetrics*, 110 (2010), 13–16.

Davies, Douglas J. and Mates, Lewis H., *Encyclopedia of Cremation* (Burlington: Ashgate Publishing, 2005).

Davies, Norman, *Europe: a History* (London: Oxford University Press, 1996).

De Dios Vial Correa, Juan and Sgreccia, Elio (eds.), *The Identity and Status of the Human Embryo. Proceedings of Third Assembly of the Pontifical Academy for Life*, 2nd ed. (Vatican City: Libreria Editrice Vaticana, 1999).

De Lugo, Juan, *De iustitia et iure* (Rome: 1663).

De Mattei, Roberto (ed.), *Evoluzionismo: il tramonto di una ipotesi* (Siena: Cantagalli, 2009).

———, *Finis Vitae. Is Brain Death Still Life?* (Soveria Mannelli: Consiglio nazionale delle ricerche, 2006).

Del Valle, Alexandre, *Il complesso occidentale. Piccolo Trattato di de colpevolizzazione* (Isola del Liri: Paesi Edizioni, 2019).

De Marco, Donald and Benjamin D. Wiker, *Architects of the Culture of Death* (San Francisco: Ignatius Press, 2004).

De Vitoria, Francisco, *Relectiones theologicae, relectio IX, De temperantia* (Lyon, 1587).

Diakonoff, Igor M., *Early Antiquity*, trans. by Alexander Kirjanov (Chicago: University of Chicago Press, 1991).

DiBaise, John K., "Euthanasia and Quality of Life. Critique of a Subjective Standard," in *NCBQ*, 17 (2017), 417–24.

Dowbiggin, Ian, *A Merciful End: The Euthanasia Movement in Modern America* (New York: Oxford University Press, 2003).

Drahos, Mary, *The Healing Power of Hope. Down-to-Earth Alternatives to Euthanasia and Assisted Suicide* (Ann Arbor: Charis Books, 1997).

Dubay, Thomas, *Faith and Certitude* (San Francisco: Ignatius Press, 1985).

DuBois, James M., "Organ Transplantation: An Ethical Road Map," in *NCBQ*, 2 (2002), 413–53.

Dulles, Avery, "John Paul II and The Mystery of The Human Person," *America*, 190 (2004), 414–29.

Durkheim, Emile, *Suicide, A Study in Sociology* (New York: The Free Press, 1951).

Engelhardt, H. Tristram, "Foreword," in Van Rensselaer Potter (ed.), *Global Bioethics. Building on the Leopold Legacy* (East Lansing, MI: Michigan State University Press, 1988), vii–xii.

―――, *The Foundations of Bioethics*, 2nd ed. (Oxford: Oxford University Press, 1996).

Erasmo, Mario, *Reading Death in Ancient Rome* (Columbus, OH: Ohio State University Press, 2008).

Eusebius, *Ecclesiastical History, Books 6–10*, trans. by J. E. L. Oulton (Cambridge: Harvard University Press, 1932).

Evans, Debra, *Without Moral Limits. Women, Reproduction, and Medical Technology* (Wheaton: Crossway Books, 2000).

Falk, Franz: *Die deutschen Sterbebüchlein von der ältesten Zeit des Buchdrucks bis zum Jahre 1520. Nachdruck der Ausgabe Köln 1890* (Heidelberg: Tenner, 1969).

Fenigsen, Richard, "Euthanasia and moral reflection," in Juan de Dios Vial Correa and Elio Sgreccia (eds.), *The Dignity of the Dying Person* (Vatican City: Libreria Editrice Vaticana, 1999), 212–18.

Fernandes, Ashley, "The Loss of Dignity at the End of Life," in *NCBQ*, 10 (2010), 529–46.

Franz, Adolph, *Die kirchlichen Benediktionen im Mittelalter*, vol. 2 (Bonn: Verlag nova & vetera, 2006).

Foitzik, Alexander, "Korrektiv," in *Herder Korrespondenz* 68 (2014), 491–92.

Fondevila, Constantino et al., "Liver Transplant Using Donors After Unexpected Cardiac Death: Novel Preservation Protocol and Acceptance Criteria," in *American Journal of Transplantation*, 7 (2007), 1849–55.

Francis, Neil, "Neonatal deaths under Dutch Groningen Protocol very rare despite misinformation contagion," in *Journal of Assisted Dying*, 1 (2016), 7–19.

Friedlander, Henry, *The Origins of Nazi Genocide. From Euthanasia to the Final Solution* (Chapel Hill: University of North Carolina Press, 1995).

Furton, Edward J., "Brain Death, the Soul, and Organic Life," in *NCBQ*, 2 (2002), 455–70.

Fye, W. Bruce, "Active Euthanasia: An Historical Survey on its Conceptional Origins and Introduction into Medical Thought," in *Bulletin of History of Medicine*, 52 (1972), 492–503.

Gerding, Jeri, "Extraordinary Means and Depression at the End of Life," in *NCBQ*, 14 (2014), 697–710.

Gerstein, Kurt, Pastore, Stephen R. (eds.), *The Nazi Slaughter of the Disabled: The Euthanasia Program T4* (New York: American Bibliographical

Press, 2017).

Gleixner, Hans, „*Wenn Gott nicht existiert...*" *Zur Beziehung zwischen Religion und Ethik* (Paderborn: Verlag Ferdinand Schöningh, 2005).

Glessner, Thomas A., *The Emerging Brave New World* (Crane: Anomalos Pub, 2008).

Golder, Barbara, et al., "Assisted Nutrition and Hydration as Supportive Care during Illness. Bedside Application of Catholic Moral Teaching," in *NCBQ*, 16 (2016), 435–48.

Gormally, Luke, "Palliative treatment and ordinary care," in Juan de Dios Vial Correa and Elio Sgreccia (eds.), *The Dignity of the Dying Person* (Vatican City: Libreria Editrice Vaticana, 1999), 252–66.

Gorsuch, Neil M., *The Future of Assisted Suicide and Euthanasia* (Princeton: Princeton University Press, 2006).

Götz, Aly Haydar (ed.), *Aktion T4 1929–1945. Die "Euthanasie"-Zentrale in der Tiergartenstraße 4*, 2nd ed. (Berlin: Edition Hentrich, 1989).

Guardini, Romano, *Die Annahme seiner selbst. Den Menschen erkennt nur, wer von Gott weiß* (Kevelaer: C.H.Beck Verlag, 2010).

―――, *Die religiöse Offenheit der Gegenwart* (Ostfildern: Matthias-Grünewald/Schöningh, 2008).

―――, *The End of the Modern World*, trans. by Joseph Theman and Herbert Burke (Wilmington, DE: ISI Books, 2001).

Guevin, Benedict M., "Ordinary, Extraordinary, and Artificial Means of Care," in *NCBQ*, 5 (2005), 471–79.

Guinan, Patrick, "Is Assisted Nutrition and Hydration Always Mandated?," in *NCBQ*, 10 (2010), 481–88.

Have, Henk ten, "End-of-Life Decision Making in the Netherlands," in Robert H. Blank and Janna C. Merrick (eds.), *End-of-Life Decision Making* (Cambridge, MA: The MIT Press, 2005), 147–68.

Heath, Ann M., "Advance Directives to Withhold Oral Food and Water in Dementia," in *NCBQ*, 16 (2016), 421–34.

Henke, Donald E., "A History of Ordinary and Extraordinary Means," in *NCBQ*, 5 (2005), 555–75.

Hester, D. Micah (ed.), *Ethics by Committee. A Textbook on Consultation, Organization, and Education for Hospital Ethics Committees* (Lanham, MD: Rowman & Littlefield Publishers, 2008).

Hillyer, Christopher D., et al., *Blood Banking and Transfusion Medicine. Basic Principles & Practice*, 2nd ed. (Philadelphia: Churchill Livingstone, 2007).

Humphry, Derek and Clement, Mary, *Freedom to Die. People, Politics and the Right-To-Die-Movement* (New York: St. Martin's Griffin, 1998).

Insa Gómez, Francisco Javier and Requena Meana, Pablo, "Is Medical Futility an Ethical or Clinical Concept?," in *NCBQ*, 17 (2017), 261–73.

Jeffrey, David, *Against Physician Assisted Suicide. A palliative care perspective*

(Oxford: CRC Press, 2009).

Jonas, Hans, *Technik, Medizin und Ethik. Zur Praxis des Prinzips Verantwortung* (Frankfurt am Main: Suhrkamp Verlag, 1985).

———, *The Phenomenon of Life. Toward a Philosophical Biology* (Evanston, IL: Northwestern University Press, 2001).

Jones, David Albert, *The Soul of the Embryo: An Enquiry into the Status of the Human Embryo in the Christian Tradition* (London: Continuum Books, 2006).

Julian, Baiju and Mynatty, Hormis, *Catholic Contribution to Bioethics. Reflections on Evangelium Vitae* (Bangalore: ATC Publication, 2007).

Kaufmann, Franz-Xaver, and Krämer, Walter (eds.), *Die demographische Zeitbombe. Fakten und Folgen des Geburtendefizits* (Paderborn: Verlag Ferdinand Schöningh, 2015).

Kheriaty, Aaron and Clark, John, *The Catholic Guide to Depression* (Manchester: Sophia Institute Press, 2012).

Kilpatrick, William, *The Emperor's New Clothes: Psychological Fashions and Religious Faith*, 2nd ed. (Ridgefield CT: Roger McCaffrey Publishing, 1998).

Klee, Ernst (ed.), *Dokumente zur „Euthanasie"* (Frankfurt am Main: Fischer-Taschenbuch-Verlag, 1985).

Kliewer, Stephen P. and Saultz, John, *Healthcare and Spirituality* (Oxford: CRC Press, 2006).

Koenig, Harold G., *Spirituality in Patient Care. Why, How, When, and What*, 3rd ed. (West Conshohocken: Templeton Foundation Press, 2013).

Kohl, Helmut, *Erinnerungen 1990–1994* (München: Droemer Verlag, 2007).

Kuby, Gabriele, *The Global Sexual Revolution. Destruction of Freedom in the Name of Freedom*, trans. by James Patrick Kirchner (Kettering, OH: LifeSite/Angelico Press, 2015).

La Barrera Villarreal, Víctor Ronald, *Il Principio di proporzionalità terapeutica nell'assistenza alla fase finale della vita*, Tesi di Dottorato di Ricerca in Bioetica (Roma: Università di Roma, 2004).

Lasnoski, Kent J., "Are Cremation and Alkaline Hydrolysis Morally Distinct?," in *NCBQ*, 16 (2016), 233–42.

———, "Burial, Cremation, and Alkaline Hydrolysis," in Edward J. Furton (ed.), *Catholic Health Care Ethics. A Manual for Practitioners*, 3rd ed. (Philadelphia: The National Catholic Bioethics Center, 2020), 25.125.15.

Lewis, Clive Staples, *The Great Divorce* (New York: Macmillan, 1946).

Lucas Lucas, Ramón, *Antropología y problemas bioéticos* (Madrid: Biblioteca Autores Cristianos, 2005).

———, *Bioética para todos* (México: Ediciones Trillas, 2003).

Lütz, Manfred, "Statement against the 'A report on cerebral death' by Prof. Corrado Manni," in Juan de Dios Vial Correa and Elio Sgreccia (eds.), *The Dignity of the Dying Person* (Vatican City: Libreria Editrice

Vaticana, 1999), 119–22.

Maio, Giovanni, *Mittelpunkt Mensch: Ethik in der Medizin. Ein Lehrbuch* (Stuttgart: Schattauer, 2012).

Manni, Corrado, "A report on cerebral death," in Juan de Dios Vial Correa and Elio Sgreccia (eds.), *The Dignity of the Dying Person* (Vatican City: Libreria Editrice Vaticana, 1999), 102–18.

Manning, Michael, *Euthanasia and Physician-Assisted Suicide. Killing or Caring?* (New York: Paulist Press, 1998).

Marker, Rita, *Deadly Compassion. The Death of Ann Humphry and the Truth about Euthanasia* (New York: William Morrow & Co, 1993).

Markette, Jo, "Three's a Crowd: An Argument Against Mitochondrial Replacement," in *Ethics & Medics*, 41 (2016), 2–4.

Marsala, Miles S., "Approval of Euthanasia: Differences Between Cohorts and Religion," in *SAGE Open*, 9 (2019), 1–11.

Marshall, Charles F., *Discovering the Rommel Murder. The Life and Death of the Desert Fox* (Mechanicsburg: Stackpole Books, 2002).

May, William E., *Catholic Bioethics and the Gift of Human Life*, 3rd ed. (Huntington, IN: Our Sunday Visitor Publishing Division, 2013).

McInerny, Ralph M., *What Went Wrong with Vatican II? The Catholic Crisis Explained* (Manchester: Sophia Institute Press, 1998).

McLean Cummings, Andrew, *The Servant and the Ladder: Cooperation with Evil in the Twenty-First Century* (Herefordshire: Gracewing Publishing, 2014).

Melina, Livio, *The Epiphany of Love. Toward a Theological Understanding of Christian Action* (Cambridge: Wm. B. Eerdmans Publishing Co., 2010).

Milano, Gianna, *Mario Riccio, Storia di una morte opportuna. Il diario del medico che ha fatto la volontà di Welby* (Milano: Galápagos, 2008).

Ministry of Law, Justice and Company Affairs, New Delhi, the 11th July 1994, The Transplantation of Human Organs Act, 1994 No.42 OF 1994.

Miranda, Gonzalo, "The meaning of life and the acceptance of death," in Juan de Dios Vial Correa and Elio Sgreccia (eds.), *The Dignity of the Dying Person. Proceedings of the Fifth Assembly of the Pontifical Academy for Life* (Vatican City: Libreria Editrice Vaticana, 1999), 297–312.

Mirkes, Renée, "The Mortuary Science of Alkaline Hydrolysis," in *NCBQ*, 8 (2008), 683–95.

More, Thomas, *Utopia* (Los Angeles: Norton, 2017).

Nair-Collins, Michael, "Brain Death, Paternalism, and the Language of 'Death,'" in *Kennedy Institute of Ethics Journal*, 23 (2013), 53–104.

Nationaler Ethikrat, *Selbstbestimmung und Fürsorge am Lebensende. Stellungnahme* (Berlin: Druckhaus Berlin-Mitte, 2006).

Nguyen, Doyen, "Does the Uniform Determination of Death Act Need to Be Revised?," in *The Linacre Quarterly*, 87 (2020), 317–33.

————, "Pope John Paul II and the neurological standard for the determination of death: A critical analysis of his address to the Transplantation Society," in *The Linacre Quarterly*, 84 (2017), 155-86.

Nolan, Marie T. and Travaline, John M., "Organ Donation and Transplantation," in Edward J. Furton (ed.), *Catholic Health Care Ethics. A Manual for Practitioners*, 3rd ed. (Philadelphia: The National Catholic Bioethics Center, 2020), 26.1-26.19.

O'Leary, Dale, *The Gender Agenda. Redefining Equality* (Lafayette: Vital Issues Press, 1997).

O'Rourke, Kevin D., "The Catholic Tradition on Forgoing Life Support," in *NCBQ*, 5 (2005), 537-53.

Paluzzi, Silvestro, *Manuale di psicologia* (Rome: Urbaniana University Press, 1999).

Paterson, Craig, *Assisted Suicide and Euthanasia. A Natural Law Ethics Approach* (Cornwall: Taylor & Francis Ltd, 2008).

Pellegrino, Edmund, "Decision at the End of Life: the Use and Abuse of the Concept of Futility," in Juan de Dios Vial Correa and Elio Sgreccia (eds.), *The Dignity of the Dying Person* (Vatican City: Libreria Editrice Vaticana, 1999), 219-41.

Perkins, Mary Anne, *Christendom and European Identity. The Legacy of a Grand Narrative since 1789* (Berlin: Walter de Gruyter, 2004).

Pieper, Annemarie (ed.), *Geschichte der neueren Ethik*, vol. 1+2 (Tübingen: A. Francke Verlag, 1992).

Pieper, Josef, *Death and Immortality*, trans. by Richard and Clara Winston (South Bend, IN: St. Augustine's Press, 2000).

Plato, *Republic*, Books 1-5, trans. by Paul Shorey (Cambridge: Harvard University Press, 1930).

Ponnuru, Ramesh, *The Party of Death. The Democrats, the Media, the Courts, and the Disregard for Human Life* (Washington, D.C.: Regnery Publishing, 2006).

Pontificia Universitas A Sancto Thoma Aquinate in Urbe, "Studia in Honorem Caroli Wojtyla," in *Angelicum*, 56 (1979), Fasc. 2-3.

Porro, Alessandro, et al., "Modernity in medicine and hygiene at the end of the 19th century: the example of cremation," in *Journal of Public Health Research*, 1 (2012), 51-58.

Potter, Jordan, "The Principle of Double Effect in End-of-Life-Care," in *NCBQ*, 15 (2015), 515-29.

Potter, Van Rensselaer, "Bioethics: The Science of Survival," in *Perspectives in Biology and Medicine*, 14 (1982), 127-53.

President's Commission for the Study of Ethical Problems in Medicine and Biomedical and Behavioral Research, *Defining Death: Medical, Legal and Ethical Issues in the Determination of Death* (Washington, D.C.: US. Government Printing Office, 1981).

Ramm, Walter, *Die Patientenverfügung*, No. 13, 6th ed. (Absteinach: Schriftenreihe der Aktion Leben e.V., 2011), 1–35.

Ravasi, Gianfranco, "It is the Lord who Gives Life and Death. Towards a Theology of Death," in Juan de Dios Vial Correa and Elio Sgreccia (eds.), *The Dignity of the Dying Person* (Vatican City: Libreria Editrice Vaticana, 1999), 287–96.

Reiss, Hans S. (ed.), *Kant, Political Writings*, trans. by H. B. Nisbet, 2nd ed. (Cambridge: Cambridge University Press, 1991).

Rohnheimer, Martin, *Christentum und säkularer Staat. Geschichte-Gegenwart-Zukunft* (Freiburg im Breisgau: Verlag Herder, 2012).

———, *Die Perspektive der Moral. Philosophische Grundlagen der Tugendethik* (Berlin: Walter de Gruyter, 2001).

Rodríguez-Arias, David, at al., "Donation After Circulatory Death: Burying the Dead Donor Rule," in *The American Journal of Bioethics*, 11 (2011): 36–43.

Russello, Gerald J. (ed.), *Christianity and European Culture. Selections from the Work of Christopher Dawson* (Washington D.C.: Catholic University of America Press, 1998).

Sandrin, Luciano, "Psychological effects of refusal of death," in Juan de Dios Vial Correa and Elio Sgreccia (eds.), *The Dignity of the Dying Person* (Vatican City: Libreria Editrice Vaticana, 1999), 53–62.

Sedgh, Gilda et al., "Abortion Incidence Between 1990 and 2014: Global, Regional, and Subregional levels and trends," in *The Lancet*, 338 (2016), 258–67.

Seifert, Josef, "A philosophical refutation of the identification of 'brain death' with human death or its criterion," in *Studia Bioethica*, 2 (2009), 19–25.

Seneca, *Ad Lucilium Epistulae Morales*, trans. by Richard M. Gummere, vol. 2 (Cambridge: Harvard University Press, 1962).

Sgreccia, Elio, *Personalist Bioethics. Foundations and Applications*, trans. by John A. Di Camillo and Michael J. Miller (Philadelphia: National Catholic Bioethics Center, 2012).

Sidel, Vitor W., "Armi chimiche e biologiche," in Giovanni Russo (ed.), *Bioetica ambientale* (Torino: Editrice Elle Di Ci, 1998), 235–50.

Singer, Peter, *Practical Ethics*, 2nd ed. (Cambridge: University Press, 1999).

Smith, Wesley J., *Culture of Death. The Assault on Medical Ethics in America* (San Francisco: Encounter Books, 2000).

Smith, William B., "Judeo-Christian Teaching on Euthanasia: Definitions, Distinctions and Decisions," in *Linacre Quarterly*, 54 (1987), 27–42.

Spaemann, Robert, "Death-Suicide-Euthanasia," in Juan de Dios Vial Correa and Elio Sgreccia (eds.), *The Dignity of the Dying Person* (Vatican City: Libreria Editrice Vaticana, 1999), 123–31.

———, "On the anthropology of the Encyclical *Evangelium Vitae*," in Juan de Dios Val Correa and Elio Sgreccia (eds.), *Evangelium Vitae Five Years of Confrontation with the Society*. Proceedings of the Sixth Assembly of the Pontifical Academy for Life (Vatican City: Libreria Editrice Vaticana, 2001), 437–51.

———, "Wann beginnt der Mensch Person zu sein?," in Manfred Spieker (ed.), *Biopolitik. Probleme des Lebensschutzes in der Demokratie* (Paderborn: Verlag Ferdinand Schöningh, 2009), 39–50.

Spieker, Manfred (ed.), *Biopolitik. Probleme des Lebensschutzes in der Demokratie* (Paderborn: Verlag Ferdinand Schöningh, 2009).

———, "The Legal Language of the Culture of Death in Europe," in *NCBQ*, 14 (2014), 647–57.

Spinello, Richard A., "Bioethics and the Human Soul. Pope St. John Paul II's Reflections on Ensoulment," in *NCBQ*, 18 (2018), 291–316.

Stiller, Calvin R., "Organ and Tissue Transplants. I. Medical Overview," in Warren Thomas Reich (ed.), *Encyclopedia of Bioethics*, 4 (New York: Macmillan Publisher, 1995), 1871–82.

Suárez, Francisco, *Opera Omnia*, E. Berton (ed.) (Paris, 1858).

Suaudeau, Jacques, "Cellule Staminali," in Elio Sgreccia and Antonio Tarantino (eds.), *Enciclopedia di bioetica e scienze giuridica*, vol. III (Naples: Edizioni Scientifiche Italiane, 2010), 103–28.

Suetonius Tranquillus, Gaius, *Leben der Caesaren (Meisterwerke der Antike)*, transl and ed. by André Lambert (München: Bertelsmann, 1972).

Thérèse of Lisieux, *Story of a Soul. Autobiography*, trans. by John Clarke, 3rd ed. (Washington D.C.: ICS Publications, 2017).

Thomasma, David C. et al. (eds.), "Introduction: Reexamining 'Thou Shalt Not Kill,'" *Asking to Die. Inside the Dutch Debate about Euthanasia* (Dordrecht: Springer, 1998), 7–16.

Toynbee, Jocelyn M. C., *Death and Burial in the Roman World* (Baltimore: Johns Hopkins University Press, 1996).

Trochu, Francis, *Le curé d'Ars Saint Jean-Marie Baptiste Vianney* (Montsiur: Résiac, 1987).

Truog, Robert and Robinson, Walter, "Role of Brain Death and Dead-Donor Rule in the Ethics of Organ Transplantation," in *Critical Care Medicine*, 31 (2003), 2392.

Ughetti, Anthony C., "A Contemporary *Ars Moriendi* for End-Of-Life Care," in *Ethics & Medics*, 44 (2019), 1–2.

United States, National Organ Transplant Act: Public Law 98–507. US Statute Large. 1984 Oct 19;98:2339–48. PMID: 11660818.

USCCB, "Ethical and Religious Directives for Catholic Health Care Services," in Edward J. Furton et al. (eds.), *Catholic Health Care Ethics. A Manual for Practitioners* (Philadelphia: National Catholic Bioethics

Center, 2009), 389-400.

Van Gool, Stefaan and Lepeleire, de Jan, "Euthanasia in Children: Keep Asking the Right Question," in David Albert Jones et al. (eds.), *Euthanasia and Assisted Suicide. Lessons from Belgium* (Cambridge: Cambridge University Press, 2017), 173-87.

Van Ittersum, Frans J. and Hendriks, Lambert, "Organ Donation after Euthanasia," in *NCBQ* 12 (2012), 431-37.

Verhagen, Eduard, et al., "The Groningen Protocol—Euthanasia in Severely Ill Newborns," in *New England Journal of Medicine*, 325 (2005), 959-62.

Vizcarrondo, Felipe E., "Medical Futility in Pediatric Care," in *NCBQ*, 19 (2019), 105-20.

Von Balthasar, Hans Urs, *Romano Guardini, Reform aus dem Ursprung* (Einsiedeln: Johannes Verlag, 1995).

Von Brandenstein Zeppelin, Albrecht, von Stockhausen, Alma (eds.), *Naturphilosophische Gegenüberstellung von Evolutionstheorie und Schöpfungstheologie (2009), Evolutionstheorie im Lichte heutiger Wissenschaften*, vol. I (Weilheim-Bierbronnen: Gustav-Siewerth-Akademie, 2009).

———, *Naturphilosophische Gegenüberstellung von Evolutionstheorie und Schöpfungstheologie (2010), „Im Anfang war das Wort" - Naturphilosophische Reflexion auf die Schöpfungstheologie*, vol. II (Weilheim-Bierbronnen: Gustav-Siewerth-Akademie, 2009).

Walder, Alphonse D., "The Artificial Prolongation of Life and the Determination of the Exact Moment of Death," in Carlos Chagas (ed.), *Pontificia Academia Scientiarum*, vol. 60 (Vatican City: Libreria Editrice Vaticana, 1985), 75-84.

Waldstein, Wolfgang, "Natural Law and the Defence of Life in *Evangelium Vitae*," in Juan de Dios Val Correa and Elio Sgreccia (eds.), *Evangelium Vitae Five Years of Confrontation with the Society*. Proceedings of the Sixth Assembly of the Pontifical Academy for Life (Vatican City: Libreria Editrice Vaticana, 2001), 223-42.

Walter, James J., Shannon, Thomas A. (eds.), *Quality of Life. The New Medical Dilemma* (Mahwah, NJ: Paulist Press, 1990).

Wang, Meiling, et al., *WTO, Globalization and China's Health Care System* (New York: Palgrave Macmillan, 2007).

Webster, Gregory, "Financial Toxicity. Treatment Expense and Extraordinary Means," in *NCBQ*, 18 (2018), 227-36.

Weikart, Richard, *Hitler's Ethic. The Nazi Pursuit of Evolutionary Progress* (New York: Cambridge University Press, 2009).

Weiler, Joseph, *Ein christliches Europa. Erkundungsgänge* (Salzburg-München: Anton Pustet Verlag, 2004).

Weimann, Ralph, *Bioethik in einer säkularisierten Gesellschaft. Ethische Probleme der PID* (Paderborn: Verlag Ferdinand Schöningh, 2015).

———, "Das Jahr des Glaubens zur Überwindung der Glaubenskrise. Der Glaube verdunstet in den Seelen," in *Die Neue Ordnung*, 66 (2012), 417–28.

———, "Il Martirio. Suprema testimonianza d'amore," in M. Graulich and ibid. (eds.), *Deus Caritas Est. Porta di Misericordia* (Vatican City: Libreria Editrice Vaticana, 2016), 123–41.

Welie, Jos V. M., "When Medical Treatment Is No Longer in Order," in *NCBQ*, 5 (2005), 517–36.

Werth, Nicolas, *Cannibal Island: Death in a Siberian Gulag*, trans. by Steven Rendall (Princeton: Princeton University Press, 2007).

White, Frederick J., "Lessons from Recent Polls on Physician-Assisted Suicide," in *NCBQ*, 17 (2017), 247–57.

Wittgenstein, Ludwig, *Notebooks 1914–1916*, trans. by Gertrude E. M. Anscombe (New York: Blackwell, 1961).

World Health Organization, *Information Sheet. Unsafe abortion incidence and mortality. Global and regional levels in 2008 and trends during 1990–2008* (Geneva: World Health Organization, 2012).

———, *Research ethics committees. Basic concepts for capacity-building* (Geneva: WHO Document Production Services, 2009).

Wojtyła, Karol, *Metafisica della Persona. Tutte le opera filosofiche e saggi integrativi*, Giovanni Reale and Tadeusz Styczeń (eds.) (Milano: Bompiani, 2003).

———, *The Acting Person*, trans. by Andrezej Potocki, in Analecta Husserliana. The Yearbook of Phenomenological Research, vol. X (Dordrecht: D. Reidel Publishing Company, 1969).

ONLINE SOURCES (ALPHABETICALLY ORDERED)

Allen, John L., Tackling taboos on Jews and Christians, the cross and deicide, in *National Catholic Reporter*, 21.1.2011, in https://www.ncronline.org/blogs/all-things-catholic/tackling-taboos-jews-and-christians-cross-and-deicide [15.1.2022].

American Foundation for Suicide Prevention, Suicide Statistics, in https://afsp.org/suicide-statistics/ [15.1.2022].

American Psychological Association, Death & Dying, in http://www.apa.org/topics/death/index.aspx [15.1.2022].

Assisted Suicide of Michèle Causse, 30.5.2014, in https://www.youtube.com/watch?v=JfyxUO4ZsDo [10.3.2019].

Austen, Ian, Brain-Dead, a Canadian Woman Remains a Silent Partner Awaiting Birth, 6.2.2014, in https://www.nytimes.com/2014/02/07/world/americas/brain-dead-a-canadian-woman-lives-on-as-a-silent-partner-awaiting-birth.html [15.1.2022].

Baklinski, Pete, Only prayer will defeat "power of darkness" called abortion: Card. Dolan at March for Life vigil, 18.1.2018, in https://www.

Bibliography

lifesitenews.com/news/only-prayer-will-defeat-power-of-darkness-called-abortion-card.-dolan-at-ma [15.1.2022].

Barron, Laignee, British People Are So Lonely That They Now Have a Minister for Loneliness, 18.1.2018, in http://time.com/5107252/minister-for-loneliness-uk [15.1.2022].

Baumann, Paul, The Truth has a Voice. The Pope vs. the Culture of Death, 8.10.1995, in http://www.nytimes.com/1995/10/08/opinion/the-pope-vs-the-culture-of-death.html [15.1.2022].

Bazzucchi, Mauro, Biotestamento, Mina Welby: Anche chi ha votato contro nel profondo del cuore la approva. Ora legge sulla morte assistita, 14.12.2017, in http://www.huffingtonpost.it/2017/12/14/biotestamento-mina-welby-anche-chi-ha-votato-contro-nel-profondo-del-cuore-la-approva-ora-legge-sulla-morte-assistita_a_23307140/ [15.1.2022].

BBC, Ethics guide. Arguments in favor of abortion, 2014, in http://www.bbc.co.uk/ethics/abortion/mother/for_1.shtml [15.1.2022].

BBC News, Italian man sparks euthanasia row, 13.12.2006, in http://news.bbc.co.uk/2/hi/europe/6174603.stm [15.1.2022].

Beals, Daniel A., The Groningen Protocol: Making Infanticide Legal Does Not Make It Moral, 23.3.2005, in https://cbhd.org/content/groningen-protocol-making-infanticide-legal-does-not-make-it-moral [15.1.2022].

Brenan, Megan, Americans' Strong Support for Euthanasia Persists, 31.5.2018, in https://news.gallup.com/poll/235145/americans-strong-support-euthanasia-persists.aspx [15.1.2022].

Bundesministerium der Justiz und für den Verbraucherschutz, Gesetz über die Spende, Entnahme und Übertragung von Organen und Geweben, in http://www.gesetze-im-internet.de/tpg/__1a.html [15.1.2022].

Bundesverfassungsgericht, Verbot der geschäftsmäßigen Förderung der Selbsttötung verfassungswidrig, Pressemitteilung Nr. 12/2020 vom 26. Februar 2020, in https://www.bundesverfassungsgericht.de/SharedDocs/Pressemitteilungen/DE/2020/bvg20-012.html [15.1.2022].

Bundesverwaltungsgericht, Urteil vom 02.03.2017 - BVerwG 3 C 19.15, in https://www.bverwg.de/020317U3C19.15.0 [15.1.2022].

Butcher, Tim, Israelis to be allowed euthanasia by machine, 8.12.2005, in https://www.telegraph.co.uk/news/worldnews/middleeast/israel/1505018/Israelis-to-be-allowed-euthanasia-by-machine.html [15.1.2022].

Cassidy, Patricia, EU Commission rejects petition to stop funding embryonic stem cell research, 2.6.2014, in http://www.bionews.org.uk/page_424657.asp [15.1.2022].

Catholic News Agency, Defying Vatican, Belgian religious brothers will continue to offer euthanasia, 12.9.2017, in https://www.catholicnewsagency.com/news/defying-vatican-belgian-religious-brothers-will

-continue-to-offer-euthanasia-97406 [15.1.2022].

Cendrowicz, Leo, Euthanasia and assisted suicide laws around the world, 17.7.2014, in https://www.theguardian.com/society/2014/jul/17/euthanasia-assisted-suicide-laws-world [15.1.2022].

Chalmers, Vanessa, Baby boy who was declared brain dead miraculously survives after his life support was switched off by doctors, 10.12.2018, in https://www.dailymail.co.uk/health/article-6478937/Baby-boy-declared-brain-dead-miraculously-survived-life-support-switched-off.html [15.1.2022].

China's Live Organ Harvests Are Happening Worldwide, 11.4.2017, in http://eng.the-liberty.com/2017/6673/ [15.1.2022].

Church denies funeral for Italian, 22.12.2006, in http://news.bbc.co.uk/2/hi/europe/6204995.stm [15.1.2022].

Connolly, Kate, Germany's opposition leader breaks from politics to donate kidney to wife, 23.8.2010, in https://www.theguardian.com/world/2010/aug/23/steinmeier-sabbatical-kidney-donation 15.1.2022].

Cremation Association of North America, An Overview of Cremation, in https://www.cremationassociation.org/page/CremationProcess [15.1.2022].

———, Industry Statistical Information, in https://www.cremation-association.org/page/IndustryStatistics [15.1.2022].

Cremation Institute. Expert Advice On Cremation, 52 Beautiful Ideas Of What To Do With Ashes, in https://cremationinstitute.com/what-to-do-with-ashes/ [15.1.2022].

Cremation Solutions, Tomorrows Traditions, Cremation Diamond Information, in https://www.cremationsolutions.com/cremation-jewelry-for-ashes/cremation-diamonds/cremation-diamond-information [15.1.2022].

———, Tomorrows Traditions, How Cremation Diamonds Are Made, in https://www.cremationsolutions.com/cremation-jewelry-for-ashes/cremation-diamonds/how-cremation-diamonds-are-made [15.1.2022].

Death with Dignity, Current as of November 6, 2019, in https://www.deathwithdignity.org/take-action/ [15.1.2022].

De Rycke, Raf, Belgian Catholic group explains switch on euthanasia, 6.5.2017, in https://www.mercatornet.com/careful/view/belgian-catholic-group-explains-switch-on-euthanasia/19757 [15.1.2022].

De Stabile, Elena, Il biotestamento è legge dello Stato: via libera definitivo al Senato con 180 sì, 14.12.2017, in http://www.repubblica.it/politica/2017/12/14/news/biotestamento_ok_definitivo_al_senato-184086928/ [15.1.2022].

Deutsches Ärzteblatt, 67 Prozent der Bundesbürger für aktive Sterbehilfe, 5.7.2019, in https://www.aerzteblatt.de/nachrichten/104419

Bibliography

/67-Prozent-der-Bundesbuerger-fuer-aktive-Sterbehilfe [15.1.2022].

Deutscher Bundestag, Basic Law for the Federal Republic of Germany, Last amended 28.3.2019, trans. by Christian Tomushat et al., in https://www.btg-bestellservice.de/pdf/80201000.pdf [15.1.2022].

Deutsches Referenzzentrum für Ethik in den Biowissenschaften, Sterbehilfe und Euthanasie, in http://www.drze.de/im-blickpunkt/sterbehilfe/module/sterbehilfe-und-euthanasie [15.1.2022].

Dignitas, Principles/Philosophy, in http://www.dignitas.ch/index.php?option=com_content&view=article&id=10&Itemid=46&lang=en [15.1.2022].

―――, Objectives and Purpose, in http://www.dignitas.ch/index.php?option=com_content&view=article&id=9&Itemid=45&lang=en [15.1.2022].

―――, Our Service, in http://www.dignitas.ch/index.php?option=com_content&view=article&id=6&Itemid=47&lang=en [15.1.2022].

Doughty, Steve, Belgian GPs "killing patients who have not asked to die": Report says thousands have been killed despite not asking their doctor, 12.6.2015, in http://www.dailymail.co.uk/news/article-3120835/Belgian-GPs-killing-patients-not-asked-die-Report-says-thousands-killed-despite-not-asking-doctor.html [15.1.2022].

DutschNews.nl, Number of official cases of euthanasia rise 10% in the Netherlands, April 12, 2017, in http://www.dutchnews.nl/news/archives/2017/04/number-of-official-cases-of-euthanasia-rise-10-in-the-netherlands/ [15.1.2022].

Eckersley, Phoebe, Brain-dead woman gives birth to a baby girl after she is kept on life support for three month following a brain hemorrhage, 27.8.2019, in https://www.dailymail.co.uk/news/article-7399705/Brain-dead-woman-gives-birth-baby-three-months-life-support.html [15.1.2022].

Engel, Matthew, More than 100 bodies found as US crematorium gives up grisly secret, 18.2.2002, in https://www.theguardian.com/world/2002/feb/18/matthewengel [15.1.2022].

Exit, Our Society, in https://exit.ch/en/englisch/who-is-exit/ [15.1.2022].

Gagliarducci, Andrea, Belgian Brothers of Charity drop board members who accepted hospital euthanasia protocol, 3.11.2018, in https://www.catholicnewsagency.com/news/belgian-brothers-of-charity-drop-board-members-who-accepted-hospital-euthanasia-protocol-81225 [15.1.2022].

Grohol, John M., Mental Health Professionals: US. Statistics 2017, 9.4.2019, in https://psychcentral.com/blog/mental-health-professionals-us-statistics-2017/ [15.1.2022].

Hallam, Mark and Prange, Astrid, German parliament: Explicit consent still necessary from organ donors, 16.1.2020, in https://www.dw.com/en/german-parliament-explicit-consent-still-necessary-from-organ-donors/a-52022245 [15.1.2022].

Hartocollis, Anemona, Hard Choice for a Comfortable Death: Sedation, 26.12.2009, in http://www.nytimes.com/2009/12/27/health/27sedation.html [15.1.2022].

Henley, Jon, At my father's bedside, I learned what death looks like, 3.2.2016, in https://www.theguardian.com/lifeandstyle/2016/feb/03/death-hospital-nhs-end-of-life-palliative-care-family [15.1.2022].

History of the Cremation Society of Great Britain, in https://www.cremation.org.uk/Our-History [15.1.2022].

In Vitro Fertilization Market is Expected to Reach $21.6 Billon, Globally by 2020, in https://www.alliedmarketresearch.com/press-release/global-in-vitro-fertilization-market-to-reach-216-billion-by-2020.html [15.1.2022].

Kapil, Rubina, 5 Surprising Mental Health Statistics, 6.2.2019, in https://www.mentalhealthfirstaid.org/2019/02/5-surprising-mental-health-statistics/ [15.1.2022].

Kim, Michelle, How Cremation Works, Cremation Regulation and Scandal, 31.3.2009, in https://science.howstuffworks.com/cremation3.htm [15.1.2022].

Kinzer, Stephen, Germans Find Mass Graves at an Ex-Soviet Camp, 24.9.1992, New York Times, in http://www.nytimes.com/1992/09/24/world/germans-find-mass-graves-at-an-ex-soviet-camp.html [15.1.2022].

Nancy Lapid, U.S. surgeons successfully test pig kidney transplant in human patient, 20.10.2021, in https://www.reuters.com/business/healthcare-pharmaceuticals/us-surgeons-successfully-test-pig-kidney-transplant-human-patient-2021-10-19/ [15.1.2022].

Laqueur, Thomas, The burning question—how cremation became our last great act of self-determination, 30.10.2015, in https://www.theguardian.com/books/2015/oct/30/burning-question-how-cremation-became-last-great-act-self-determination-thomas-laqueur [15.1.2022].

Mainwaring, Doug, Facebook blocks ad for pro-life movie telling the true story about Roe v Wade, 14.1.2019, in https://www.lifesitenews.com/news/facebook-blocks-ad-for-pro-life-movie-telling-the-true-story-about-roe-v-wa [15.1.2022].

Mayo Clinic, Resomation, in https://www.mayoclinic.org/body-donation/biocremation-resomation [15.1.2022].

Mayr, Gesa, Ternieden, Hendrik, Sterbehilfe-Debatte in Deutschland. Der gewünschte Tod, 11.2.2014, in http://www.spiegel.de/panorama/fragen-und-antworten-zur-sterbehilfe-debatte-in-deutschland-a-945147.html [15.1.2022].

Bibliography

Menon, Malini and Mohanty, Suchitra, India's top court upholds passive euthanasia, allows living wills in landmark judgment, 9.3.2018, in https://www.reuters.com/article/us-india-court-euthanasia/indias-top-court-upholds-passive-euthanasia-allows-living-wills-in-landmark-judgment-idUSKCN1GL0MF [15.1.2022].

Müller, Sabine, Wie tot sind Hirntote? Alte Frage—neue Antworten, vom 9.5.2011, in http://www.bpb.de/apuz/33311/wie-tot-sind-hirntote-alte-frage-neue-antworten?p=all [15.1.2022].

Naghavi, Mohsen, "Global, regional, and national burden of suicide mortality 1990 to 2016: systematic analysis for the Global Burden of Disease Study 2016," in *The British Medical Journal*, 6.2.2019, in https://www.bmj.com/content/364/bmj.l94 [15.1.2022].

Newhaven Funerals, Ocean Funerals, in http://newhavenfunerals.com.au/other-services/ocean-funerals/ [15.1.2022].

Pacholczyk, Tadeusz, Should I Have a Living Will, in https://www.catholiceducation.org/en/science/ethical-issues/should-i-have-a-living-will.html [15.1.2022].

Pasolini, Caterina, Biotestamento: da oggi i desideri dei malati sono legge, 31.1.2018, in https://www.repubblica.it/cronaca/2018/01/31/news/bioestamento_da_oggi_i_desideri_dei_malati_sono_legge-187697062/ [15.1.2022].

Patience, Martin, China's black market for organ donations, 11.8.2015, in http://www.bbc.com/news/world-asia-china-33844080 [15.1.2022].

Pontifical Council *Cor Unum*, Questions of Ethics Regarding the Fatally Ill and the Dying, 27.6.1981, in http://www.academyforlife.va/content/dam/pav/documents/papi/documentisantasede/ENGLISH/fatally_ill_and_dying_ENG.pdf [15.1.2022].

Position Paper of the Abrahamic Monotheistic Religions on Matters Concerning the End of Life (Casina Pio IV, 28 October 2019), in http://press.vatican.va/content/salastampa/en/bollettino/pubblico/2019/10/28/191028f.html [15.1.2022].

Potapov, Victor, Thou shalt not kill—Euthanasia, in https://stjohndc.org/en/orthodoxy-foundation/thou-shalt-not-kill-euthanasia [15.1.2022].

Ray, Mark, Addressing Loss on Social Media, 7.8.2019, in https://www.nextavenue.org/addressing-loss-on-social-media/ [15.1.2022].

Resultaten Perspectief—onderzoek naar ouderen met een doodswens aangeboden, 30.1.2020, in https://www.zonmw.nl/nl/actueel/nieuws/detail/item/resultaten-perspectief-onderzoek-naar-ouderen-met-een-doodswens-aangeboden/ [15.1.2022].

Samuel, Henry, Belgium authorized euthanasia of a terminally ill nine and 11-year-old in youngest cases worldwide, 7.8.2018, in https://www.telegraph.co.uk/news/2018/08/07/

belgium-authorised-euthanasia-terminally-nine-11-year-old-youngest/ [15.1.2022].

Shiel, William C., Medical Definition of Hippocratic Oath, in https://www.medicinenet.com/script/main/art.asp?articlekey=20909 [15.1.2022].

Statista, Durchschnittliche weitere Lebenserwartung in Deutschland nach Geschlecht und Altersgruppen laut der Sterbetafel 2017/2019, in https://de.statista.com/statistik/daten/studie/1783/umfrage/durchschnittliche-weitere-lebenserwartung-nach-altersgruppen/ [15.1.2022].

Stockenström, Tone, Is Dying a Pro-Choice Issue? The Right to Die Movement Gains National Attention, 22.12.2014, in https://thehumanist.com/magazine/january-february-2015/features/is-dying-a-pro-choice-issue [15.1.2022].

Ratzinger, Joseph, Homily *Missa pro eligendo Romano Pontifice*, 18.4.2005, in http://www.vatican.va/gpII/documents/homily-pro-eligendo-pontifice_20050418_en.html [15.1.2022].

The Cremation Society, Progress of Cremation in the British Islands 1885-2018, in https://www.cremation.org.uk/progress-of-cremation-united-kingdom [15.1.2022].

Telegraph Reporters, Preacher locked up for hate crime after quoting the Bible to gay teenager, 5.2.2017, in http://www.telegraph.co.uk/news/2017/02/05/preacher-locked-hate-crime-quoting-bible-gay-teenager/ [15.1.2022].

The Royal Dutch Medical Association (RDMA), Euthanasia in the Netherlands, 16.8.2017, in https://www.knmg.nl/actualiteit-opinie/nieuws/nieuwsbericht/euthanasia-in-the-netherlands.htm [15.1.2022].

The World Federation of Right to Die Societies, Our beliefs, in https://wfrtds.org/beliefs/ [15.1.2022].

―――, Our history, in https://wfrtds.org/history-of-the-world-federation-of-right-to-die-societies/ [15.1.2022].

―――, Manifesto, in http://www.worldrtd.net/manifesto [15.1.2022].

United Network for Organ Sharing, Stories of hope, in https://unos.org/transplant/stories-of-hope/ [15.1.2022].

United States Postal Service, How to Package and Ship Cremated Remains, Publication 139, September 2019, in https://about.usps.com/publications/pub139.pdf [15.1.2022].

USCCB, Advance Medical Directives: Planning for Your Future, 2014, in http://www.usccb.org/about/pro-life-activities/respect-life-program/2014/advance-medical-directives.cfm [15.1.2022].

―――, Living the Gospel of Life: A Challenge to American Catholics, in http://www.usccb.org/issues-and-action/human-life-and-dignity/abortion/living-the-gospel-of-life.cfm [15.1.2022].

US. Department of Health & Human Services, General Donation

Bibliography

Questions, in https://www.organdonor.gov/about/facts-terms/donation-faqs.html [15.1.2022].

US. Government Information on Organ Donation and Transplantation, Organ Donation Statistics, in https://www.organdonor.gov/statistics-stories/statistics.html#glance [15.1.2022].

Vatican Radio, Pope orders Belgian Brothers of Charity to stop offering euthanasia, 11.8.2017, in http://en.radiovaticana.va/news/2017/08/11/pope_orders_belgian_brothers_to_stop_offering_euthanasia/1330120 [15.1.2022].

Walker, Peter, Organ donation presumed consent could be adopted in England, 30.6.2017, in https://www.theguardian.com/society/2017/jun/30/presumed-consent-organ-donation-could-be-adopted-england [15.1.2022].

Walsh, Fergus, Vegetative patient Scott Routley says "I'm not in pain," 13.11.2012, in https://www.bbc.com/news/health-20268044 [15.1.2022].

Welby, prosciolto il medico Riccio, 23.7.2007, in http://www.repubblica.it/2007/07/sezioni/cronaca/welby-medico/welby-medico/welby-medico.html [15.1.2022].

With cemeteries almost full, Mexico City pushes cremation, threatening Day of Dead traditions, 11.12.201, in http://www.foxnews.com/world/2014/10/28/with-cemeteries-almost-full-mexico-city-pushes-cremation-threatening-day-dead.html [15.1.2022].

World Medical Association, Modern Physicians' Pledge Approved by World Medical Association, 14.10.2017, in https://www.wma.net/news-post/modern-physicians-pledge-approved-by-world-medical-association/ [15.1.2022].

————, WMA Declaration of Geneva, The Physician's Pledge, 6.11.2017, in https://www.wma.net/policies-post/wma-declaration-of-geneva/ [15.1.2022].

Zúñiga-Fajuri, Alejandra, Increasing organ donation by presumed consent and allocation priority, 3.12.2014, in https://www.who.int/bulletin/volumes/93/3/14-139535/en/ [15.1.2022].

ABOUT THE AUTHOR

RALPH WEIMANN was born in 1976. After studying in the USA, Italy, and Germany, he obtained a diploma in humanities and a bachelor in philosophy, followed by a licentiate in theology. After his ordination to the priesthood, he earned a doctorate in theology in 2010 on the thesis "Dogma and Progress in the Theology of Joseph Ratzinger." He earned a second doctorate in 2013 on the thesis "Bioethics in a Secularized Society." He has worked as a military chaplain since 2015. Rev. Weimann lectures at various colleges and universities in Rome, in particular the Pontifical University of St. Thomas Aquinas (*Angelicum*) and the International Online University *Domuni*.